BEYOND ENDURANCE

BEYOND ENDURANCE
Survival at the Extremes

Glin Bennet

St. Martin's/Marek
New York

BEYOND ENDURANCE. Copyright © 1983 by Glin Bennet.
All rights reserved. Printed in the United States of America.
No part of this book may be used or reproduced in
any manner whatsoever without written permission except
in the case of brief quotations embodied in critical articles
or reviews. For information, address St. Martin's/Marek,
175 Fifth Avenue, New York, N.Y. 10010

Library of Congress Cataloging in Publication Data

Bennet, Glin.
    Beyond endurance.

    "A St. Martin's/Marek book."
    1. Stress (Psychology) 2. Judgment. 3. Accidents—
Psychological aspects. 4. Disasters—Psychological
aspects. I. Title.
BF575.S75B38 1983   155.9   83-3172
ISBN 0-312-07783-1

First published in Great Britain by Secker & Warburg

First U.S. Edition

10 9 8 7 6 5 4 3 2 1

This book
is
dedicated to the memory
of
Brian Cooke
Mike McMullen
David Blagden

three brave lone sailors
who died
at sea

Acknowledgements

I am grateful to the following publishers for permission to reproduce extracts of their works:

Allen and Unwin (from *A Woman in the Polar Night* by Christiane Ritter), William Collins, Sons & Co. (from *Ice Bird* by David Lewis and *Eiger Direct* by P. Gillman and D. Haston), Essex Record Office Publications (from *The Great Tide* by Hilda Grieve), Hamish Hamilton Limited (from *Fetch Felix* by D. Patrick), Hart-Davis MacGibbon Limited (from *Red Mains'l* by Peter Pye), William Heinemann Limited (from *Last Voyage* by Ann Davison), Her Majesty's Stationery Office (from *Railway Accidents: Moorgate Station*), Hodder and Stoughton Limited (from *Camp Six* by Frank Smythe), Allen Lane (from *Scott's Men* by David Thomson), Mockingbird Books (from *Life After Life* by Raymond A. Moody), Penguin Books Limited (from *Everest, The Hard Way* by C. Bonington), Thames and Hudson Limited (from *The Informed Heart* by Bruno Bettelheim), *Yachting Monthly* (from 'The Loneliness of the Long Distance Sailor' by Frank Mulville), George Weidenfeld and Nicolson Limited (from *Prisoner Without A Name, Cell Without A Number* by J. Timerman).

Contents

PART IV COPING AND PREVENTING

Illustrations

Preface

This is a book about what happens to people when the psychological demands made upon them become too great, and how they cope or fail to cope when pressed to their limits, and beyond. A sailor alone in a small boat on the ocean, the pilot of a jet airliner, a climber on the south-west face of Everest, a woman at home with small children, a motorist driving home from work, a man taken hostage by terrorists, a woman out alone on a polar night, the driver of the local train — these are some of the people who will feature here.

To develop these themes, the book is divided into sections. First, there is an introduction indicating my main lines of interest and how I became involved with the subject. In *Part I*, examples are given of how human factors can lead to errors and accidents. The working environments of airline pilots, train drivers, high altitude climbers, sailors and others are then described briefly, and the more extreme environments afflicting those in natural disasters, under interrogation or expecting sentence of death. In *Part II* certain circumstances are given special mention, such as isolation, isolated groups and physical hardships of various kinds including cold, oxygen lack and hunger.

The central part of the book is *Part III*, dealing with the personal attributes of adventurers, and individual reactions to different conditions. These vary from simple errors caused by tiredness, to depressions and moments of ecstasy, to hallucinations and misinterpretation of surroundings, to complete psychological disintegration.

Part IV is about coping with the crises and, where possible, preventing them. Different calamities call for different strategies: there are occasions when clear thinking and resolute action save the day, and others when the only survivors are those who can accept their predicament with passivity and resignation.

The investigations conducted after accidents have occurred are painstaking with regard to the mechanical factors but naive where the human ones are concerned. The psychological expertise is available, but is seldom utilised.

No one writes a book like this alone, and I am indebted to the great many adventurers and others who have shared their experiences so honestly with me. Especially, I think of the three superb sailors, Brian Cooke, Mike McMullen and David Blagden, who contributed so richly to my studies, and who each died tragically at sea in a small boat. The book is dedicated to their memory with affection and admiration.

I owe much to Professor Derek Russell Davis for his interest and advice throughout. To a considerable extent he laid the foundations for the subject matter of this book through his experimental studies on fatigue during the Second World War – work which is as relevant today as when it first appeared nearly forty years ago. I am deeply grateful to Jackie Barton who did a large part of the initial research and helped with the planning. I also want to thank Rosemary Hayward who prepared the entire manuscript, Sue Phillpott for her meticulous editing, and Linda Bennet who created the setting in which the book could be written.

Superscript numbers indicate references to sources which have been arranged by chapters at the end of the book. Statements or accounts not accompanied by references have been given personally by their authors.

Introduction

A ship goes down with all hands, a jet airliner crashes on take-off with hundreds killed, a train driver misses a signal and plunges into the back of another train. An official inquiry follows in which every detail of mechanical functioning is meticulously analysed. In the great majority of cases no mechanical fault is found, and so the explanation offered is that 'human factors' were to blame.

I want to know more about these human factors, not only as they apply to ships' captains, pilots and train drivers, but also to adventurers into the natural environment such as small-boat sailors, climbers and explorers of all kinds; and to ordinary people when their routines break down and they find themselves under excessive strain.

Four strands of personal experience and interest are interwoven in this book: my work as a clinical psychiatrist, studies of human behaviour in disasters, studies of singlehanded ocean sailors, and the lessons learnt from experimental psychology. I will explain how they relate to the general theme of how people behave in extreme conditions of various kinds. Trying to understand how and why people act as they do is a central part of my work as a psychiatrist, and the approach is broadly the same whether I am trying to make sense of individual behaviour in a small boat or on a mountainside, or else of the problems of someone whose life has become unmanageable because of intractable personal conflict.

When someone comes to see me who is, say, depressed to the degree that he (or she) can no longer cope with the demands of work and family, I will try to understand what is happening to him (in addition, of course, to trying to share some of the burden of his suffering) by exploring the current circumstances of his life and considering various antecedent factors. Once the relevant factors are reviewed systematically, the hitherto inexplicable depressive behaviour usually not only becomes intelligible but can appear as an almost inevitable consequence of pressures the individual has been bearing but which he has been unable to deal with or adapt to in a positive manner. People may also present who have been making ruinous decisions or acting irrationally, or who have been involved in drinking bouts, inappropriate love affairs, overdoses of drugs and uncharacteristic acts of various kinds. All these behaviours can begin to make sense once they are seen in relation to the main themes in a person's life.

An airline pilot, ship's captain or mountaineer may be confronted with a challenge or a crisis which, in the short term at any rate, it is beyond his abilities to cope with. This may be because of the sheer magnitude of the challenge, or because he is somehow sensitised and rendered more vulnerable to any given event or crisis by a number of remote or antecedent factors. That is to say, some crises are so great that they may overwhelm the most experienced and best prepared of people: others are not so great in themselves, but the individual involved is, at the moment at any rate, in a less than optimum state to deal with them.

For example, the experienced sailor in heavy seas has his mast snap off. The broken end is smashing a hole in the side of the hull; being entirely on his own, he is powerless to prevent this, and he knows that it could sink the boat. He needs to be able to think calmly and logically, but this is a situation of extreme danger which would be likely to impair the judgement of the coolest sailor. In due course the side of the hull is smashed in and the boat sinks. On another occasion the same sailor has gone off on a solo cruise to take his mind off the pain of the breakup of his marriage and his home. When his rudder is broken off by a large piece of timber which he failed to notice in the water, he is unable to act effectively, even to set up the large oar he always carried on deck against this very eventuality. Nor does he seem able to steer by trimming the sails. The boat yaws around broadside to the wind and eventually fills with water and founders, and he takes to his life-raft. Although probably not conscious of it at the time, he was clearly functioning below his optimum in failing to meet a serious, but not yet catastrophic, emergency in a rational and purposeful manner.

In psychiatric practice one encounters people of both categories: an ordinary person overwhelmed by a massive personal tragedy, or someone with pre-existing and unresolved problems who is brought to a standstill by an event which is not in itself shattering but may be perceived so by this extra-vulnerable person. Who is going to crack up and who is going to surmount the most impossible conditions is beyond anybody's power to predict with certainty, because, apart from anything else, some people seem to thrive on crises and only come into their own when conditions are really bad. Nevertheless, there is a broad average area into which most people will fall, and for whom this book is mainly intended.

I have outlined an approach to psychological problems and mental disorder which relates the reactions (i.e. symptoms) to the immediate and to the remote circumstances of a person's life, and I used the same approach when studying the effects of flooding on the health of people in Bristol in 1968. Had the Bristol floods been an overwhelming disaster, it would not have been possible to carry out much in the way of research, which was mainly into the effects on health.[1] Yet a number of examples of unexpected behaviour were observed among the victims and others — reactions such as shock and apathy, aggression against officials and helpers, an apparent need to find people or organisations to blame for what had happened, and, of course, the increased sickness and death rate from all kinds of illnesses, not merely those which might have been connected with physical exposure.

This stimulated in me a more general interest in the whole question of human reactions to disasters and other catastrophes, public and private. The phenomena seen in Bristol proved to be entirely characteristic and entirely predictable, as numerous subsequent disasters have shown. When the expected reactions occur, say, after an earthquake, the authorities concerned still feel hurt and affronted by them, and totally surprised at how the victims could react so harshly and ungratefully towards those who are trying valiantly to give assistance.

On 27 July 1969 I read an account in the *Sunday Times* by Nicholas Tomalin about the abandoned trimaran belonging to Donald Crowhurst which had been found intact and drifting in mid-Atlantic. Crowhurst, it seemed, had suffered a complete mental breakdown while about one thousand miles from home after an apparently successful singlehanded non-stop circumnavigation of the world, and it seemed he had been set to win the *Sunday Times* round-the-world sailing contest.

Tomalin's preliminary assessment brought about a full-scale investigation of what had led up to Crowhurst's disappearance – an investigation made possible by the large amount of material found on board in the form of tape-recordings, film, details of radio messages, navigational logs, and twenty-five thousand words of his own writing. Together with Ron Hall he reconstructed what had happened, and I was involved in this reconstruction with regard to the psychological issues and the interpretation of some of the stranger writings in the log-books. The resulting story was tragic, engrossing, and of great psychological importance for, almost as never before, it chronicles events leading up to final psychological disintegration. The story has been told[2,3] and does not need to be repeated here, but certain details will be referred to from time to time.

After working on Donald Crowhurst's log-books, I wondered to what extent this experience was unique, or were psychological breakdowns of greater or lesser degree perhaps quite common on the oceans, especially among singlehanded sailors in small boats? It was a pure fluke that Crowhurst's yacht was found intact. Had there been any strong winds, all that might have been found would have been a capsized hull which would have been left to its fate to be broken up at sea, or dashed to pieces on reaching land. More likely, if the boat had capsized nothing more would ever have been heard of Donald Crowhurst, who would then have joined the countless sailors who have disappeared at sea.

I did not have to talk with many sailors or read many accounts of ocean voyages in small boats before it was clear that psychological disturbances are far from rare at sea. Not only that, but they seemed to be equally common in other hard environments such as mountains and the polar regions.

The next step in this investigation, then, was to try to make some systematic observations, because so far I had only had access to individual reports from or about highly unusual and doubtless atypical individuals. As it happened, the 1972 *Observer* Singlehanded Transatlantic Race was soon to take place, and that could provide an ideal opportunity to make just such observations. With the great cooperation of the English-speaking competitors, who completed a daily record of the general level of function and well-being, together with interviews with them and others at the finish in Newport, Rhode Island, it was possible to obtain interesting information about how highly-motivated people may function under arduous (though not extreme) physical and psychological conditions for up to five weeks in isolation on the Atlantic ocean. This work has been published in the medical and nautical press,[4,5] but being a rather novel kind of investigation it raised many more questions than it answered.

The singlehanders, as I shall call the competitors in the 1972 Singlehanded Transatlantic Race who participated in my study, will feature throughout the book, along with other sailors who have had interesting experiences. The sea will provide the setting for many of the examples, partly because I have elected to study behaviour at sea, and partly because I know of no other circumstances where it is possible to endure such physical and psychological hardship in isolation for such long periods yet with the possibility of keeping some sort of a record.

Examples will also be drawn from major transport accidents, and tragedies on mountains as well as at sea. Investigating these can be a delicate matter: the principal figures are no longer available to be interviewed and no one wants to intrude upon the grief of bereaved relatives. Nevertheless, a gread deal more could be learned from a study of these events than is being learned, and this knowledge could save lives in the future.

I have been fortunate in being able to work in the Department of Mental Health in Bristol University, headed by Professor Derek Russell Davis. In the Second World War he did important fundamental research into pilot error,[6] and after the war continued his interest in this area by investigating non-fatal train accidents.[7,8] This work introduced me to the contribution of experimental psychology to the study of human behaviour under arduous conditions, and has provided a conceptual framework which can help make sense of the disturbances of perception and judgement and the abnormal behaviours which at first sight appear quite inexplicable. There is also a great deal of experimental work to draw on from laboratory and field studies, which shows how the best ordered people can become totally disorganised when frustrated, isolated, kept without sleep, or made anxious or afraid for their lives.

In experimental psychology all the conditions and variables are controlled with utmost rigour; but studies in hostile environments or in 'real life' cannot be so well controlled, or indeed controlled at all, so that a neat sequence of cause and effect can seldom be identified. There are two reasons for this.

First, causes and effects become confused; take a simple domestic example. A man is kept awake at night by the barking of a dog. Next morning he is feeling out of sorts and he snaps at his wife. She snaps back and a row ensues. He is angry by the time he leaves the house, and drives the car rather aggressively. In a fit of impatience he tries to overtake another car on a corner and collides with it. What is the cause of the accident? Is it enough to say that he was in an angry mood? What was the cause of that? Was it the row he had with his wife, the sleeplessness or the barking dog?

The process can be represented schematically:[9]

cause: dog barking
effect: sleeplessness
cause: sleeplessness
effect: row with wife
cause: row with wife
effect: bad temper
cause: bad temper
effect: aggressive driving
cause: aggressive driving
effect: *collision*

In other words, each effect becomes the cause of the next stage, and so the two elements become very easily confused. This is especially so where sleep deprivation is concerned.

The second reason why the simple cause-and-effect model will not serve is that real life is never that straightforward. There are always a host of factors affecting every action that we take. In the example given, what was making the man sleep badly? Was there some issue which made his wife extra-likely to pick a row with him? What were the weather conditions like on the roads? What kind of condition was the car in?

Environmental conditions (weather on the roads in this example) and mechanical or equipment factors (state of the car) will feature a good deal in these pages, even though they are responsible for only a small minority of transport accidents.

In our example the human factors are the reasons for sleeping badly and for the man's relationship with his wife. There may be other factors – his attitude towards dogs in general, something awaiting him at work which might have intensified his agitation from the moment he woke that day, a previous near-accident on the roads the week before. There may also be remote matters which will affect the man's (and perhaps also his wife's) general attitudes. If the man's father had lost his job so that his family had suffered considerable privation, the man might be in an extra-nervous state if that day he was about to have a meeting in which his own future was at stake. Again, the man might have lost his mother in early childhood, a factor which would increase the likelihood of psychological difficulties in later life.

There are thus precipitating or provoking factors which contribute directly to the accident, and remote or vulnerability factors which sensitise the individual in a general way. It is difficult and fortunately not normally necessary to separate these out. What matters when studying accidents and personal misfortunes is that we learn to recognise a network of factors in a constant state of interaction.

These factors fall into three main groups: human, environmental and mechanical. The interaction between them is all-important. It can sometimes make human behaviour seem enigmatic and paradoxical, but that is how it is in reality, so no apology is needed. The simple cause-and-effect models are extremely useful when it comes to disentangling specific processes, but when we want to get some grasp of the broader issues we have to think in an interactional way.

I have brought together various approches and interests in order to learn more about the vagaries of human functioning under adverse psychological and physical conditions, whether the potential disaster happens in a yacht, in a sailing boat, in the cockpit of a jumbo jet, on the south-west face of Everest, or simply during the drive home through the rain after a hard day at the office. The extreme environments give us dramatic examples, but the principles apparent in them apply equally to ordinary people in the course of their daily lives. A person can, for want of a better word, go mad isolated in a small boat on the ocean, but the underlying processes are not fundamentally different from those leading to the breakdown of a suburban housewife who feels rejected and unvalued. The difference is one of intensity, just as tragedy acted out on the stage is more intense than silent tragedies occurring privately in the home.

Under sufficiently severe environmental conditions, the most manifestly stable people can crack and display signs usually associated with mental disorder – incapacitating anxiety or depression, paranoid ideas, auditory or visual hallucinations. This potential for 'mad' behaviour is within all of us. We should acknowledge it and not suppose that people who are labelled by society as mentally ill are in some way different in kind. It can be convenient to treat as outsiders those who are an embarrassment or who do not easily seem to fit in with social conventions, but it is cruel and a fundamental mistake to do so. People who talk in a disparaging way about those who have suffered a psychological breakdown, and act as though they would like to extrude them from ordinary society, should reflect that they too have limits to their endurance, and that once pushed beyond them they would behave indistinguishably from those they affect to despise.

The study of people in harsh environments can make us more humble about our own ability to withstand adversity.

My main theme throughout this book is that environmental conditions and the individual's state of mind play decisive roles in his or her overall efficiency. The theme will be illustrated with a multiplicity of examples. Some will call this merely anecdotal reporting and claim that a case can only be made on the basis of controlled studies. That is true, but only up to a point. There are very few controlled studies of human behaviour under adverse conditions, mainly because such studies are very difficult to set up; but even if there were many available they could at best only give us a picture of the average and the collective, and would miss the essential individual perception and experience. The personal examples on the whole are more illuminating. Inevitably I have selected examples to emphasise a point, but I hope in order to illustrate some well recognised psychological principle rather than to act as bricks in a wall of argument. The same stories will crop up in different parts of the book, according to the particular topic under consideration. It could be distracting to insert cross-references into the main text, but reference to the name or to the topic in the index will indicate all the other entries for the same story.

Lastly, I want to stress that the examples will indicate what *may* happen, not what invariably *does* happen, because no one can ever predict what a given person will do. At best, an outcome can be expressed in terms of probability, and for the same reason nothing about human behaviour can ever claim finally to have been 'proved'.

PART I

Activities

1

How Things Go Wrong

In February 1975, a crowded morning rush-hour train was driven at 40 miles per hour (64 kph) past Moorgate station in the City of London, where it should have stopped, and into a dead-end tunnel. Forty-three people were killed and seventy-four injured. The driver was variously reported by witnesses waiting on the platform to have been accelerating while passing through the station, to have had a 'glazed look', and to be sitting motionless at the controls. At all events, when his body was reached five days later at the far end of the tunnel jammed with the wreckage of the train, he was found to be seated with his hands on the controls.[1,2]

The commission of inquiry judged that *human factors* were involved, but no serious attempt seems to have been made to find out what these factors might actually be and by what processes the driver's behaviour had become so disastrously disorganised.

According to an unpublished London Transport report, 209 drivers on the London underground system committed serious errors during 1973.[3] Over half of these involved passing signals set at danger. The report described the main causes of these incidents as 'faulty judgement' and 'lack of attention'.

A British European Airways Trident crashed 106 seconds after take-off on an afternoon in June 1972 at Staines, Middlesex, killing all 118 people on board.[4,5,6] The Trident has devices called 'droops' and 'flaps' which extend the width of the wing to give greater lift at slow speeds. Seventy seconds after take-off, at a lower altitude and airspeed than normal, the droops were withdrawn. The aircraft was now in serious danger of stalling and the automatic stall recovery device was activated. This pointed the nose of the Trident downwards so that the air speed would increase rapidly and control could be re-established. To make sure the pilot and co-pilot are aware of the danger of a stall in such a situation, both control columns are made to shake, and if no corrective action is taken the control columns ram forward – in effect simulating automatically the movement the pilots should be making. These safety devices were operating, and in addition there was a flashing red light and an audible warning to each pilot.

Because of the still inadequate speed, this whole cycle repeated itself eight seconds later, and again three seconds after that. One second after that, for reasons we shall never know for sure, the stall recovery system was manually inhibited by pulling an override lever. The aircraft was now doomed; the nose pitched up, it lost speed and height, entered a deep aerodynamic stall and crashed in a field three and a quarter miles (5.2 km) from the airport. Post-mortem examination of the captain showed that he had suffered a tear in the lining of the wall of one of his coronary arteries, which was judged by the pathologist to have occurred not more than two hours and not less than one minute before death.

This disaster attracted widespread interest and publicity, largely because of a fierce argument the captain was said to have had in the crew-room an hour and a half before take-off. Also, possibly significant graffiti (described on p. 222) were later found on the flight deck of the Trident.

The committee of inquiry found that Captain Key's 'abnormal heart condition' led to 'lack of concentration and impaired judgement sufficient to account for his toleration of the speed errors and his retraction of, or order to retract, the droops in mistake for the flaps'. They did not feel that the crew-room incident or the graffiti were of much consequence.

Similar experiences with Tridents on take-off, two years and four years before the present disaster, came to light at the official inquiry. The same captain (not Captain Key) was assumed to have been involved in both of them, but as there was no crash or near-crash nothing more happened than the filling in of an incident report. Unlike the railway authorities, the airline authorities do not (or did not) investigate every incident, but only the major accidents, when the relevant witnesses are liable to be unavailable.

In 1974, two years after the Trident disaster, a Lufthansa jumbo jet crashed thirty-five seconds after take-off from Nairobi. Fifty-nine people were killed; ninety-eight, including the pilot, co-pilot and engineer, survived. It was all painfully similar to what had happened over London airport in the Trident – particularly, juddering of the aircraft, which was evidence of an impending stall but was misinterpreted by the captain and crew for reasons which have not adequately been explained. The 'corrective' action they took (raising the undercarriage, which they had thought was responsible for the juddering) was entirely inappropriate, since it slowed the aircraft and so precipitated the actual disaster.[7]

Owing to a bomb explosion at Las Palmas airport in the Canary Islands on 27 March 1977, two Boeing 747 jumbo jets loaded with holiday-makers were diverted to a neighbouring, and often foggy, airport, on Tenerife. One belonged to KLM, bringing 234 passengers with fourteen crew from Amsterdam, and the other was a Pan American with 380 passengers and sixteen crew on board on a flight from Los Angeles. The trouble began when these two aircraft were eventually allowed to resume their journey to Las Palmas, one of them having refuelled in the meantime. Both aircraft were on the same runway at the same time because of the unusual congestion of the airport. The KLM was taxiing to the end of the runway prior to take-off, and the Pan Am was therefore ordered to leave that runway at a named intersection.

The KLM turned round 180° at the end of the runway and prepared to take off. The Pan Am missed the intersection and so remained on the runway. Fog came down and reduced visibility to 300 metres so that the two aircraft and the air traffic controllers could no longer see one another. The KLM thought they had take-off clearance and so began their run, and by 17.06 and 35 seconds the KLM had attained a speed of 100 knots. Here is what happened over the next few seconds according to one of the Dutch reports, with 'KLM' and 'Pan Am' substituted for the official designations:

At 17.06.40 the captain of Pan Am saw through the fog, at a distance of approximately 700 metres, the landing lights of KLM; he has stated to have realised after a few seconds that KLM was coming towards them and was taking off. He immediately increased power on all engines and started to turn the aircraft to the left, in order to clear the runway as soon as possible.

At 17.06.44 the captain of KLM initiated the rotation. At 17.06.47 the captain gave an exclamation and pulled the control column fully aft, because of which the aircraft over-rotated and its tail scraped over the runway over a distance of 22 metres.

At 17.06.50 both aircraft collided; KLM was at that moment fully airborne. Meanwhile Pan Am had turned at least 34° to the left relative to the runway heading.

The nose section and the nose wheels of KLM passed over the

fuselage of Pan Am while the wing gears and body gears collided with the right wing of Pan Am in the area of engine no. 3. The fuselage and the engines nos 2, 3 and 4 passed through the cabin section of Pan Am. KLM subsequently fell back on the runway and skidded over a distance of approximately 450 metres, while the aircraft gradually disintegrated. Because of the spillage of fuel from the ruptured tanks, both aircraft and the whole area in between immediately caught fire.

All 248 people on board the KLM were killed, plus 326 on the Pan Am – a total of 574 which makes it easily, to date, the worst aircraft accident of all time. It will also be the most expensive in terms of insurance claims. The captain, first officer and flight engineer of the Pan Am survived and were able to give evidence at the inquiries, but unfortunately there have been disagreements in the Spanish[8] and Dutch reports, particularly about how much weight to give to human factors.

The agreed facts seem to be: the KLM pilot probably thought he had clearance to take off when in fact he had only clearance to line up from the air traffic controllers, who also believed the KLM was stationary on the runway when in fact it was preparing for take-off; the Pan Am missed the intersection and so failed to clear the runway for the KLM. Contributing factors were: fog, confusion on the radio-telephone links, and irritation experienced by the flight crews, especially the Pan Am crew, over the delay; some kind of hierarchical conflict between the captain and co-pilot of the KLM; unusual pressures on the air traffic controllers because Las Palmas airport had been temporarily closed to traffic on account of the bomb; and possible distraction of the air traffic controllers by a radio broadcast of a football match which was claimed to have been audible in the background of messages from the control tower at Tenerife airport.

Whether any more satisfactory explanation will be forthcoming remains to be seen, but I would think it unlikely. Airlines, like insurance companies, do not feel obliged to reveal information, however helpful it might be in saving lives in the future, if it might interfere with their commercial operations.

On 18 March 1967, the master of the *Torrey Canyon* drove his ship with 117,000 tons of Kuwait crude oil on board at its full speed of about 15.75 knots onto the Seven Stones rocks, which lie between Land's End and the Isles of Scilly. It was the consequence of a course laid 1,400 miles (2,600 km) further back, in the region of the Canary Islands, when the master had set his ship on automatic pilot which would take it to the north and west of the Scillies. On 17 March an astronomical fix showed that the ship had 'apparently been set over to eastward by the prevailing current'. To change back to the original course would, in the master's view, have lengthened the duration of the voyage by twenty-nine minutes, which in turn would have caused him to miss the tide and so have to wait another five days until his deeply-loaded tanker would be able to enter Milford Haven. This opinion was disputed at the inquiry. The *Torrey Canyon* continued, still on automatic pilot, south of the Scillies with a view to passing between them and Land's End.

One third of the way across this 25 (statute or land) mile (40-km) gap is the dangerous reef, the Seven Stones, but if these rocks are left well to the west the channel is reasonably safe. However, the officers on deck were not satisfied about the ship's heading and made repeated checks on their position. According to the Liberian government inquiry:

> The master, realising that he was closer to the Seven Stones than expected (only about 2.5 miles), decided to come left to 000 degrees [directly north]. He testified that he was prevented from any further alteration of course to the left by the presence of one of the fishing boats (identity unknown) on his port side. He also testified that there was no vessel on his starboard side which would have prevented a right turn at that point.

> About 08.48 another position was obtained by the third officer, using radar range and visual bearing to the light vessel. The distance was only about 2.78 miles.

> The master knew that his vessel was perilously close to the Seven Stones and he shouted to the helmsman to come hard left. The helmsman immediately went to the steering stand and put the wheel over hard left, but saw there was no response. The vessel remained on course 000 degrees.

> He promptly called out to the master, who ran to the wheel and saw that the selector switch was in the control position, not 'hand'. The master immediately turned the lever to 'hand' and the bow of the *Torrey Canyon* began to swing left. According to the course recorder graph she reached a heading of 350 degrees when at 08.50 the vessel struck Pollard Rock and came to a sudden stop, hard and fast aground. The main engines were stopped and tank soundings indicated that all six starboard tanks were ruptured, possibly others as well.

> There had been no orders to the main engines prior to the stranding, and the *Torrey Canyon* hit at full speed of approximately 15.75 knots.

The inquiry found that 'the disaster was caused entirely by human error' on the part of the captain. No explanation was offered for his keeping the ship on automatic pilot in treacherous coastal waters with fishing vessels about, for maintaining full speed right up until the time of the stranding, and for failing to alter course ten minutes before the stranding even though the third officer had warned him that they were dangerously close to the part of the Seven Stones reef which they eventually hit.[9]

The *Torrey Canyon* affair set off a huge debate about how to stop this kind of thing happening again, but it is now remembered as the prelude to the modern era of pollution disasters. Three years later two more Liberian-registered tankers collided off the Isle of Wight following a muddle about whether the 95,000-ton *Allegro*, with a Greek crew, was overtaking or crossing the path of the 78,000-ton *Pacific Glory*, with a Chinese crew. The two ships were in sight of one another for a good hour and a half on a clear October night, but each held to its original course. The *Pacific Glory*, travelling at 15 knots, altered course slightly to port (left), away from *Allegro*, in order to avoid a distant ship that was approaching. *Allegro*, coming in on *Pacific Glory*'s starboard side at 15.50 knots, made no such alteration until the very last moment, when it was too late. She then swung hard away, but the sterns of the two ships collided. There was later an explosion on board *Pacific Glory*. Fourteen people died and six thousand tons of oil were spilled.

In addition to the usual charges of poor lookouts, there seems to have been poor communication between the two ships. The Liberian board of investigation found that the *Allegro* had been crossing, not overtaking, and therefore the *Pacific Glory* should have given way, but the captain of the *Allegro* was criticised for travelling at over 15 knots if, as he said, he had had difficulty in seeing the other tanker. The story may sound more characteristic of our overcrowded roads than of the sea, but this is how the English Channel can become with three hundred ships a day passing through the Strait of Dover, not to mention the two hundred and fifty daily ferry crossings back and forth across their tracks. The pile-up a few months later, in January 1971, may therefore come as less of a surprise.

The Panamanian tanker *Texaco Caribbean* was in collision with the Peruvian freighter *Parcas* on the English side of the Varne sandbank off Folkestone. The empty tanker exploded and sank, breaking up into at least four pieces which proved remarkably difficult to locate on the sea-bed. A few days later *Texaco Caribbean*'s submerged bow was struck by the German freighter *Brandenburg*, which then sank. A few weeks after that the Greek coaster *Niki* had her bottom ripped out on what was probably the sunken *Brandenburg*. The wrecks had been brilliantly illuminated and there was a 250,000-candlepower lightship – and later a second lightship was brought up – but even after the loss of the *Niki*, vessels continued to sail through the danger area,[10] presumably because of the difficulty of interpreting such a novel kind of hazard as a whole group of wrecks in a region of sandbanks and heavy traffic. Notices of dangers are published regularly, but they have to be read; hazards are marked, but they have to be looked out for. If they are met unexpectedly and at the last moment they become urgent crises which call for not only rapid but also carefully reasoned and well informed action. This is unlikely to be forthcoming, say, from an officer roused hastily from his slumber, who may also be generally inexperienced, unfamiliar with the region, and possibly preoccupied with personal concerns.

The United States used to lag behind Northern Europe in experience of the new style of shipping accidents, but their moment came over a five-week period in 1976–7 during which seven ships (five of them sailing under flags of convenience) were involved in collisions, groundings or explosions which led to the spillage of oil. The most conspicuous of these was the *Argo Merchant*, a 29,000-ton tanker with Greek officers and a 'mixed bunch' as a crew. The ship was *en route* from Venezuela to Salem, Massachusetts, with a cargo of heavy fuel oil, and a faulty gyro compass was being used for which certain corrections were allowed. The ship also had on board a magnetic compass which later it was decided to use, but it seems that no account was taken of the fact that the magnetic variation (the difference between true and magnetic north) alters from eight to fifteen degrees as one proceeds north along the eastern coast of the United States. These and other navigational errors caused the ship to sail inside the Nantucket light vessel, which was probably the cause of the echo noted on the radar screen by the master and the second officer, but since it was on the 'wrong' side – to the east, not west – they both assumed it was a tanker going the other way.

They were heading straight for dangerous shoal waters and in due course they grounded about half-way between the Nantucket light vessel and Nantucket Island, spilling 28,000 tons of oil. At the Liberian inquiry the accident was put down to bad navigation, but the level of incompetence was such – including no lookouts, no depth soundings – that there was a suspicion that the twenty-three-year-old vessel might have been stranded on purpose, since it was well insured.[10]

Eleven years after the *Torrey Canyon* disaster, almost to the day, but this time at the southern 'gatepost' to the English Channel, the *Amoco Cadiz* ran aground. In the intervening years the main progress had been in the size of ships, so that almost double the amount of oil was spilled – 223,000 tons of Arabian and Iranian crude oil. Sailing round Ushant in heavy but not exceptional conditions, the *Amoco Cadiz* lost the use of its rudder through a failure of the hydraulic control system. There happened to be a German ocean-going tug in the vicinity, the *Pacific*, which, hearing the distress call, immediately headed for the stricken ship. There then followed an interchange of messages which would have made for high farce had not the issues been so serious. While this enormous and helpless ship (1,096 feet (334 m) overall) drifted out of control towards the coast of Brittany, the Italian captain of the *Amoco Cadiz* haggled, mainly via intermediaries, with the German captain of the tug about whether taking a line on board from the tug would constitute a tow (since *Amoco Cadiz* still had engine power, only the control of direction having been lost) or salvage, and if the latter, what kind of contract might be involved. A towage contract would involve thousands of pounds; a salvage award could run into millions. The captain also had to communicate with the ship's owners in Chicago, which was difficult since it was still the middle of the night there.

The *Amoco Cadiz* lost the use of its rudder at 9.45 in the morning. By 2 p.m. the tug had a cable on board and had started towing, but soon after threatened to release the tow unless a Lloyd's open salvage agreement was signed. At this point the supertanker was 5.7 miles (10.5 km) from the shore. The French government, of course, knew nothing about this private altercation, which was causing an immediate and colossal threat to the coast of France and to the livelihoods of the people who lived there. The tow line was not released, it broke spontaneously. Then the *Amoco Cadiz* dropped anchor, but supertankers cannot just drop anchor and expect to stop like small boats can. The anchor flukes were torn off by the rocks, but the anchor did control the ship to some degree until the steam winch, which had been taking the strain off the anchor chain on board, blew up and let the chain run free. It was now past 8 p.m. and sea conditions were still bad. The *Pacific* by then had fixed another line to the stern of the tanker, now little more than a mile from the rocks. The tug requested the *Amoco Cadiz* to run her engines slow astern: the captain of the tanker insisted on running full ahead. The tug wanted to pull to port: the tanker wanted to be pulled to starboard.

This argument was short-lived as at 9.04 p.m. on 16 March 1978 the *Amoco Cadiz* ran aground at high water on the Rocks of Portsall, and the oil spillage began. Two hundred and forty-five miles (392 km) of coastline (far more if the convolutions of the Brittany coast are taken into consideration) were polluted with tenacious black oil. It was eventually cleared, but before the year was out the Standard Oil Company of Indiana and its subsidiaries were facing claims totalling 1.6 billion dollars.[10]

Being wise after the event, one might say that the *Amoco Cadiz* disaster could probably have been avoided if laden supertankers did not have to sail inshore around the dangerous coast of Brittany, if really powerful tugs (the *Pacific* was not really up to the job) could be stationed near the potential danger points, and most of all if machinery could be devised to aid stricken vessels, which would take account of human and environmental needs and not merely the financial interests of owners and insurers.

These accidents befalling aircraft and large ships have variously involved errors of judgement and decision-making, and problems of communication of one kind or another. Despite boards of inquiry it can be extremely difficult to discover what actually happened, let alone *why* it happened, or even the sequence of events which led up to the final catastrophe. The actual stories are complicated and often involve highly technical arguments, but one of the main problems preventing elucidation, especially of the human factors, is their enormous scale. So much personal suffering may be involved, and such immense sums of money, that quiet reflection on the human factors is impossible. In some of the examples given, human factors have been identified at the inquiries, sometimes not; and I do not wish to imply that human factors were necessarily central to all of them, although in some degree they may have been. Where obvious human error has not been an issue, individual decisions were nevertheless made under conditions of tremendous psychological strain; and even in an age where the importance of safety control systems is recognised, there will always be occasions when one man's decision taken in the heat of the moment will determine the fate of hundreds, even thousands of lives. It is important that this man is functioning under the best conditions that circumstances will allow.

In trying to make sense of the apparently erratic way people can act under certain circumstances, I prefer to look at the responses of individuals or of small groups where there are no large-scale economic or financial considerations. In fact, the greater part of this book will be devoted to individuals or small groups in a variety of difficult circumstances.

Here is a simple story of how things can go wrong on a small scale. One April evening, seven adults (four of them experienced sailors) set sail in a yacht from the Solent to Cherbourg. Fourteen hours later, although weather conditions remained moderate throughout, they sent up the red distress flare, as they were incapable of handling the boat.

At 6.15 p.m. they set off in light winds and rain, and with 'visibility very poor'. No written log or track on the chart was kept at this stage. There were also 'fumes' from the engine which they had used to clear the Solent. Once out to sea the wind freshened and they began to keep a written log. At forty-five minutes past midnight they altered course to pass astern of a ship, and the boom inadvertently slammed over in a gybe, splitting the mainsail right across. As the boom was unsupported it fell down on deck. By this time the crew were already cold, tired and seasick. They had a new mainsail on board but they did not set it. They decided to abandon their cruise and sail for home, but they did not record their position at the time of the mishap.

At 6 a.m., while off the south-east coast of the Isle of Wight, they considered setting the new mainsail but for some reason did not get round to doing it. Therefore, when by 7 a.m. they rounded the eastern end of the Isle of Wight and met the full wind with tide against them, they found they could not sail with headsail alone. Nor could they start the engine as the battery was flat – which they had recognised during the night as their navigation lights would not work. They attempted to set a storm sail, but these able-bodied and experienced men were unable to manage it; the cold, wet and seasickness had weakened them too much. They had eaten no food all night.

Shortly afterwards they sent up the distress flares and made a distress call on their radio. An hour and a half later a submarine, of all things, arrived and offered assistance, but it was the local lifeboat that towed them in.

This little story illustrates how capable people in an adequately equipped boat can rapidly become reduced physically and mentally by really quite modest adverse circumstances, to the point where they collectively fail to take elementary precautions. The only fault subsequently found in the boat was that one of the batteries was not holding its charge. The fumes were not due to any engine defect; the burning off of surface oil and fresh paintwork from the recently refitted engine seemed the most likely explanation.

2

Working Environments

Some working environments are physically so hard that survival is always an immediate consideration; others will be severe only intermittently; and there are many which in the ordinary way are completely comfortable. In all these we assume that there is a task to be performed, and a fairly special task at that, one in which there is personal investment as well as some degree of motivation to succeed.

The selection of environments for study has to be somewhat arbitrary. My choice has been determined by personal interest and experience, by the amount of information available and by the general lessons which can be learned. The main examples of behaviour in natural environments come from the sea, mountains at high altitude and polar regions. What could be called technological environments are represented by the experiences of pilots, train drivers and motorists. By way of contrast a third area of activity has been included – positions of authority held by leaders and decision-makers.

Small boats on the ocean
Conditions on the ocean can be tranquil and delightful, but the small-boat sailor always lives with apprehension of the kind of 'knock down' that Dr David Lewis described on 29 November 1972 during his circumnavigation of the Antarctic continent:

> Veritable cascades of white water were now thundering past on either side, more like breakers monstrously enlarged to perhaps forty-five feet, crashing down on a surf beach. Sooner or later one must burst fairly over us. What then?
>
> I wedged myself more securely on the lee bunk, clutching the tiller lines, my stomach hollow with fear . . .

My heart stopped. My whole world reared up, plucked by an irresistible force, to spin through giddy darkness, then to smash down into daylight again . . .

Ice Bird had been rolled completely over to starboard through a full 360 degrees and had righted herself thanks to her heavy lead keel – all in about a second. In that one second the snug cabin had become a shambles.

. . . I stumbled over rolling cans, felt the parallel rules crunched underfoot and pushed aside the flotsam of clothes, mattresses, sleeping bag, splintered wood fragments and charts . . .

Sure enough the lower seven feet of the mast leaned drunkenly over the starboard bow and the top twenty-nine feet tilted steeply across the ruptured guard wires and far down into the water, pounding and screeching as the hulk wallowed . . .

Then I stumbled back aft to observe, incredulously, for the first time that eight feet of the starboard side of the raised cabin trunk had been dented in, longitudinally, as if by a steam hammer. A six-inch vertical split between the windows spurted water at every roll . . .

What unimaginable force could have done this to eight-inch steel? The answer was plain. Water.[1]

Not everyone suffers the extremes of the Southern Ocean, but even in the English Channel Ann Davison could write of being

. . . worn out by the bellowing assaults of the sea. One of the most subtle tortures and unrecognised contributory factors to fatigue on a small ship in heavy weather (if it goes on long enough) is the utter inability to relax. For all the time muscles are in play, flexing, working, contracting, whether you are awake or asleep, upright, moving or sitting down. On they go, automatically, relentless, never letting up for an instant – until you could scream.[2]

Even in ordinary sea conditions, hours in the cockpit can leave the helmsman stiff and numb with cold, and soaked with salt water which penetrates everywhere, stinging the eyes and often causing painful sores on wrists and buttocks. Everything inside the boat eventually becomes saturated and will remain so for the duration of the voyage because the damp will not disappear until the salt can be rinsed out. Robin Knox-Johnston even used to trail his salty clothes in the sea so as to reduce their salt content merely to that of sea water.[3]

Proximity to land, icebergs, fog, merchant ships, oil rigs and other hazards require the sailor to remain awake and alert for prolonged periods, and if weather conditions are bad it is impossible to do more than grab occasional mouthfuls of food, that is, if he is not feeling too sick – when the thought of food will be abhorrent. Part of the sailor's environment is the boat itself; failure of gear or structural damage in bad sea conditions further increases the strain. Nor are things much better when it is flat calm. For many highly motivated and energetic men, forced inactivity can generate more acute distress and frustration than fighting for survival; but, storm or calm, an invariable factor affecting the singlehanded sailor is isolation.

The physical and psychological factors form the background against which he has to function. He must sail his boat across miles of ocean, and handle it intelligently. He must make numerous careful and rapid judgements about how much sail to set, how the boat should be headed in relation to the wind, and what to do in a variety of crises. He must navigate – psychologically, much the most complex task the yachtsman has to perform.

Descriptions of conditions at sea can make it sound so unpleasant that one may wonder why anyone ever sails on the ocean at all. But people do, and in very large numbers. Bad conditions are emphasised here because they may prevail for prolonged periods during which the sailor has to go on functioning effectively.

Large ships

The bigger the ship the more comfortable the ride, until in the very largest, one is hardly aware of being at sea at all. The bridge, the control centre of a large ship, looks to the uninitiated more like the interior of a power station or an air traffic control tower, where all around are dials, visual display screens and computer terminals. The predominant task in such an environment is to monitor the function of a complex system, and this requires a sustained high level of vigilance.

So much of the navigation on the high seas and of routine ship control is automatic that there is relatively little for the small crew to do, so an overriding problem can be boredom. From fifty feet up, the feeling of relatedness with the ocean, which means so much to small-boat sailors, is lost: it is more like being marooned at the top of a high-rise apartment block for several weeks at a time. Family groups may be together on board and the food can be excellent, but nothing can quite overcome the monotony. Because of the enormous costs at sea and in port, time schedules are vital. They hang implicitly over the captain throughout every voyage, and may tempt him to take short cuts, delay maintenance or overlook hints of mechanical failure in order not to miss a tide or a rendezvous at a terminal.

In 1980 there were about seven hundred ships like the *Amoco Cadiz* with a dead weight of 200,000 tons or over, and about a hundred of these are in the 300,000-tons class – the ultra-large crude carriers: it can be convenient on board them to use a bicycle when visiting the bow from the living quarters at the stern.

Under water

Diving is one of the most dangerous of the non-combatant occupations, but it can bring great rewards to the adventurous. There are wrecks to be explored, but a good deal of the work is on underwater structures such as oil rigs which may be in inhospitable regions like the North Sea. This contrasts sharply with the holiday image of scuba (self-contained underwater breathing apparatus)-diving in turquoise waters, observing brightly coloured fish.

At a depth of 200 feet (60 m), even off the coast of southern California, little sunlight filters down and the abundant marine life, as well as any silt stirred up from the bottom, further reduces visibility. The temperature will range around 50°F (10°C), which is debilitatingly cold, and the pressure will be about six times atmospheric. There may also be venomous marine creatures which can administer painful and almost incapacitating stings through a diver's clothing.[4]

Moving around under water can present problems, because visual perception and spatial orientation can be severely distorted, so that the diver can fail to realise which way up he is and can swim straight down while intending to return to the surface.[5] Any disturbance of the gas supply will aggravate these problems by generating anxiety and by producing the direct physiological effects of oxygen deprivation. At any depth the breathing gases must be delivered at a pressure equal to that of the surrounding water, and that necessitates the addition of inert gases such as helium and nitrogen which can produce effects similar to those of oxygen lack. According to their temperaments, divers speak of the 'raptures of the deep' or the 'narks' to describe the kind of euphoria and overconfidence that are associated with the use of these gases, and which can lead to them trying to remove their breathing apparatus and to lose sense of time and spatial orientation.[6]

Submarines in the nuclear age involve a hundred or so men immured together for weeks or months at a time, with every possible physical comfort but with an ever-present tension that comes from their vulnerability, not to mention their political significance.[7,8]

While everything is functioning well, they are merely a totally enclosed isolated group (Chapter 5) with a particularly boring routine. If anything really serious goes wrong there is probably nothing much that anyone can do to save them.

Aircraft

Piloting an aircraft is intensely enjoyable; it also routinely generates more powerful anxiety reactions than any other working activity, apart from space flight.

Although in many ways it is an adventurous occupation, because of the large numbers of aircraft about and the inherent risks of flying, rules and procedures have been evolved for every aspect. Elaborate checking routines are carried out before each flight, and even on a short hop there may be many predetermined changes of course in order to remain within meticulously defined air corridors. In the air, and even more just before landing, continual checks must be made. The crew must have the temperament to maintain these repetitive routines without becoming careless, but they must not become automatons. The one chance in ten thousand crisis, which an individual pilot might meet only once in three lifetimes, demands the ability to make rapid decisions and to act with resolution according to his own interpretation of events: the rule book cannot help here.

The complexity of aircraft engines demands many monitoring devices – usually four times over. Navigation equipment fills the rest of the available space in the cockpit. But this is not all. In the interests of safety, automatic warnings – visual, auditory, or involving some physical movement – will signal the malfunction of any system, a navigational error, or a deviation on the part of the pilot from approved handling procedures. The result is a bewildering array of knobs, dials, lights, screens and levers, so that a pilot switching from one aircraft to another has to undergo a familiarisation programme with the new cockpit layout. (In a small way the same is happening with the more expensive new cars, which have warning lights for more and more functions.) At accident inquiries suggestions are often made for yet more warning devices or for the rearrangement of instruments or controls.

On the longer flights, especially those in west-easterly directions, the flight crew are crossing time zones, with the result that body rhythms become disturbed. It is not always realistic to maintain people abroad in a 'time-free' environment, that is, eating and sleeping according to their home time, and flight crews suffer accordingly.

Home life is fragmented. Not only are wives alone for much of the time, but when the men return they may be tired and 'jet-lagged' and so be little company for their families. They may not feel like sex either, and the wives are left wondering whether that is because of fatigue or because of the air stewardesses whose attractions they regularly see displayed on posters or in colour magazines. Divorce rates for pilots are high, and – this may be another index of the strain under which they live – they have an increased likelihood of dying in accidents on the ground, especially in car crashes.[9]

The modern airline pilot enjoys high status and high income; his work is demanding, irregular and sometimes dangerous. Nevertheless he seldom wants to give it up, even when perhaps he should. There is a kind of emotional attachment to flying, plus the excitement of change, which make land-based occupations seem dull by comparison. Therefore, as with any job which confers a powerful identity, air crews can sometimes make out that they are fitter than they really are, and so pose a problem for airline medical officers who want to meet the needs of the travelling public as well as those of the men and women who will fly them.

Air traffic control

Air traffic controllers are taken for granted until there is an accident or a near miss, when they become potential scapegoats in the controversies generated by the media or in delicate international rivalries. They have an unenviable task, as air traffic is increasing but runway capacity, on the whole, is not.

Their main duties concern the separation of aircraft, flow management, the monitoring of traffic, and responding to requests from pilots. They must observe the aircraft directly, or monitor their blips on radar or on a computer-generated plan view display, and they must operate the related controls.[10] Their work is highly automated but the very systems which make flying relatively safe, and without which no large airport could operate at all, also lead to secondary problems. Instead of controlling each aircraft directly, the air traffic controller is monitoring the function of machines, but he must be sufficiently in touch with what is going on to be able to take over effectively at a moment's notice if something unexpected occurs. Thus he must be able to switch rapidly from a possible state of boredom and inattention to one of impeccable concentration.

Air traffic controllers have accreted quite a literature concerning their proneness to 'stress-related' conditions such as high blood pressure, peptic ulcers and diabetes,[11,12] hence the familiar joke about the family-size box of antacid tablets left out on the counter in many control towers. One of the causes of the problems is simply information overload.

However efficient the air traffic controllers and the flight crews may be in their own right, the interrelationship between them is crucial. The official language for communication is English, so the Egyptian pilot has to speak to the Brazilian air traffic controller in a language foreign to both of them, although the native language will be used for domestic flights. Communications are of course very stereotyped and procedures formalised, but when something unforeseen happens so that the stock phrases and procedures cannot be used, the scope for error increases dramatically.

Spaceflight

Getting up into space and coming down again after a few days calls for prodigious physical and psychological stamina, and has led to a new breed of super-stable person. The astronaut, or cosmonaut, has a physiology that can withstand the physical stresses and not respond catastrophically to high anxiety. Space itself, or the surface of the moon, does not seem to be an inherently attractive environment; the fascination is mainly that of being there at all. Space is on a par with the bottom of the ocean, as a totally impossible environment for humans without very special clothing and equipment. The low pressure would cause the body's blood to boil within seconds, because the gases contained in the blood would come out of solution and appear as bubbles. There is constant bombardment by high-energy particles of various kinds with essentially unknown effects. Weightlessness causes the calcium to disappear from the bones (as does prolonged recumbency in illness when there is no weight on the legs) and doubtless other consequences as well, which will only emerge with the development of long-range spaceflight.[13]

The principal factors affecting astronauts are: tremendous acceleration and deceleration forces, dangers at the beginning and end of flights, living in a confined space, monitoring instruments and carrying out numerous observations; and, on longer flights, boredom, anxiety about the functioning of the vehicle, distress about separation from families, and living in an isolated group.

Trains

The train driver's job, though just as important, is altogether simpler than the pilot's. His machine travels in one dimension instead of three, his life is much more regular, he remains in his own country and he will never have to deal with anything as complex as the routine landing of a large aircraft. Because of this greater simplicity, because rail accidents are less likely to kill the major witness and because they are all investigated, it should be possible, in theory, to study the human errors very thoroughly.

The train driver's scope for decision-making has diminished with the advent of safety warning devices and automatic braking systems, so the skills of train driving are above all skills of timing. The driver is guided along his track by a series of external signals, which almost always will appear as expected. He must know what these are, know the gradients of the track and his speed, and when to apply power or brakes according to the load and gradient. Most train accidents involving driver error result from failure to brake sufficiently or in time, or from running at speeds greater than conditions will allow.

Motor cars

Cars are everybody's business, so that each one of us that ventures anywhere near a road has a predictable chance of being run over or involved in a crash. In terms of numbers the United States probably leads the world, with sixteen million motor vehicle accidents in 1975, killing 8,600 pedestrians and 37,400 passengers and drivers, and leaving nearly two million seriously injured. Road accidents are the principal cause of death for Americans under the age of forty and the principal cause of accidents for all ages. More Americans are killed *each year* on the roads than in the ten years of the Vietnam war. All the same, the *rate* for accidents in the United States is not as high as in some places: 361 fatalities for every million vehicle-miles as compared with 7,500 in Kenya.[14] Thus road accidents are collectively much more serious than air crashes, but since they occur in a steady 'stream' rather than as occasional 'floods', searching inquiries are never held, nor do they attract as much research attention as they deserve.

People buy cars and motor cycles for all kinds of reasons beyond those overtly stated. Associations with elegance, power and sexuality are claimed,[15,16] and the majority of car manufacturers are evidently more influenced by these considerations than by a desire to produce the safest possible vehicle, although there are some notable exceptions to this generalisation. Nevertheless, the interior of most cars is a pretty satisfactory working environment.

Ideally, the motorist should be scanning the whole 360° around the car during all of every journey, as other vehicles or road hazards can appear from any direction at any time. Even with wide-angle mirrors this ideal can seldom be achieved, so that there will always be blind spots, and the field can further be diminished when rain, snow, dust or fog obscure the view.

Extremely complex calculations have to be made almost instantaneously: the speed, direction and likely changes of direction of other vehicles have to be estimated, as well as the distances between vehicles. As many as ten vehicles could easily be involved in these computations. Bearing in mind that at the moderate speed of 60 miles per hour the car covers 88 feet every second (at 100 kph, and 28 m per sec.) and that the slightest contact between vehicles can lead to disaster, it is surprising how efficiently the human brain functions and that accidents are not even more common than they are.

Good visibility, clearly written and illuminated road signs, well laid out roads with distinctly painted edges, and other vehicles obeying the rules and giving proper signals, are all vital to safe motoring. Inside the car there may be distracting passengers, such as fractious children or someone choosing a car journey for a domestic row. The radio may be troublesome but can also soothe the harassed or aggressive driver so that he reduces speed a little. Too often the driver brings his latest row with him, whether it is before leaving home in the morning or the office in the evening or after the last business encounter. Thus motoring can become either a relaxation or a way of working off anxieties or aggression – and this may be more likely if the vehicle in question is endowed (unconsciously maybe) by its owner with attributes which make it possible in fantasy to transcend the limitations of mundane daily existence.

The driver also needs to be rested to be efficient, to be free of the influence of alcohol or drugs of any kind, to have good visual acuity for daytime and night-time levels of illumination and for moving as well as static objects, and good peripheral vision (abilities not normally tested for); he must have some understanding of how a car works and be familiar with the road, but not so familiar that he becomes overconfident and careless.

Mountains at high altitude

High altitude climbing can bring moments of ecstasy and well-being alternating with terror and appalling discomfort, and these changes can occur even more rapidly than they do at sea.

Rock climbing demands physical strength, an ability to tolerate heights, technical expertise not only in climbing but in handling and keeping control of ropes and associated hardware, and the ability to work things out calmly while in conditions of great personal danger.

The direct route up the north face of the Eiger in winter is just about the ultimate in rock climbing. Dougal Haston and his companions pioneered this route, and here is part of his account of the final stages of that historic climb.

Sigi and Roland kept shifting uncomfortably on their stance. They could not even take their crampons off. A vague greyness was the signal of day. Staying on the bivouac hadn't been too easy but preparing to leave it was really unpleasant. My gloves and gaiters were frozen solid. My numb fingers pulled ineffectually on the crampon straps. To add to my troubles, one of the straps broke. I then had painfully to extract a cord from my ice-coated rucksack and fix it to the crampons. This simple manoeuvre took over an hour.

Slowly my mind began to face up to the day. I started painfully prusiking up [method of climbing fixed ropes] the ropes again. I hadn't thought it possible that the storm could get worse, but somehow nature managed to drag up her last reserves and throw them at the five miserable figures fighting for fulfilment of a dream. Half-way up the first rope my fingers started to freeze. There was nothing I could do to stop it. The hostile forces were insidiously beginning to win. I pulled off my gloves at the stance and was confronted with ten white wooden objects . . .

The next hour was one of the most testing of my climbing career. It was 60° water-ice. The steps of the previous rope had been wiped out. I had no axe or hammer. My left crampon was wildly askew on my boot. The right one was loose. Armed with one dagger ice-peg, I moved off the stance. The wind was crashing the snow into my face with such force that it stuck in huge masses on my eyelids making it impossible to see ahead. My movements were cautious and groping. I would search around for traces of a step, scrape it out, then make a breath-holding move up on my wobbly crampons. The pitch went on and on and I became increasingly aware of the extremeness of the situation. Sigi and Roland were on a very poor belay. There just could not be any question of falling. Yet in a strange way I was enjoying this test. I knew the odds were stacked with the house, but I felt in perfect control. There was no panic, only well-planned movement.[17]

When it comes to high altitude climbing, as in the Himalayas, all the skills of rock climbing are called for, plus a few others as well. Coping with altitude is the most important of these. Around 11,000 feet (3,350 m) the effects will be apparent in the majority of those normally living at sea level, and at lower levels in some if the ascent has been rapid. Many Peruvians work in mines at 19,000 feet (5,800 m), but they prefer to return to a lower level to sleep. Above 22,000 feet (6,700 m) Himalayan climbers generally climb and sleep using oxygen, although certain individuals in earlier expeditions seemed to manage at higher altitudes than these without it, the heavy old-fashioned equipment may have been an even greater inconvenience than the lack of oxygen.

Temperature generally decreases with altitude, but it is the winds on high mountains that bring the effective temperature right down. Temperatures of $-35°C$ ($-30°F$) are common on Everest, but with a wind of only 15 mph (24 kph) the effective temperature drops to $-50°C$ ($-60°F$). At such levels exposed fingers will become frostbitten in minutes and will freeze hard on to any metal that they touch, but it is not possible to rock climb (as was required on the upper part of the south-west face of Everest) or to handle the special hardware needed, while the hands are fully protected.

The large and spectacular Himalayan expeditions of recent years can give an impression of climbing as a kind of communal activity. Thus Reinhold Messner's solo ascent of Everest, and without oxygen too, can seem quite exceptional, which of course it is, but smaller expeditions to scale the higher Himalayan peaks are becoming commoner. Under normal circumstances no climber climbs on his own for much of the time because he is in a close relationship with the man at the other end of the rope. However, the mountains are so large and the snowy terrain at times so featureless, that two men can almost be regarded as one when considering the effects of isolation.

Polar regions

Polar exploration is at once the cleanest and most isolated way of having a bad time which has been devised. It is the only form of adventure in which you put on your clothes at Michaelmas and keep them on until Christmas, and, save for a layer of the natural grease of the body, find them as clean as though they were new. It is more lonely than London, more secluded than any monastery, and the post comes but once a year. As men will compare the [wartime] hardships of France, Palestine, or Mesopotamia, so it would be interesting to contrast the rival claims of the Antarctic as a medium of discomfort. A member of Campbell's [a member of Scott's expedition] party tells me that the trenches at Ypres were a comparative picnic. But until somebody can evolve a standard of endurance I am unable to see how it can be done. Take it all in all, I do not believe anybody on earth has a worse time than an Emperor penguin.[18]

This account by Apsley Cherry-Garrard dates from Scott's Antarctic expedition of 1910–13. These early experiences can be very illuminating about an individual's responses to a harsh environment. The modern polar resident or traveller is materially so well equipped that it is only when something goes wrong that he is confronted with the full ferocity of his surroundings.

For sheer misery from cold, I doubt if anything can compare with Cherry-Garrard's description of what he called 'the weirdest bird's-nesting expedition that has ever been or will be'. He and two others set off in the middle of the Antarctic winter to search for emperor penguins' eggs. They regularly endured temperatures of −60°F (−50°C), which sometimes fell to as low as −77°F (−60°C). He went out of his tent one morning, raised his head to look around, and found himself frozen into that position for the rest of the day. 'From time to time, he wrote, 'we all took care to bend into sledge-pulling position before being frozen in.' At night it took them an hour to kick and thaw their way into frozen sleeping bags, where they forced themselves to stay for seven miserable shivering hours. On the other hand, it is quite possible to sunbathe naked at temperatures of −40°F (−40°C) when there is no wind.

The unique attribute of the polar environment, which depends on its high latitude, is the extremes of light and dark. During the short autumn the hours of darkness grow longer and longer until the sun finally disappears altogether.

> ... the coming of the polar night is not the spectacular rush that some imagine it to be. The day is not abruptly walled off: the night does not drop suddenly. Rather, the effect is a gradual accumulation, like that of an infinitely prolonged tide. Each day the darkness, which is the tide, washes in a little farther and stays a little longer; each time the day, which is a beach, contracts a little more, until at last it is covered ... The going of day is a gradual process, modulated by the intervention of twilight. You look up, and it is gone. But not completely. Long after the horizon has interposed itself, the sun continues to cast up a pale and dwindling imitation of the day. You can trace its progress by the glow thrown up as it makes its round just below the horizon.[19]

Admiral Richard Byrd, a daring American aeronautical explorer of both polar regions, wrote this in April 1934 as he settled down to spend a winter in the Antarctic entirely alone. He was in a hut 600 miles (960 km) from the South Pole and 123 miles (197 km) from his base, where he had volunteered to go and man a weather observation post.

Nowadays the Antarctic continent is ringed with observation stations of various kinds. Although these may have every comfort that the different countries can provide, the residents still have to cope with living in relatively isolated groups through the four months of winter darkness. The problems are those of human relationships, as Roger Banks described in 1962:

> If you are lively and gay, try living with someone who never responds to your jokes. If on the contrary, you are not, try living with people who make endless witty allusions above your head. If you are a non-smoker, try sharing a double bunk with somebody who smokes in bed and drops endless stubs and a rain of ash on your pillow. If you smoke heavily, on the other hand, live with someone fussing about it continually. If you take even an occasional bath, wake up continually to someone treading on your bunk in socks which you know they haven't removed in weeks. Do it unremittingly month after month, shut up in a tiny hut in the worst possible weather, then say you are neither intolerant nor snobbish.[20]

The winter routine is also monotonous, engendering a general intellectual inertia, poor concentration and absent-mindedness. Sleeplessness, known as 'big eye', is common; so also is depression, and suicide attempts are not infrequent.

In the circles of power – leaders and decison-makers

This is something of a sidestep from physical hardship to conditions of material luxury where people appear to be pampered and protected but yet in the end work under considerably greater strain than practically anyone. These are the leaders and decision-makers.

Doctors daily have to make decisons which can fundamentally alter the course of a person's life. The head teacher of a school, or the manager of a factory, a power station or a large chemical plant, for example, can all make decisions which may affect, directly or indirectly through the social consequences of management decisions, whole communities and neighbourhoods. In times of conflict, generals can affect the lives of even greater numbers, and at the top of the tree, political leaders may be promoting policies which will determine the fate of whole countries or of millions of people.

The greater scrutiny of the media and the prompt publication of political diaries and memoirs, as well as intimate revelations by doctors and others of the health of those in high office, should dispel the illusion that our leaders determine our fate as a result of cool decisions made after painstaking consideration of all the relevant facts. All too often major decisions are taken hurriedly, under great pressure from opponents, and always with the awareness that each decision is part of a larger chess game of power politics, with all kinds of interests needing to be satisfied.

The demands made on civil and military leaders and holders of high office are quite simply intolerable. Whether they seize power by force or by democratic election, they have to work under conditions which will break down practically all of them in time. Yet there are exceptions, remarkable and diverse men who have remained in power for unusually long periods, such as Stalin, Mao Tse-tung and Fidel Castro; elected leaders such as Franklin Roosevelt and, bearing in mind his total time as prime minister, possibly also Harold Wilson.

Without being drawn into the trap of listing the qualities required of a good leader, it is clear that in modern 'jet-age politics' quite extraordinary physical and mental qualities are called for. A leader requires a redoubtable physique that can tolerate broken routines, irregular meals and crossing time zones without any apparent loss of mental efficiency. Such people ordinarily often need only three or four hours' sleep a night, which greatly extends what they can accomplish in one day. They also must possess that charisma – easily recognisable but hard to define – which enables them to inspire others to work for them and to adopt their ideas. Such leaders may also possess outstanding intellectual gifts, so that high positions of responsibility seem quite natural to them. Others, unfortunately, occupy high positions because of driving ambition; this activates them and fuels their great energy, but it is all-important to understand what lies at the root of their ambition – be it simple power or a desire to improve the lot of the underprivileged. There may, for instance, be varying degrees of paranoia. A certain suspicion of the motives of others can have great survival value in a competitive society, but when suspicion dominates and when plots are perceived all around, then maintaining one's position takes priority over the task of ruling or managing, as was probably the case with Stalin in his later years.

Most of the British prime ministers in this century, *while in office*, have had serious identifiable physical diseases which are quite likely to have affected their efficiency, in particular their decision-making ability. Most notable in this respect was Ramsay MacDonald, who was prime minister during the 1931 financial crisis and depression. He suffered from a bladder infection (possibly due to stones or an enlarged prostate), from glaucoma which made reading difficult, and from a degree of dementia which would lead associates to make such remarks as: 'He [MacDonald] was already no longer in a mental and physical condition to be capable of the continuing and exacting responsibilities of high office', or 'He has lost his grip and moves from one vagueness to another.'[21] On one occasion MacDonald clasped his head and said: 'My brain is going.'[22] Politicians are unlucky, when they begin to fail, in having all their public utterances recorded verbatim. Company chairmen, senior civil servants, bishops, professors and the like, function more privately and so are spared having their ramblings and rantings publicly recorded.

Winston Churchill's latter years in office were clouded by the physical and psychological effects of his cerebral arterial degeneration, but for years before that he was blighted with periodical depressions which he called his 'black dog'. Anthony Eden, who followed him at No. 10, suffered badly from his gall bladder and subsequent bouts of high fever from bile duct inflammation. This debilitating condition, plus the effects of the stimulants and sedatives he was reported to be taking at the time, must have impaired his appreciation and response to the Suez crisis of 1956, if only by reducing the flexibility of his thinking. He fell back on earlier, almost stereotyped, attitudes towards dictators, which had served him well enough twenty years earlier but which were not relevant to the understanding of the aspirations of President Nasser.

Following a prostate operation necessitated by acute retention of urine, Harold Macmillan resigned abruptly in 1963, thereby throwing his Conservative party in temporary disarray. However, for some time before that he had been experiencing the effects of poor kidney function, which probably accounts for these retrospective comments of his about his state of health during his latter months in office: 'I felt nervous, uneasy and with a curious lack of grip, combined with a tendency to drowsiness at inconvenient moments. This I put down to fatigue and did little about it.'[22]

The United States has fared little better. Woodrow Wilson suffered illnesses throughout his life, but during his last year and a half of office he was totally incapacitated by a stroke, and the presidency seems to have been maintained by his wife, his doctor and his secretary. Franklin Roosevelt was crippled with polio a decade before he was elected president, and he was an ailing man through much of the Second World War. During his disastrous negotiations with Stalin at Yalta he was dying, succumbing gradually to the effects of heart disease, high blood pressure and possibly – although never officially confirmed – malignant melanoma. Eisenhower suffered intermittently from coronary artery disease, small bowel obstruction (regional ileitis) requiring surgery, and spasm or thrombosis of the cerebral blood vessels, causing a stroke with the attendant physical incapacity (temporary) and quite likely with a significant degree of intellectual impairment. During his last year in office he collapsed in Kabul, in Afghanistan, which is at 6,000 feet (1,800 m), but his secret service aide had brought along an oxygen cylinder just in case.

John F. Kennedy's famous back trouble has been claimed to have been due variously to football and to war injuries, but others maintain it was due to a congenital defect carefully kept secret.[23] Certainly his adrenal insufficiency (Addison's disease) was a long-guarded secret despite the conspicuousness of some of the complications of treatment, such as the puffy moon face and possibly his continued youthful appearance. He was dependent on regular steroid injections throughout his presidency and for a good long time before, when the therapeutic agents (only available since about 1948) were less well developed and more likely to cause disturbances of mood and thought processes. There is also evidence that from time to time he used amphetamines, which can induce a beguiling sense of superior power. Lyndon Johnson had a severe coronary thrombosis years before assuming office. He had no further trouble with his heart while at the White House, but during his second term he was regarded by some as suffering from paranoid delusions.

Two years elapsed between the Watergate break-in and President Nixon's final resignation. It must have been an intolerable burden for the man who had his finger on the button, as we say, but even before that there had been signs of psychological strain, of his appearing depressed or incoherent in public, not to mention his tendency to develop clots in his veins, possibly at times of particular crisis.[22]

Despite all their pathology, these leaders were outstanding, and while they laboured with ailments of varying severity they did initiate important legislation. The crucial question, and the one which relates to the main theme of this book, lies in their ability to make reliable decisions; but it is very difficult to relate a given decision (subsequently regarded as bad, although possibly quite reasonable at the time in the light of the available information) to a leader's ill health. However, it is highly unlikely that Roosevelt would have been so blind to Stalin's motives before the beginning of his final decline around 1944, or Anthony Eden so hopelessly wrong in his interpretation of the background to the Suez crisis if he had not been suffering from disabling gall bladder disease and feeling the need for amphetamines to keep himself going. Roosevelt never seemed to grasp that Stalin was a totally implacable and unscrupulous tyrant and not a basically kind generous man who could be won over with demonstrations of good will. Eden, similarly, could never realise that Nasser was a potential friend and not another Hitler, and that the

British Empire no longer had effective sway over other nations. Both these men were unable to modify their preconceptions in the light of current information: their ailments had probably rendered them less flexible than they might otherwise have been. These and other civil and military leaders have been alarmingly scrutinised by Hugh L'Etang in his book *Fit to Lead?*,[22,24] which leaves the reader with the impression that leaders of all kinds, even if they are fit in mind and body when they assume office, are seldom so by the time they relinquish it.

It is all rather absurd. We choose our leaders, we hope, with great care, and then subject them to working conditions that are bound to wear them out before their time. While in office they are under constant attack, overt and covert; they have to travel the world, crossing the time zones and appearing before television cameras immediately on arrival in a foreign country, to answer complex questions when their body rhythms may be at their lowest ebb. They must manage with minimal sleep, and eat and manifestly 'enjoy' all manner of unfamiliar food and drink. They must keep going despite personal tragedies, and will be expected to make major decisions even while in hospital awaiting an operation. All this applies not only to the person at the top but to all those in precarious positions of authority and power.

It is of rather dubious value, though tempting, to compare such diverse groups as adventurers into the natural environment with political and military leaders. Both are exposed to physical and psychological strains of a high order, but I suspect that those afflicting leaders are usually more damaging to the human system.

The principal factors affecting leaders are constant demands from supporters and assaults from opponents throughout their terms of office, disruption of all regular habits including rest periods, crossing time zones, threats to life, frequent lack of a confidant sufficiently knowledgeable to be a support without being a threat.

3

Extreme Predicaments

The unsuspecting traveller is caught in an earthquake, a housing estate is inundated by floodwater, a school building collapses, a tower office block catches fire, an airline passenger is taken hostage by a group of terrorists, a suspected person is arrested in the street and subsequently interrogated and tortured, another suspect finds himself before a firing squad. Most of the examples in this chapter are of ordinary people who did not seek out danger or adventure in the first place, but who, often with very little warning, found themselves pressed to their very limits, and beyond.

Major disasters – natural and man-made

A major disaster obliterates just about everything that gives people their identity and their lives meaning. In seconds an earthquake can totally alter the landscape of a lifetime. Floods and high winds can devastate whole communities and vast tracts of land. Famine and epidemics decimate populations which may subsequently never come together again. Pollution from the accidental or deliberate release of toxic chemicals can ravage crops and wildlife, injure adults, children and unborn babies, and leave large areas unusable for years.

Increasingly, there is a human hand in disasters. A flood may be the consequence of neglected sea walls, or, in the case of Buffalo Creek in West Virginia, of an inadequate dam at the head of a valley which, as had been predicted, gave way in early 1972 and wiped out the community of miners and their families who lived below it.[1,2] Famines and epidemics so often follow in the wake of wars, as populations flee from good land which is being destroyed or are so dislocated by conflict that they cease to be able to take the simplest measures to care for themselves and their families.

The common factor in all disasters is the total disruption – often sudden and unexpected – of everything familiar, together with the loss of loved ones and material possessions. Daily routine is impossible and now irrelevant, except that the need for food and shelter becomes more intense. There may be no one the survivor can recognise, the house may have vanished and the rest of the family with it, all landmarks obliterated. With such a total annihilation of reference points, it is not surprising that survivors tend to wander around aimlessly in a state of shock, not even taking trouble to look for food or to protect themselves from common dangers.

Every month there is a major natural disaster somewhere in the world. Mostly they afflict the poorer countries and are on a scale which Westerners find hard to imagine, even if they want to. I will give one example of a disaster that would not have earned more than five lines in a newspaper if it had occurred in Bangladesh but which made world news because it affected people in England (and also in Holland). This was the sea flooding in the winter of 1953 in which 307 lives were lost on the east coast of England, and which showed how easily the life of the average affluent Westerner can be disrupted owing to our total dependence on external services for fuel and food.

Here is how one mother of eight-year-old twins described her experience on 31 January. It was a stormy night but there was absolutely no warning about what was to come:

> We were both awakened by a terrific crash, which we thought must be our T.V. aerial coming down, but in matter of fact, it was our front door bursting open with the force of the water. We automatically switched on our bed light, which did not come on. We dashed out of bed to the top of the stairs; there was water gushing and swirling round our kitchen, with pots and pans clattering round. Of course our only thought was for the children, so we went into the water without a moment's hesitation in our night attire, and the water was up to my armpits immediately. My husband disappeared into our daughter's room, while I tried to get to the boy. He had a sliding door which was jammed tight; I just could not move it. I kept calling to him, but I could not hear what he was saying owing to the noise. The water dragged me into another room, but I managed to pull myself back again. After what seemed an age, my husband brought our daughter out and stood her on the dresser. He was a long time getting her because a very large chest

of drawers had fallen over, and he had his foot trapped. I managed to get her on the stairs and take her to our bedroom. Then my husband with a superhuman effort managed to force our son's door open and brought him up.

My husband paced the room, and when he looked out of the back window he saw that a large bungalow had lifted completely off its foundations, and he feared it might hit our bungalow. We felt extremely dry in the mouth and sipped some water from the hot water bottle out of a vase. When I looked out of the window, the moon was shining and I could see the water rapidly getting higher up the bungalow opposite, and there was water as far as you could see, and I thought we could never get out of it alive, so I told the children to pray with me and ask God to save us.[3]

Earthquakes, volcanoes, hurricanes, tornadoes, tropical cyclones and other totally unpreventable natural disasters occur in regions prone to these afflictions for geological or climatic reasons. For the rest of the world, especially the industrialised West, the greater threat is from the ill effects of technology.[4] If the BEA Trident (p. 11) had crashed three or four hundred yards further on it would have landed in the centre of Staines, Middlesex, causing a really massive social and economic disaster.

The terrible technological disaster has not yet happened, but it will. Buildings collapse regularly, often because of materials or constructional methods which are either not properly understood or else treated casually in order to save costs in building or maintenance.[5] High buildings may catch fire, as happened to the Joelma office block in São Paulo, Brazil, in 1974, where 227 out of the eight hundred employees died in the blaze. The fire engine ladders could only reach to the fourteenth of the twenty-five floors, and the roof was too fragile to allow helicopters to land.[6] On the Isle of Man, pressure was put on the builders to have the Summerlands Leisure Centre open in time for the 1971 season. For this and other reasons, many combustible materials were used, and there were also design flaws which aggravated the fire which destroyed the building two years later, killing fifty-five people.[7]

Potentially more serious is chemical pollution, and again we are still awaiting the massive conflagration. When a petrol road tanker with 5,000 gallons (23,000 l) on board skidded in the main street of the Bedfordshire village of Westoning in 1976 and exploded, ten shops in the village and several houses were destroyed, but luckily it was seven o'clock on a Saturday morning before the shoppers had arrived. There are many more lethal substances than petrol being transported on the roads and through towns. A tanker was in a slight collision in fog on the M6 motorway earlier the same year and its load of fuming sulphuric acid, called oleum, began to leak on to the road. A woman who went to investigate did not see the fumes because of the fog. She was overcome by the fumes, fell into the strong acid, and seems virtually to have been dissolved by it; at least there was no way subsequently of identifying the body.[8]

In 1974 an explosion at Flixborough in Lincolnshire of cyclohexane (used in the manufacture of nylon), from some faulty pipe work used to make a temporary connection, led to the deaths of twenty-eight men. Fortunately, again, it was a Saturday, when there were only seventy on site instead of the usual 550.[9] There was no such luck at Seveso in northern Italy. In 1976 dioxin leaked from the plant there, causing widespread and long-lasting pollution of the surrounding countryside, as well as, among the local population, chloracne (disfiguring skin eruptions) and possible cancers and genetic damage.[10] Dioxin had been used by the American forces in Vietnam as a defoliant some years before, and a higher than expected rate of certain cancers and congenital malformations had already been reported from the affected regions. Even so, it was not until eight days after the discharge of dioxin at Seveso that the authorities admitted the leakage.[11]

Far and away the worst possible catastrophes would be those involving nuclear energy. The safety record of nuclear power stations has been anything but reassuring, despite the official denials of danger. Mishaps with nuclear armed rockets are equally disturbing, not to mention the false alarms that have gone out about impending nuclear attack which could so easily provoke a real retaliatory strike. These accidents have nearly all been due to human errors, even though no effort and expense has been spared to try to eliminate human failure.

When it comes to the bomb itself, there are difficulties even in reacting intelligently to it. We are dealing with a scale of potential devastation and suffering which is quite beyond our powers of imagination. The effects of blast, heat and radiation can be described with the aid of maps indicating how many millions will be killed or merely badly burned, but we cannot comprehend the significance of the deaths of millions of people in a few minutes. It is hard enough even to imagine that a chunk of uranium no bigger than a medium-sized orange caused the deaths of 140,000 people at Hiroshima, and the later deaths of two or three times that number from radiation effects. When faced with the implications of nuclear war, we are in danger of responding to that which we cannot comprehend by denying its seriousness, lapsing into a helpless apathy, or even developing a vague admiration for bomb technology.[12]

Sudden captivity

Being taken hostage

Terrorist groups make the world headlines but most 'sieges' and hostage-taking episodes are domestic issues, with the people involved known to or related to the captor. The remainder are criminal or political, or the actions of cranks or the mentally sick. Money may be sought, or the release of certain people from prison, or the act may simply be designed to draw attention to a cause.

Between 1950 and 1972 over four hundred 'skyjackings' were reported.[13] To begin with they were nearly all successful; towards the end of this period they mostly failed, with a consequent reduction in frequency. Nevertheless, they provide good examples of captivity without warning.

The initial assault shocks people, especially if there has been shooting or bombing. Then there is a period of frightening uncertainty until they all settle down to wait. For wait they will, as the policy of most police and other forces is to 'play it cool'. These forces will stall for time, avoid taking up any definite position, negotiate interminably while they get to know the assailants. All the while the captives wait. The first crisis may come at the time when the aircraft should have reached its original destination. Some passengers will become agitated, fearing that they may never see their loved ones again, and will swap addresses in case they 'don't make it'.[14]

Conflicts may break out among the captives. For example, if there are Israeli passengers on a plane hijacked by an Arab group, the Israelis can become objects of suspicion, since they may be thought to be endangering the lives of the others. Sub-groups are likely to form, young children may become a source of irritation, and active men may feel guilty because of their inability to do anything to help themselves or others.

Food supplies, cigarettes, the presence of sick passengers, the young and the old, all become bargaining counters in the tedious negotiations between the captors and the outside world, and individual hostages may be shot from time to time to stress a point. After several days of this and of looking into the muzzles of loaded firearms and perhaps at sticks of (presumably real) explosive wired up ready for detonation, agitation steadily rises.

Hostages quite often form close relationships with their captors, a phenomenon now called the 'Stockholm effect'[15] after an incident in

Sweden where one of the female hostages fell in love with and married one of her captors.

Unexpected arrest

Unexpected arrest is a regular fact of life in totalitarian regimes, be they of the right or of the left. Terror can precede arrest, followed by blank disbelief when it actually happens, but once under arrest the mood changes again dramatically. Archbishop Anthony Bloom has described his arrest by the Gestapo while entering the Paris metro: 'I began to think very quickly, feel very intensely, and to be aware of the whole situation with a relief and a colourfulness which I had never before perceived, on the last steps of the Métro Étoile . . . I realised that I had no past, because the real past I had was the thing for which I should be shot.' He also realised that he had a future 'only to the extent to which you can foresee a minute before it happens, or an inch before you reach it, what will come next'.[16] Thus he was intensely alert and totally in the present, which presumably enabled him to function optimally – at any rate he lived to describe his experiences.

Solzhenitsyn, writing of arrest in his novel *The First Circle*, says: 'Their manners were a bit rough, but being arrested wasn't nearly so frightening as he had imagined. He even felt a certain sense of relief – no more need to fear, to resist, to think of a way out – it was like a pleasant numbness spreading through a wounded body.'[17] Less robust people may experience an initial panic in the face of the unknown, but this is likely to be replaced by a kind of shock that may last for hours or days; and the same kind of experience can follow a serious accident or any emotional shock, rendering the victim for a time totally helpless.

Concentration camps

There are many forms of harsh, arbitrary imprisonment without trial for those who either oppose a totalitarian regime or who are perceived as a threat to it. Sadly, the literature on such prisons is huge, and it continues to accumulate because these barbaric places still seem to multiply. Coercive detention is practised on the largest scale by the Russians, and has been majestically chronicled by Alexander Solzhenitsyn in *The Gulag Archipelago*.[18] In Soviet Russia the labour camps had for years been part of the background to the culture. The German concentration camps, on the other hand, were a totally new kind of horror following a totally new kind of regime in that highly developed society. I have, therefore, chosen here to use the Nazi concentration camps as examples. In the late 1930s ordinary people who opposed Hitler or who happened to belong to the wrong religious or cultural group were removed suddenly from their comfortable existence to the vilest horrors in the camps.

Curt Bondy was a professor of social psychology in Hamburg when he was caught up in the holocaust.

> In November, 1938, the Nazis carried out one of their big actions against the Jewish population in Germany. Nearly all synagogues in Germany were set on fire on one night, and tens of thousands of men between 18 and 65 years of age were taken to concentration camps. The pretext for these acts was the assassination of an officer of the German legation in Paris by a young Polish Jew.
>
> I was among those arrested and sent to Buchenwald. Mistreatment started at the railroad station in Weimar. We were driven into an underpass where stormtroopers senselessly cudgeled the defenseless mass with all kinds of instruments. The old men, not being able to run fast, were those who came in for most injury. They looked horrible with their bleeding wounds, which were never dressed. Each prisoner received a number and had his hair clipped. The mistreatment continued and was particularly bad during the first days and nights. Sometimes the prisoners had to stand up for many hours or sit on a hard stone floor, or they were not allowed to go to the toilet, all unbearable torture. One day the prisoners had to sit for hours around two whipping racks and watch while various captives were flogged with different kinds of whips. During one of the first nights the stormtroopers were permitted to vent their rage freely. Water was distributed in the night after a long period without any beverage. I suppose that a laxative was mixed in the water. The poor chaps who then ran out of the barracks were pitilessly tortured, shot at, strangled, and mistreated in other ways. I cannot guess how many captives died in that horrible night, but it was a considerable number. I know from an absolutely reliable source that a few weeks after I had left the camp, a prisoner, who had killed a sentry while trying to escape, was publicly hanged. All the prisoners, insufficiently dressed for the cold, had to walk in line into the courtyard and be present while the man was hanged.[19]

Interrogation and thought reform

Techniques of thought reform have been developed mainly by the totalitarian countries of the left, because they have an interest not only in obtaining information but also in modifying attitudes and ideological viewpoints. The main interest of right-wing dictatorships is in obtaining information and suppressing opposition.

Victims are liable to be exposed to practically all the physical and psychological hardships so far described in this book, plus the deprivation of almost everything that gives life meaning to most people – contact with home, family and friends, freedom of choice and some kind of purposeful activity.

The aims of the captors are twofold: first, to break down individual resistance in order to obtain (possibly real) information and/or a (probably false) confession, and to render the victim more pliable and susceptible to the implantation of new ideas;[20] second, to implant those new ideologies so firmly that they will be incorporated into the individual's fundamental belief system and form the basis of a new sense of identity. These techniques have been most highly developed by the Chinese, but they are employed in all total institutions to some degree.

The term 'total institution' has been coined by the American sociologist, Erving Goffman,[21] to describe institutions and organisations which control every aspect of a person's life, including, inevitably, thinking and values. Mental hospitals were Goffman's prime example, but the concept applies equally to prisons, ships at sea, armies, boarding schools, general hospitals (to varying degrees) and religious orders. To emphasise that there is nothing very new in these processes, here is a description of conditions in an Augustinian monastery in the sixteenth century:

> The novice is assigned a cell a little more than three metres long, three wide. The door cannot be locked and has a large opening for inspection at any time. There is one window, too high to allow one to see the ground. There is a table, a chair, a lamp; a cot with straw and a woollen blanket. The room cannot be heated. No ornamentation of any kind, no individual touch is permitted . . . Outside his cell, the whole monastery is a chequer-board of times and places where silence is or is not mandatory. Special permission is required for private conversation, and must be overheard by a superior so that it does not become an escape valve for boast or banter, flattery or gossip. Above all, laughter is to be avoided. During meals . . . the monks must listen and not talk, a lectio is fed into their ears while the food enters their mouths.[22]

Individual resistance is weakened during interrogation by three processes: isolation, so that there is no reassuring contact with any friendly person; maintenance of anxiety by the constant fear of physical maltreatment or execution and a general state of uncertainty; and actual physical hardship in the form of interrupted sleep, inadequate food, exposure to excessive heat or cold, absence of exercise, brutal beatings, and exhausting interrogations which fluctuate between the harsh and aggressive and the benign and solicitous.

Torture

The reason for including this section is simple: anyone who reads it may one day have to undergo the horrors described, and this story may help. Jacobo Timerman was editor of a Buenos Aires newspaper, apparently steering a middle course, since on a single day he received death threats from both right-wing and left-wing groups. Then he was arrested by an extremist faction of the Argentine army, and without any charge being brought against him apart from that of being Jewish, he was brutally tortured and kept in captivity for thirty months.

In the long months of confinement, I often thought of how to transmit the pain that a tortured person undergoes. And always I concluded that it was impossible.

It is a pain without points of reference, revelatory symbols, or clues to serve as indicators.

A man is hunted so quickly from one world to another that he's unable to tap a reserve of energy so as to confront this unbridled violence. That is the first phase of torture; to take a man by surprise, without allowing him any reflex defence, even psychological. A man's hands are shackled behind him, his eyes blindfolded. No one says a word. Blows are showered upon a man. He's placed on the ground and someone counts to ten, but he's not killed. A man is then led to what may be a canvas bed, or a table, stripped, doused with water, tied to the ends of the bed or table, hands and legs outstretched. And the application of electric shocks begins. The amount of electricity transmitted by the electrodes – or whatever they're called – is regulated so that it merely hurts, or burns, or destroys. It's impossible to shout – you howl. At the onset of this long human howl, someone with soft hands supervises your heart, someone sticks his hand into your mouth and pulls your tongue out of it in order to prevent this man from choking. Someone places a piece of rubber in the man's mouth to prevent him from biting his tongue or destroying his lips. A brief pause. And then it starts all over again. With insults this time. A brief pause. And then questions. A brief pause. And then words of hope. A brief pause. And insults. A brief pause. And then questions. . . .

When electric shocks are applied, all that a man feels is that they're ripping apart his flesh. And he howls. Afterwards, he doesn't feel the blows. Nor does he feel them the next day, when there's no electricity but only blows. The man spends days confined in a cell without windows, without light, either seated or lying down. He also spends days tied to the foot of a ladder, so that he's unable to stand up and can only kneel, sit or stretch out. The man spends a month not being allowed to wash himself, transported on the floor of an automobile to various places for interrogation, fed badly, smelling bad. The man is left enclosed in a small cell for forty-eight hours, his eyes blindfolded, his hands tied behind him, hearing no voice, seeing no sign of life, having to perform his bodily functions upon himself.[23]

Prison

In many parts of the world just being in prison is tantamount to living with the possibility of death at any moment, and Arthur Koestler's experience in prison in Seville in 1937 during the Spanish Civil War is typical:

We heard everything. On the nights of the executions we heard the telephone ring at ten o'clock. We heard the warder on duty answer it. We heard him repeating at short intervals: 'ditto . . . ditto . . . ditto . . .'. We knew it was someone at military headquarters reading out the list of those to be shot during the night. We knew that the warder wrote down a name before every 'ditto'. But we did not know what names they were and we did not know whether ours was among them.

The telephone always rang at ten. Then until midnight or one o'clock there was time to lie on one's bed and wait. Each night we weighed our lives in the balance and each night found them wanting.

Then at twelve or one we heard the shrill sound of the night bell. It was the priest and the firing squad. They always arrived together.

Then began the opening of doors, the ringing of the sanctus bell, the praying of the priest, the cries for help and the shouts of 'Mother'.

The steps came nearer down the corridor, receded, came nearer, receded. Now they were at the next cell; now they were in the other wing; now they were coming back. Clearest of all was always the priest's voice. 'Lord, have mercy on this man, Lord, forgive him his sins, Amen.' We lay on our beds and our teeth chattered.

On Tuesday night seventeen were shot.

On Thursday night eight were shot.

On Friday night nine were shot.
On Saturday night thirteen were shot.
Six days shalt thou labour, saith the Lord, and on the seventh day, the Sabbath, thou shalt do no manner of work.
On Sunday night three were shot.[24]

More than forty years on, the same tragic drama is being re-enacted more often and in more countries than ever before: men awaiting death by execution with 'the same leaden, hollow-eyed gaze, the same flickering, hunted look of brute fear'.[24] The innumerable accounts all tell the same story, whether the setting is a Nazi extermination camp or a prison of the right or of the left.

Risking death – bomb disposal

There is no activity quite like this one – going carefully up to a bomb which might blow up at any moment, knowing that the explosion may be set off by the slightest disturbance. Yet this is what is being done several times a day in, for example, Northern Ireland.

Derrick Patrick was a bomb-disposal expert until he retired from the army. During his tour in Northern Ireland there had been a number of bombs planted in petrol road tankers, as the petrol and petrol vapour could greatly augment the power of any explosion. Lt.-Col. Patrick had already successfully disposed of two such devices, but he could not have felt too easy when he heard of a third one awaiting his intervention.

Patrick's plan was to climb up on top of the tanker, at that moment containing 1,000 gallons (4,500 l) of petrol plus an explosive mixture of petrol and air in the 'empty' compartments. He would open no. 5 compartment, where the bomb was known to be, lower a rod and hoist out the bomb on the end of it. To make matters more awkward he had to climb wearing a heavy bomb suit, to give him some protection. Cumbersome, but, as one of his officers said to him, it would 'help hold you together if the bomb goes off'.

The day was dry and clear [wrote Patrick] but once I began my trek to the tanker I wouldn't have noticed if it had snowed. In my left hand I clutched the rod, in my right the disruption device. Despite the gaggle of experts who were watching me there was no point in looking back. I simply kept on heading for the tanker, watching the letters 'FINA' growing larger and larger.

I left the disruption device on the pavement and then began my slow ascent up the ladder, once again a most difficult climb in a bomb suit.

Once on top I went straight to no. 5 tank and unlocked the lid with the driver's key. The rod I laid beside me. The bomb was just as the driver had described it. The light was good and I had no need of a torch to see it lying on its side at the bottom of the tank with a splash of white paint beside it. The handle, to which the lowering string was attached, was clearly visible and I had little difficulty in reaching it with the hook on the end of the rod. Carefully, hand over hand, I brought it up and then walked to the side of the tanker to lower it. Problem! The rod which had been long enough to reach the bottom of the tank could not reach the pavement . . . naturally enough. Now what the hell was I to do with the thing? I bent forward as far as the heavy bomb suit would let me without plunging over the side and froze in a position which one of my old sergeant-majors used to call a 'constipated duck'.

To stay in this ludicrous position for ever was clearly impossible. Had I felt flexible enough, I could of course have pulled back the rod and carried the bomb down the ladder in one hand – but it didn't strike me as a great idea. I then reasoned that if the paint tin had been driven from the Falls [Road] to Dunmurry on its side, it must have rolled about considerably. Conclusion: there was no tilt switch and whatever else was inside was fairly robust. If I dropped it the remaining foot or so the chances of it being activated were almost nil. It was just possible that the time set for detonation had been reached but it had failed to work because of a poor contact. A jar might theoretically re-establish the contact, but the possibility seemed remote. So I dropped the thing, hook, rod and all. It clattered to the ground and that was all. Just a clatter.

It was an action I would not expect to be taken by any but the most experienced operators and no training manual should recommend it. I can only say that deductions were right in the given circumstances.

Closing the lid of no. 5 I retraced my clumsy steps down to the street, unhooked the device from the rod and lined up the disruption device before retiring to the safety of the Pigs [a public house] and the incident control point 100 yards away.[25]

Bomb disposal calls for patience, intelligence and the ability to think logically on a problem where the slightest error will lead to one's instant annihilation. Things can go badly wrong in this work, as will be discussed in the section on errors.

Expecting death

What do you think about when you are falling to your certain death? A friend of mine fell 45 feet (14 m) from the mast of his trimaran one Christmas Eve in the English Channel. Because of the width of the trimaran he was bound to strike some part of the boat, break his back or his limbs and then perhaps be bounced into the icy sea. What were his thoughts besides his analysis of his various possible fates? They were simply calm and matter-of-fact thoughts about a girl he loved. There was no distress, just acceptance. When he landed on the deck he did break his back, and he survived to sail again, though his next long sail was his last.

The expectation of death is very different from the fear of the possibility of it. I found hearing shots fired in anger at fairly close range initially much more frightening than when on another occasion I was sitting in the rear cockpit of a light plane that seemed to me to be falling, out of control, with the engine cut out. That kind of falling evoked in me the feeling of calm acceptance that has been described by many in the face of death, especially by falling in the course of a mountain climb.

A Swiss geologist, Albert von St Gallen Heim, collected in the 1890s a number of experiences of climbers who survived falls which they had expected to be fatal:

> In nearly 95 per cent of the victims [Heim wrote] there occurred, independent of the degree of their education, thoroughly similar phenomena experienced with only slight differences. In practically all individuals who faced death through accidental falls a similar mental state developed. It represented quite a different state than that experienced in the face of less suddenly occurring mortal dangers. It may be briefly characterised in the following way: no grief was felt, nor was there paralysing fright of the sort that can happen in instances of lesser danger (e.g. outbreak of fire). There was no anxiety, no trace of despair, no pain; but rather calm seriousness, profound acceptance, and a dominant mental quickness and sense of surety. Mental activity became enormous, rising to a hundredfold velocity or intensity. The relationship of events and their probable outcomes were overviewed with objective clarity. No confusion entered at all. Time became greatly expanded. The individual acted with lightning quickness in accord with accurate judgement of his situation. In many cases there followed a sudden review of the individual's entire past; and finally, the person falling often heard beautiful music and fell in a superbly blue heaven containing roseate cloudlets. Then consciousness was painlessly extinguished, usually at the moment of impact, and the impact was, at the most, heard but never painfully felt. Apparently hearing is the last of the senses to be extinguished.[26]

So you may *hear* your bones breaking but not feel the pain.

Denying death

Eighteen men and one woman were in the 'death house' at Sing Sing Prison awaiting execution for murder. They were studied by two New York psychiatrists[27] who found that they displayed one or more types of reaction. Seven denied the true reality of what was going to happen to them by detaching themselves emotionally – 'So, they'll kill me; and that's that.' Four assumed that a pardon would be granted, and one believed his pardon had actually been granted. Four denied any past or future reality for themselves; they could block out the future by living totally in the present.

Seven of the condemned were convinced that they had been unjustly persecuted; and eight distracted themselves with the minutiae of their appeals or with religious, intellectual or philosophical matters.

Most people suffering a life-threatening illness want to know what is the matter with them, but a proportion do not and will simply fail to register any statements concerning diagnosis, however explicitly given.[28] There is even evidence that denial may actually improve survival rates for certain people suffering from cancer of the breast[29] or coronary artery disease.[30]

Accepting death

When Captain Scott and his companions settled down exhausted and frozen to face their deaths in the Antarctic, Scott was able to write in his diary: 'We took risks, we knew we took them; things have come out against us, and therefore we have no cause for complaint.'[31] They were resigned and accepting.

The question is often asked: 'What is dying like?' The answer depends on the circumstances and on the awareness and attitude of the person who is dying. When someone slips quietly out of this life in mature years with his ambitions fulfilled and with a full awareness and acceptance that he is dying, the occasion is quiet and beautiful, and profoundly moving to all who witness it. Even when someone is fighting and denying an inevitable death from serious illness, the final moments are peaceful. Non-violent death is not painful, and the moment when life slips away is always ultimately calm.

Albert von St Gallen Heim himself had a fall which at the time he was almost certain would be fatal. He recalled the 'flood of thoughts' he had about how he would fall and land, and:

> I considered how the news of my death would arrive for my loved ones and I consoled them in my thoughts. Then I saw my whole past life take place in many images, as though on a stage at

some distance from me. I saw myself as the chief character in the performance. Everything was transfigured as though by a heavenly light and everything was beautiful without grief, without anxiety, and without pain. The memory of very tragic experiences I had had was clear but not saddening. I felt no conflict or strife; conflict had been transmuted into love. Elevated and harmonious thoughts dominated and united the individual images, and like magnificent music a divine calm swept through my soul. I became ever more surrounded by a splendid blue heaven with delicate roseate and violet cloudlets. I swept into it painlessly and softly and I saw that now I was falling freely through the air and that under me a snow field lay waiting. Objective observations, thoughts, and subjective feelings were simultaneous. Then I heard a dull thud and my fall was over.[26]

With modern resuscitation techniques more and more people are returning to good health who to all intents and purposes had died. Raymond Moody has collected a remarkable number of such experiences, including some from people actually pronounced dead.[32,33] In a foreword to Moody's first book, Elisabeth Kübler-Ross, who has herself made an important study of death and dying, wrote that they 'experienced a floating out of their physical bodies, associated with a great sense of peace and wholeness. Most were aware of another person who helped them in their transition to another plane of existence. Most were greeted by loved ones who had died before them, or by a religious figure who was significant in their life and who coincided, naturally, with their own religious beliefs.'

Such experiences are by no means the exception. Rather, they are sufficiently common to be a source of consolation to us all.

Accepting death may be tolerable if it is the only possible outcome, and for a person or a group lost, exhausted and starving in some hostile environment, sitting down to die can become almost attractive. Apathy comes over people in the later stages of exhaustion, when bodily discomfort is no longer a problem and no more effort is made to search for food. Then, great determination and a consciousness of the dangers of apathy are needed if behaviour that will fulfil the fatal expectation is to be avoided.

PART II

Circumstances

4

Isolation

To a great extent our ideas about personal identity and the reality of
things come from other people and from our physical surroundings.
Take those people and the surroundings away, and our grasp on
reality weakens. Rational, conscious control depends on a continuous and reassuring stimulation from outside. Without such a
steadying input, any sensory cues that remain are liable to be
misperceived and misinterpreted; and all kinds of psychological
material, ordinarily unconscious, is free to erupt into consciousness.

Thus, a truck driver can swerve off an empty, straight and
featureless road at night because through lack of variety in the visual
field he begins to misinterpret signals, until a small bright stone is
perceived as a major hazard which must be avoided. Yachtsmen have
been known to take drastic evasive action on seeing a large light
directly ahead, which later turns out to be the moon. All kinds of lone
adventurers may find phantom companions when conditions are
extreme. People blindfolded after eye operations can have terrifying
experiences of being chased and tortured, and sentries at night can
fire shots into the nothingness which becomes alive in their
imaginations.

To provide more information about such experiences, laboratory
experiments have been devised; two main conditions have been
produced, called sensory deprivation and reduced patterning.

Sensory deprivation
Here the subjects are suspended in a tank of water at body
temperature, with their heads, eyes and ears totally covered with a
mask, so that the only sounds are their own breathing and faint water
noises. At first subjects find this environment relaxing, but after an

hour or so they begin to seek some stimulation by making slow swimming movements or rubbing one finger against another. Directed thinking about, say, the previous day's events soon gives way to reveries and fantasies, and after about three hours some subjects report simple visual imagery, for example, 'small, strangely shaped objects with self-luminous borders'. The attempt here is to try and abolish all sensory input, so that the subject is deprived of all outside cues. Few people can tolerate this deprived environment for more than about three hours.[1]

Reduced patterning

Reduced patterning describes an earlier experimental approach which aimed not so much to abolish all input as to render the input so monotonous and featureless that the subjects were really without any effective stimulation.[2] The subjects sat in a soundproofed cubicle wearing goggles which let in only diffused light with no clear vision of objects, and gloves with cardboard cuffs extending from the elbows to beyond the fingertips so as to limit tactile stimulation. Then the continuous hum of the fans and air conditioner was fed into the cubicle to create a satisfactory masking noise. It was planned that the subjects should remain there for four days, being allowed out only for eating and toilet, and they were provided with a bed in the cubicle.

An environment of reduced patterning is less severe than one of total sensory deprivation, but, even so, few of the subjects remained in the experiment for more than three days. In both environments the subjects felt apathetic and found it hard to concentrate, and they performed poorly in verbal and numerical tests. They also described similar visual experiences, which varied from random dots, lines, patterns and flashing lights, to fully formed images of other people, sometimes with malevolent intent towards them. Strange bodily sensations, like electric shocks, were experienced. One man reported that he saw a rocketship and felt the pellets it was firing at his arm. Several reported feelings of detachment or 'otherness', or that there were two bodies (instead of one) lying on the bed.

Since these early studies a great deal of work has been done on the effects of artificial isolation,[3,4] but the early findings have been broadly upheld.

Venturers into harsh environments are likely to fare better than the subjects of experiments because they are more powerfully motivated and better prepared for the hardships. Also they are generally people who are used to a measure of isolation, and who have developed a relationship with the natural environment so that they may feel at their best in conditions which would render more outgoing and sociable types acutely frustrated and apprehensive. However, few people would choose the kind of sudden isolation which may follow an air crash, a shipwreck, or being thrown into solitary confinement in prison.

Sensory deprivation and reduced patterning outside the laboratory

The polar regions, being alone in a cave, solitary confinement in prison, isolation in small boats at sea and certain intensive care units in high technology hospitals all provide examples that reflect to some degree the conditions created in the laboratory.

Polar regions For total and unrelieved solitude, I know of no experience equal to that of August Courtauld who spent five months of winter, from December 1930 to May 1931, in complete isolation on the Greenland ice cap, a lifeless area about the size of Western Europe. He was twenty-six at the time, with a record of Arctic and desert exploration behind him, and was part of an expedition engaged in weather-recording. With two companions, he had just relieved two others who had been manning the weather station – a double-layered tent, ten feet (3 m) in diameter with a ventilator pipe at the top. These others were glad to be able to get away, especially as the weather was worsening. Courtauld wanted to stay. He argued that the weather observations should be continued, since no one had previously spent a winter on the ice cap, but as there was only food for one, he said he would like to stay on alone. Furthermore, he had bad frostbite at the time and needed rest, and was in no state for a long sledge journey back to base. There was nothing his companions could do to dissuade him.

To begin with, the days passed uneventfully. He read a great deal, and six times a day he dressed in the full heavy Arctic clothing of those days to go outside to read the weather instruments, after which he had to thaw himself out. He continued to do this for three months until a blizzard finally defeated him in his battle to keep the exit free, and from that time on he was forced to stay underground. He had started off with only three months' supply of food and fuel, but in the laconic style favoured by explorers, he merely remarked that 'the food situation was . . . becoming interesting'. The next month passed uneventfully until his lamp fuel ran out, so that the last month was spent in darkness.

Tobacco was completely exhausted, so tea was used as a substitute. Food consisted of a little oatmeal, just warmed up for breakfast, and, thereafter, uncooked pemmican, biscuit and margarine. The most unpleasant part was the frozen condensed moisture which covered the whole inside of the tent, which, hanging down in long icicles from the roof, used to drop off in one's face. It also condensed inside my sleeping bag, and so froze any part of it that I was not in contact with.

The only external incident of interest which happened during the time I was there was the occurrence of a curious and very terrifying phenomenon, of which I have been unable to find an explanation. It was a sound beginning as a distant rushing noise, which rose quickly in a crescendo to end in a crash, rather as if an avalanche had buried the house [his tent]. It happened twice, in February and April.[5]

Such sounds have been described by other polar explorers, and are probably due to cracking of the ice or snow crust.[6]

Courtauld adapted very well to this extreme degree of isolation, and after his rescue – which came just as his food and cooking fuel had run out – he continued his adventurous style of life.

Caves   The inside of a cave is a natural environment providing pretty minimal sensory input,[7] and it may seem rather odd for anyone to spend a long time alone inside one. In 1962 Michel Siffre,[8] at the age of twenty-two, spent sixty days down a cavern in the region of the French Alps. The temperature was always below freezing, the humidity was high, and the only light was one dim electric light bulb. There were no sounds except running water and periodic rock falls. He wrote that he was 'almost entirely lacking in thought of a higher order', although, surprisingly, he recalled 'having many long meditations of a philosophical nature'. Towards the end of his time in the cave his memory weakened, and he could not remember, for instance, whether he had played both sides of a record or not. 'The symphonies that had once charmed me became merely chaotic noise. And the popular songs by the best café singers seemed only to increase my feeling of loneliness.'

He lost his sense of colour, confusing green with blue, and he also lost his sense of distance: 'Above my head, space and solid rock blended together in the same way that sky and sea often blend. Sometimes I had unusual hallucinations: I saw, usually for an instant, a multitude of flashing lights when I shut my eyes or peered intently into the darkness.' And he developed quite a severe squint.

When the time came to return to the surface, his limbs were weak and his movements uncoordinated. As he neared the top he collapsed in despair and began to cry: he was convinced the rope was fraying and would not hold him. When he finally did reach the open air he blacked out, but he recovered and by the end of five weeks or so all the disturbances described had resolved themselves.

Prison Solitary confinement in prison involves being alone except for contact with warders who are potentially hostile. People who have endured it look back on the experience variously, according to their temperaments and the precise conditions in the cell and in the prison around them. They may be on their own but with their isolation tempered by clandestine communications, or by the sounds of torment or of executions. Alternatively, the solitude may be almost total. This was the experience of Edith Bone, a Hungarian-born British doctor, who was arrested as a spy in Budapest in 1949 at the age of sixty-one. She spent the next seven years in solitary.

> In my specially isolated cell I was, to a very considerable extent, undisturbed, especially in the first five months after the sentence when I was in the dark and therefore necessarily inactive physically. In the dark there is little one can do except think, and the absence of anything to divert one's thoughts gives them an intensity seldom experienced in normal conditions.
>
> While I was in the black hole underground [this seems to have been a temporary but even more extreme form of privation], there was little else I could do [but compose poetry]. There was not even the prisoner's eternal resource – walking to and fro – because I had a horror of treading in the stinking muck on the floor.
>
> For certain reasons ... I did not eat at all during the nine days I spent down there, and found that I was not hungry. I experienced instead a strange lightness of the body and clarity of thought.[9]

Edith Bone had read widely, including many prison memoirs, and these helped her prepare herself for her prolonged incarceration. Her durability was quite remarkable. By some standards, though, her experiences would be considered mild: she was not moved around, beaten, starved, cruelly interrogated or indoctrinated. Her ordeal was primarily one of isolation, which is why it has been mentioned here.

Isolation increases suggestibility, a fact that is used by interrogators and indoctrinators of all kinds, whether the motive is religious, military or political. The process can be illustrated by a simple experiment conducted in the United States in the early 1960s, when there was a great deal of anxiety there about the effects of 'brainwashing' and communist indoctrination. Two groups were selected who were quite neutral in their attitude to the country of

Turkey. Each member of one group spent twenty-four hours isolated in total darkness in a soundproofed room, while those in the control group were allowed to spend the time as they pleased. Then members of both groups heard, under identical and isolated conditions, 'a tape which contained propaganda favourable to Turkey'. Those who had been confined showed a change of attitude in favour of Turkey that was 'over eight times as large as that of the non-confined group', and the 'concrete thinkers' (those who take things at their face value) were more effectively swayed than the 'abstract thinkers' (those who evaluate things in the light of their total experience).[10]

Oceans   The regular splash of the waves, the whistle of the wind in the rigging, the creaking of the boat, become so repetitive under ordinary conditions that they create a 'good' background of reduced patterning. The sailors I studied in the 1972 Singlehanded Transatlantic Race commonly reported consequences of this monotonous environment, such as imagining they had left their radio on, hearing a voice calling their name, or various disturbances of visual perception.

Generally, the experience of being alone at sea is pleasurable for people who have deliberately set out on solitary voyages. William Willis' experience is typical:

> The solitude continued to affect me. It had a sort of fascination that grew and grew. I began to feel more and more at home in it, and had no desire for a change. I am content with the sea and the sky. It is easy to see how men who have lived in solitude seek it always and resent any intrusion of human beings. But there are moments of suffering too; a vague uneasiness which comes when one realizes that he lives on the edge of an abyss. Man must talk to someone and hear the sound of human voices.[11]

Some lone voyagers find that solitude is not quite what they had expected, especially on the ocean. Alain Bombard, who crossed the Atlantic in an inflatable dinghy and trying to live off plankton, wrote:

> I had begun to understand the difference between solitude and isolation. Moments of isolation in ordinary life can soon be ended. Isolation is merely a matter of isolating oneself, but total solitude is an oppressive thing and wears down its lonely victim. It seemed sometimes as if the immense and absolute solitude of the ocean's expanse was concentrated right on top of me. It was a vast presence which engulfed me. I talked aloud to hear my own voice, I only felt more alone, a hostage to silence.[12]

Hospitals Modern medical technology has led to the development of special environments in hospitals which are admirable from the point of view of saving life but which may impose intolerable strains on the patients. The main strain comes from isolation with, of course, the added factor of the anxiety at being ill enough to need to be in such a special unit in the first place.

Intensive care units abound with monitoring equipment and machines for supporting life. Signals of heartbeat and breathing flash regularly, and there may be visual displays of other bodily functions. There are repetitive sounds from respirators, air mattresses and oxygen flow. The room is permanently lit so there is little distinction between night and day, and the staff are made anonymous by their white uniforms and masks. All this makes an intensive care unit an environment both monotonous and difficult to interpret, so it may come as no surprise to learn that patients there quite often have psychological disturbances, for example, hallucinations or convictions that they are being poisoned or otherwise slowly killed.[13,14,15] After certain eye operations both eyes are blindfolded, which can lead to serious disorientation in the elderly patients who are the ones most often requiring such surgery (usually for cataract).[16]

Isolation is such a central issue that it is worth looking at it more closely, and differentiating it from loneliness. The loneliness of an elderly or a handicapped person, or someone living alone in the middle of a big city, is never experienced at sea or in other natural environments – at least not by those who have sought such isolation. As David Lewis wrote in October 1972, one week out of Sydney on his circumnavigation of the Antarctic continent:

> I was not in the least lonely. This solitude was a different thing altogether from the lonely emptiness you suffer in a strange city where, knowing no one, you are surrounded by uncaring men and women, all supported by their own human ties. I for one am not particularly self-sufficient – I am peculiarly susceptible to loneliness among crowds. The sea or, for that matter, the desert or the mountains are companionable – or at least they are neutral once you have learned to respect their ways.[17]

Being alone in the natural environment involves a relationship with that environment. The lone sailor talks about his feeling for the sea and all the abundant life in it, the climber about the mountain and its ever-changing moods. The lone venturer is totally at the mercy of the environment, but by knowing its ways and bending to them it is possible to survive most natural hazards. Nevertheless, 'nature' will always have the last word, and the venturer knows never to take her for granted.

This chapter opened with the statement that our sense of identity and reality derives to a great extent from other people and from our physical surroundings. Other people and the environment provide a steady input of information which reassures and stabilises us. But this input also performs another function – it keeps under control all kinds of thoughts and emotions which in normal waking conditions never reach consciousness. In psychoanalytic terms, this is the unconscious mental activity which ordinarily manifests itself in dreams and slips of the tongue. When the stabilising conscious inputs are removed, this mental activity and energy is able, as it were, to come to the surface and so into consciousness. This means that the individual may now be able to make contact with inner parts of his being. This is the kind of experience that is sought in many forms of meditation, where the outer preoccupations are stilled so as to make contact within.

Some people go off for a singlehanded ocean trip and swear that they will never do it a second time: for others it is a revelation, an opening of doors to a totally new realm of experience. This is presumably what William Blake meant when he wrote:

> If the doors of perception were cleansed,
> Everything will appear to man as it is, infinite.

In other words, if we can cleanse ourselves of all the clutter, prejudices and distractions of ordinary living, we can see the world more accurately and more fully. Blake was able to maintain his pure vision while living in the middle of eighteenth-century London, but most people need to withdraw from the daily round to some degree. Others may take certain drugs (cannabis, LSD and other hallucinogens) to enhance their perceptions. Indeed, Aldous Huxley entitled his book about his experiences under mescaline *The Doors of Perception*,[18] after the same quotation. In it he described how for the first time he felt he was perceiving the external world as the visual artist does, and saw, for example, not only the chair but at the same time the very essence of the chair.

Christopher Burney was a British agent in France when he was arrested by the Gestapo in the early 1940s. Amazingly, he was not executed but left in solitary confinement for eighteen months:

> So many months of solitude, though I had allowed them to torment me at times, had been in a sense an exercise in liberty. For, by absolving me from the need either to consider practical

problems of living or to maintain the many unquestioned assumptions which cannot conveniently be abandoned in social life, I had been left free to drop the spectacles of the near-sighted and to scan the horizon of existence. And I believed that I had seen something there but it was only a glimpse, a remote and tenuous apprehension of what lay behind the variety and activity of life, and I was afraid that I would lose sight of it as soon as I was forced to turn my attention back to my immediate surroundings.[19]

Much of the joy of solitude comes from making some contact with one's inner being. In stripping away the jumble of distractions, or society's expectations, or the professional mask (persona), the individual makes contact with something which is uniquely himself. This does not have to lead on to lofty states of awareness, simply to a profound sense of tranquillity and sense of meaningfulness.

The risks of solitude
If the external circumstances are too threatening, if the individual is experiencing a high degree of anxiety or is of an unstable temperament (to use that term rather loosely), then removing the reassuring presence of others may be catastrophic. The most tragic example I know of this kind was Donald Crowhurst's last voyage in 1968.[20,21] He had faked a singlehanded voyage round the world and was returning to Britain hoping to come in an unnoticed third or fourth in the *Sunday Times* contest, but events turned on him so that he was to become the inevitable winner who would have all his log-books minutely scrutinised, thus revealing the deception. Entirely alone in the calm of the mid-Atlantic, he was unable to make radio contact with anyone or to find any way out of his predicament. He thus did what people do in such unresolved circumstances, especially if in isolation: he retreated into the private world of madness. Without the constraints of the outside world, his imagination (or unconscious mental processes) burgeoned uncontrolled, so that in his own mind he had attained a point of superior insight where he had the power to control all events in the world and thus transcend all his practical difficulties. The story is more complicated than I have indicated, and I cannot comment on his ordinary mental stability (although I have no reason to believe that he was any more or less stable than most adventurers), but I do not believe he would have broken down as he did had he not been so utterly isolated.

An extreme sense of isolation and abandonment is probably too much to expect any ordinary person to bear. Joseph Conrad describes the plight of such a man in his novel *Nostromo*, and I think he catches the essence of the problem of isolation. Here Decoud, an outwardly successful man, finds himself totally alone on a small island after a series of disturbing events. The isolation proves too much for him and he kills himself:

> He was not fit to grapple with himself singlehanded. Solitude from mere outward condition of existence becomes very swiftly a state of soul in which the affectations of irony and scepticism have no place. It takes possession of the mind, and drives forth the thought into the exile of utter disbelief. After three days of waiting for the sight of some human face, Decoud caught himself entertaining a doubt of his own individuality. It had merged into the world of cloud and water, of natural forces and forms of nature. In our activity alone do we find the sustaining illusion of an independent existence as against the whole scheme of things of which we form a helpless part. Decoud lost all belief in the reality of his action past and to come ... the truth was that he died from solitude, the enemy known but to few on this earth, and whom only the simplest of us are fit to withstand.

5

Isolated Groups

Accidental isolation

Most of the elements of accidental isolation can be found in the story of the Andes air crash of 1972. It is something that could happen to anybody who flies over remote or hostile terrain, and demonstrates how quickly a carefree outing can change into a desperate struggle for survival. The story also made cannibalism respectable in modern times.[1]

Fifteen rugby football players from well-to-do families in Uruguay, plus some of their friends and relatives, were flying to Santiago in Chile for a match. The pilots of the Fairchild F-227, probably against their better judgement, were flying in storm conditions through a gap in the Andes (since the plane could not clear the highest peaks there), when through some error of navigation they turned into an area of rocky peaks which in due course ripped off one of the wings. The aircraft crashed in soft snow at 11,500 feet (3,500 m), killing seventeen and leaving twenty-eight stranded with minimal food and little warm clothing (it was October). Some of the survivors were badly injured and soon died, but the fit ones were effectively organised by the captain of the rugby team into groups in charge of medical care, cleaning the fuselage of the aircraft in which they now lived, and melting snow to drink. They managed to make the radio receiver work, but on the tenth day they learned from it that the search for them had been called off. The captain wept at this news, it broke his spirit and he soon withdrew as leader. A few days after that he and seven others were killed when an avalanche hit the aircraft.

The question of eating the flesh of their dead comrades was discussed as soon as the fourth day, and only a short time after that they broke this taboo, which enabled them to survive. (Eating human flesh raises a number of difficult issues, which I would like to discuss in the next chapter, when dealing with hunger.)

After the captain's withdrawal as leader, a new optimism about escape developed, and soon an escape group of the fittest and most resourceful men was formed who would have extra meat and be excused routine duties. Another leadership was evolved – this time a group of three cousins who collectively held benign sway over the others and coordinated activities, which inevitably were mostly concerned with food. There were many tribulations and doubts about whether the escape group would ever make it down out of the mountains to the valleys of Chile. There were minor aggravations, the usual scapegoats, and all along a number who were injured and unable to contribute to the melancholy tasks of 'collecting' food.

The escape group set off on the final attempt sixty days after the crash. Ten days after that, after a pretty desperate descent of the mountain, they encountered some Chilean peasants. In a little while helicopters were on their way and the remaining survivors were rescued from the mountain. In the end, only sixteen out of the original forty-five on the plane came out alive.

All in all, the survivors coped well with their adversity. They appraised their circumstances and chances accurately, and were realistic in their decisions. The group held together, changing leaders as conditions changed, and morale never deteriorated too much nor did divisive factions arise. Those who survived were mostly the fit and young, although only five of them belonged to the rugby team. Why this group managed as they did must be a subject for speculation: there was homogeneity of age and social background, and a common interest in rugby, yet there were divergent political and religious views. However, they somehow managed to avoid focusing too much on sensitive areas, and they also steered clear of painful discussion of families and girlfriends. Piers Paul Read[1] has written a graphic and detailed account of the whole episode, and it is one of the key books for adventurers into harsh environments, as it challenges everyone to ask how they would cope in similar circumstances.

A number of other isolated groups have been described in other sections, according to the particular topic under discussion and most of these occur in Chapter 14 dealing with survival, but they can be briefly mentioned here.

Shackleton's retreat in 1915 from his stricken ship, *Endurance*, and the subsequent hardships through which he successfully brought himself and twenty-seven men safely back from the

Antarctic during eighteen months of living on ice floes, small boats and a desolate island, are described as an epic of leadership. In 1942 Walter Gibson was one of four survivors out of 135 crammed into a lifeboat after his ship was torpedoed in the Indian Ocean, and he exemplifies the value in the right circumstances of an attitude of passivity and acceptance. Then there are two family groups: Dougal Robertson and his family who were found in good condition in July 1972 after drifting for thirty-seven days after their yacht had been sunk by a whale, and Maurice and Maralyn Bailey who survived 117 days after a similar accident in March 1973. By contrast, we have the detailed record of how nineteen Canadian coal-miners coped with being trapped at the bottom of their mine for eight days, and how they selected different leaders according to their current needs. And of course there are hostages, taken on aircraft, trains or in buildings.

Planned isolation

Most adventures and expeditions involve groups of people living in isolation, and some of these have been the subject of systematic observation. There are examples from Alpine[2] and Himalayan[3] climbs, from American nuclear submarines[4,5] and from the Sealab II project – groups of ten men living for two weeks at a time in a steel cylinder 205 feet (63 m) below the surface of the Pacific, a mile off San Diego in California.[6]

A great deal of work was commissioned in the 1960s when it was envisaged that men would be spending months, possibly years, cooped up together on long-range space voyages. This even included a study of the British navy in the age of sail and world exploration, when isolation was extreme, conditions appalling, and the groups held together only by means of harsh discipline.[7] However, most of the work on isolated groups has been done on Antarctic stations, and what follows will be based in part on these accounts.[8,9,10]

People make a positive choice to go to the Antarctic, sometimes because it is a desirable thing to do in their, usually military, careers; and there is a lot to be said in favour of it. Life is simplified on an Antarctic station. There is no money, no ordinary social hierarchy, no need for fine clothes, and the pursuit of possessions becomes meaningless. There are no conflicting obligations between family and work, and a man can devote himself wholeheartedly to his job, undistracted by social engagements, travel or holidays. Most important for many is that a man is judged by his companions largely on the basis of his efficiency at his job.[11]

On the other hand, there are disadvantages. The environment is inevitably hostile. There is intense cold, prolonged darkness (leading to the troublesome insomnia called 'big eye'), continuous light in summer, high winds with snow storms and 'white-outs'.

Confinement can present problems, too. Although each man will have his own living space and the opportunity for some solitude outside, the level of involvement with others is still pretty high and may have to continue for a year or more. However, confinement with others here is nowhere near so intense as on fully crewed ocean-racing yachts, where there are only sufficient bunks for those off watch, there is constant buffeting from the waves, and the whole vessel may be heeled at an angle of 20° for days on end. Intense confinement can also be experienced on mountaineering expeditions when the members are cooped up in tiny tents for the duration of bad weather.

Monotony and repetitive routines can weigh heavily after the first few weeks, especially when there is little environmental stimulation. If the requisite amount of stimulating input cannot be obtained from the surroundings then it will be sought through interactions with others, sometimes with rather acrimonious results. In all but the most energetically organised groups, a measure of boredom is inevitable, since here are men deprived of most of their usual opportunities for leisure and enjoyment. Furthermore, mental inertia is liable to overtake the majority (as is does in individual isolation), so that the big books are never read and languages go unlearned. Any variation in the routine is welcome, even dangerous activities, but best of all is the arrival of people from outside.

The United States Navy Department makes a close scrutiny of personnel who winter over in their Antarctic bases. In general the men adapt well to the physical privations and dangers of polar life: what troubles them more is adjustment to the isolated group, to the sameness of the environment, and to the absence of customary sources of gratification. In one survey a kind of 'winter-over' syndrome was reported[12] in which 72 per cent recorded a 'significant depression', and 65 per cent had 'problems with hostility and anger'. These usually led to withdrawal, but one or two 'episodes of actual or attempted physical aggression' occurred each year in the winter months. Sixty per cent had difficulty getting off to sleep or staying asleep, especially in mid to late winter; and 41 per cent described 'difficulty in concentration and memory, absent-mindedness and general slowing of intellectual activities'.

These problems, though a nuisance, were not disabling, but they could easily become so in a vulnerable personality. When psychological breakdown did occur it generally took the form of clinical depression of an incapacitating kind, or of alcohol abuse which would tend to be linked with depression – drinking to relieve the depression, and so on. There was only one instance of paranoid psychosis in their groups, but these explosive reactions are reported from time to time in other isolated groups when conditions become psychologically difficult, and they usually occur in people who have displayed similar reactions in the past. A number of men reported sick with bodily complaints of emotional origin, and these often seem related to events, real or imagined, that were occurring back home.

Long-duration spaceflight would represent the most extreme kind of planned isolation for a group, but the issue is less real than it was in the early 1970s when trips of years' duration were being contemplated; how people would cope under such conditions remains a matter for speculation and extrapolation from studies in laboratories, and polar and other regions.[6,13]

The Russians isolated a small group in a capsule at ground level for a year or so. The impression given is that there were considerable psychological problems, but as far as I know these experiences have not been reported in detail.[13] The current interest is in stations in earth orbit, where it should be possible to break up a group if relationships become too destructive.

Weightlessness and bombardment with cosmic rays cannot be reproduced on earth, and most studies have not been able to maintain a background of danger. So I would suggest to anyone wanting to take this line of research further that they put their proposed group on a yacht and have them sail round and round the Southern Ocean for a year or more, and if they have not thrown their observing psychologists – and each other – overboard by the end of the voyage, we may have some interesting data.

Groups in general

Most people live in groups (families, communities) and may come together in other groups for particular purposes (football matches and other sporting events, political demonstrations).[14] A group generally possesses an identity and an ethos which add up to more than the sum of the attributes of its members. Thus it can confer a sense of security, identity and freedom from individual responsibility which is valuable, especially when external conditions are threatening and the members realise that they have an interest in keeping the groups efficient and harmonious.

There is always likely to be some tension between the needs and desires of the individual and the interests of the group – a potential conflict which pervades all human and animal societies. In the dangerous circumstances with which we are concerned here, the issues tend to be simpler: if the group is going to offer the best chance of survival, or of achieving a particular objective, then the individuals will subordinate their independent wills to the collective. The group demands a measure of conformity. A structure will develop or be imposed in which members have their special tasks and responsibilities. Norms will evolve about what kind of behaviour is permitted and what is not, and all of this will be readily accepted, since belonging to a group or to ordinary society meets deeply felt needs for most people. This readiness to conform can be demonstrated by two simple psychological experiments.

In the first of these, subjects were placed in a darkened room and asked to look at a single point of light. In such circumstances the light will appear to move (as will all small objects seen in the distance), and the subjects had to estimate the amount of movement. When they made their estimates alone in the room they gave much more varied answers than when they were all together and could hear the judgements of the others.[15]

In the second experiment, subjects were required to judge which of three lines shown to them was the same length as a standard line. When on their own, the subjects hardly ever made a mistake. Then they were placed in a group, not of fellow subjects but of people primed to give a wrong answer. In these circumstances, up to one third of the answers given by the subjects were incorrect but conformed to the voice of the majority – the group. Some, of course, resisted the majority verdict, others succumbed every time, but few failed to show signs of tension and discomfort either from making a false observation to keep in with the group, or from risking alienation from the group by adhering to their beliefs.[16]

Group disintegration

The worst thing that can happen to a group is that it will fall apart and cease to function as a whole. The experienced leader is always alert to this danger, which may occur at the most improbable times.

There can hardly have been a more foolhardy act under desperate conditions than when Harry McNeish, the carpenter on Shackleton's *Endurance* expedition, refused to go on pulling the sledges over the ice floes on the grounds that Shackleton had no jurisdiction over him once the *Endurance* had sunk. It was a quite absurd situation. They were a good thousand miles from human habitation, and one man on his own would not have the slightest chance on the treacherous ice floes, so his 'mutiny' soon collapsed. But Shackleton presumably perceived that the cohesiveness of the group was threatened, as he mustered all hands – that is, the twenty-seven exhausted and bedraggled men – and read to them the articles they had signed which obliged them to obey his orders: an authoritarian act maybe, but it worked.[17]

If Shackleton's group had collapsed, they would all have been dead within a week, and that was doubtless an important factor in its holding together. When conditions are less extreme a group can fall apart and still survive, as Roger Banks, a meteorologist on an Antarctic expedition some forty years later, describes. His ship was calling at an isolated Antarctic station, and instead of the usual ecstatic welcome:

> ... we realised with a shock that though we were anchored within sight of the base hut, no dinghy had put out from the shore to greet us, so a dozen of us piled into our own boat and poled our way towards the beach through the fringe of pack [ice] which lay offshore.
>
> The atmosphere of the place was utterly forlorn and with no people bursting out of the hut to come and meet us in the usual way. Only when we opened the front door of the hut and called down the long corridor did doors start opening and faces begin to appear. We didn't know them.
>
> They were all pale and sickly-looking in a way scarcely credible to us in our ruddy good health. As we talked, we gradually took in their unkempt appearance. The airless smell of the hut made itself felt and, as we looked around, we discovered in the different rooms little animal dens where, as base life had broken down and they had become no longer on speaking terms with each other, each man had retired to make himself a little corner in the wreck of his personality.[18]

This tendency to retreat physically from the group and to establish one's territory can happen in families where communications have broken down. It was described in extreme conditions after the wreck of the *Medusa* – a French sailing ship carrying passengers from France to Senegal in West Africa in 1816 – when seventeen men remained on the abandoned ship which subsequently did not sink. Forty-two days later, a boarding party found four of them still alive, 'very weak and half-crazed. Each had his separate den, which he never left except in search of something to eat, and then only with knife in hand.'[19]

The party making the first direct assault of the Eiger in 1965 and the 1971 International Himalayan Expedition attempting Everest each lost a man. In the first Whitbread Round the World Sailing Race a man was lost overboard from Chay Blyth's boat *GBII*, and also from a French yacht. In the Eiger party and on Chay Blyth's boat, the groups held together and the missions were brought to a successful conclusion. In the others the enterprises were abandoned. The issues are discussed further in Chapter 13.

Successful groups

The most important member of an isolated group is the leader, and the next most important may well be the cook. As far as the ordinary members are concerned, to list the desirable qualities is rather like listing the qualities which might make for a successful marriage. So it includes, rather obviously, unselfishness, tolerance, optimism, humility of opinion, sufficient intelligence to be able to work out verbally interpersonal problems and conflicts of interest, courage, a sense of adventure and tenacity of purpose, specific skills, a degree of self-sufficiency and autonomy, and a sense of humour. In addition to individual qualities there is the equally important issue of the interrelationship of qualities. There should be a homogeneity of intellectual and educational levels, cultural values, social backgrounds and attitudes towards the enterprise in general. The range of ages should be such that they are not so close as to provoke rivalries yet not so spread out as to be a source of irritation amongst members.

If the right balance can be struck, there is room for complementary attitudes and skills. A few dominant types can be counterpoised against others of a more submissive disposition. Where skills are concerned, it is important that each member contributes some useful talent for which he can be respected by the others.

Married men seem to do better than single men, provided they have been married for more than a year and do not have high sex drives, and that their career ambitions take precedence over their affectional needs. A person might sign on for an Antarctic or other expedition in order to get away from an intractable marital or work problem, or after the breakup of a relationship, but it is an open question whether the icy open spaces and the company in a hut would provide what he really needs at such a time. The presence of women is likely to be stabilising, provided they are of a caring disposition rather than the type that generates powerful tensions in men.

Very few personal qualities constitute an absolute bar, but the ones most likely to cause trouble are rigidity and unwillingness to compromise, and the tendency to react to difficulties by displays of aggression and vituperation.

6

Physical Conditions[1]

Along with isolation, there are numerous physical influences which can affect overall functioning. The most important of these are high altitude, cold, heat, changes of time zone and body rhythm, hunger and thirst, noise and vibration, the effects of drugs and alcohol, and lack of sleep. This chapter has inevitably a medical and physiological bias. No more than an outline is given of the various factors, but there are plentiful references for those who want to pursue the subject further.

High altitude[2,3,4,5]

Oxygen lack

The pressure of oxygen in the air, and thus the amount of available oxygen, falls with altitude, so that at 18,000 feet (5,500 m) the oxygen pressure is only half of that at sea level. At the top of Mount Everest (29,028 ft., 8,848 m) it falls to one third of the value at sea level.

Oxygen lack is a problem for high altitude climbers, and for air crew in the event of accidental decompression of the aircraft. For the former group the effects are gradual; for the latter they are sudden and more dramatic.

Measurable impairment of efficiency in picking out dark objects against a dark background can be demonstrated as low as 5,000 (1,500 m). Thus pilots are advised to use oxygen whenever flying at night.[1] At this altitude and up to 8,000 feet (2,500 m) most people feel slightly euphoric, with increased energy and alertness. A few, however, will become mildly depressed, drowsy, lethargic or emotionally indifferent to what is going on around them. Up to 15,000 feet (4,600 m) these phenomena will become more marked, but there will be considerable variation according to personality, rate of acclimatisation and previous experience at high altitudes.

By 18,000 feet (5,500 m) definite changes will be apparent, although the subject may be quite unaware of his impairment. Movements are likely to become laborious, with a general laziness and slowness in thinking, forgetfulness and increased touchiness. Food fads can develop, with a particular fondness for sweet things. Some people can function quite effectively at 20,000 feet (6,100 m) without oxygen, and Michael Ward, medical officer on the 1953 Everest expedition, has reported that at this altitude a man completed the *Times* crossword in normal sea-level time, and the physiologists could carry out their examinations of the constituents of the blood of the climbers for six hours a day with relatively few mistakes in the calculations. He also reported that publishable prose and poetry have been composed at this altitude, although a little higher the handwriting itself would start to become uncoordinated.

Above 23,000 feet (7,000 m) without oxygen all physical and mental activity is slowed. Judgement is likely to be severely impaired, as well as the ability to comprehend and to react to new situations. Misperceptions of various kinds can be expected. The most serious defect can be the lack of insight into one's condition. Michael Ward observed that after three days at 26,000 feet (7,900 m) John (now Lord) Hunt's 'condition had deteriorated a great deal and despite a reeling and drunken gait he considered he was quite fit to lead the party on the descent'.[3]

At upwards of 26,000 feet (7,900 m) without oxygen, almost all bodily and mental functions will be impaired to some degree. Movement will be laborious, with stops perhaps for several complete respirations after each step. The eyes may not focus correctly, with consequent double vision, and visual misinterpretations of the environment or hallucinations may occur. Emotional blunting and general apathy become more conspicuous so that, for example, the collapse of a fellow expedition member can be treated with indifference.

Climbers are usually quite unaware of the extent of their impairment until they breathe oxygen. They then experience a great increase in general awareness and enjoyment of their surroundings. They become less fatigued and find within themselves greater powers of endurance, and the warmth returns to cold extremities. They also can sleep much better with oxygen at these high altitudes.

Very considerable differences exist in the ability to tolerate hypoxia. Everest has now been climbed without oxygen[6] and a number of climbers have reached 28,000 feet (8,500 m) without it –

none with any long-term after-effects. However, no one has been able to last more than a very few days at these altitudes without oxygen.

Useful consciousness This refers to the state in which an individual is conscious and can function effectively, well enough at any rate to aid his chances of survival.

The concept of useful consciousness is relevant mainly to the sudden decompression of aircraft. At 25,000 feet (7,600 m) the pilot has between two and six minutes of useful consciousness, at 35,000 feet (10,700 m) he has one minute, and at 50,000 feet (15,250 m) only 15 seconds. At altitudes above 35,000 feet (10,700 m) even breathing pure oxygen will not lengthen the period of useful consciousness much, as not only does the oxygen have to be delivered under pressure but the body must be pressurised also – as with the suits worn by astronauts.

Other effects of altitude

Cold (to be discussed next) and *dehydration* increase both discomfort and the effects of oxygen lack. After some time at high altitude people lose weight and suffer a loss of appetite, and their sleep tends to be disturbed. *Mountain sickness* is a condition characterised by headache, lassitude, nausea, vomiting, and irregular breathing which can occur quite rapidly above 14,000 feet (4,300 m) or so.

Cold[7]

This is what happens when the core body temperature falls:[8]

°C	°F	
37–34	98.5–93	shivering
35–34.5	95–94	disorientation, confusion
34–33	93–91.5	loss of memory, apathy
33–30	91.5–86	semi-consciousness, heart irregularities, muscular rigidity (instead of shivering)
32–30	86–89.5	Unconsciousness, dilated pupils, no tendon reflexes
30–28	89.5–82	ventricular fibrillation (ineffective heart contraction)
below 26	below 79	death

These figures must be treated as approximations, especially as many of the people who get into extreme conditions will be fundamentally very fit. Severe core temperature loss in climbers can show itself by a gradual slowing in the rate of progress, clumsiness in placing the feet, and a tendency to stumble and fall. There may be failure to understand and respond to questions and directions, with outbursts of violent language and bursts of unexpected energy. There may be sudden shivering fits of great intensity, and sometimes a feeling of 'central coldness' (especially at high altitude) as opposed to the commoner peripheral feelings of cold. Abnormality and failure of vision are said to occur quite often, and are serious signs.[3]

Even half an hour of watch-keeping at night on the open bridge of a ship during an Arctic winter can lead to a significant deterioration in efficiency in visual vigilance, and also to a drop in body temperature (measured in the mouth) of 0.7°C (1.2°F). A fall in the skin temperature of the hands to 15°C (60°F) leads to a measurable impairment of manual dexterity and tactile discrimination, but this will also occur if the hands are kept warm while the skin temperature of the rest of the body is allowed to fall, so the mechanism is more complex than cold fingers losing their sensation.

The body's initial response to cooling is to increase energy output by muscular activity in the form of shivering, but this is an unpleasant kind of muscular activity. Better to increase the work rate and consequently the oxygen intake as well. Thus a cold, wet hill walker can maintain his body temperature by increased activity. The trouble is that such high energy expenditure is extra-tiring and only the very fit can maintain it for any length of time. When the physical activity slows, the body temperature then begins to drop quite rapidly.

Wet cold

Water seriously diminishes the insulation properties of virtually all garments except closed-cell foam wetsuits which do not take up water, so that someone floating in water or saturated on a hillside is virtually without heat insulation.

In water at 5°C (41°F) an unclothed man of average body build will become helpless from hypothermia after about 20–30 minutes, and with thick conventional clothing after about 40–60 minutes. In water at 15°C (59°F) he would last unclothed about 1½–2 hours, and from 4–5 hours if clothed.[9] English Channel swimmers may have twice the average body fat and will not cool while swimming (i.e., while producing some heat),[1] and very fat men, if warmly clothed, can survive almost indefinitely in water at 0°C (32°F).

Seasickness hastens loss of body heat (through the dilatation of surface blood vessels) and so increases the risk of hypothermia.[10] It can quite rapidly reduce people to such a state of misery that they no longer care whether they live or die, and many errors of judgement can be made before this point is reached.

Dry and high-altitude cold

When the air is thin it is necessary to breathe harder to obtain the same amount of oxygen, and this leads to extra loss of heat and moisture in the expired air. The atmosphere anyway is very dry, so there is an outpouring of body fluid to keep the air passages and the lining of the mouth moist. This leads to loss of weight as the protective subcutaneous fatty tissues get thinner, which further encourages heat loss. More oxygen is then required to maintain heat production, so an even greater respiratory effort is needed, which is very fatiguing. The blood becomes thicker and so flows less readily to the hands and feet and increases the likelihood of clotting.[3]

Acclimatisation to cold

Acclimatisation to cold does occur but only to a small degree, and there is no physiological reason to suppose that the body could survive very low temperatures for long. Heat is required to maintain body processes, and this heat is bound to be lost through the surface. Ultimately, food is the source of body heat, but it would not be possible to maintain body temperature in very cold conditions simply by a huge food intake. Insulation in the form of clothing is of course vital, but that can only retain what heat is there already.

Despite all this, there are holy men who live and travel in the Himalayas who can be seen making their way barefoot over snow-covered passes clad only in light cotton garments.[11] They show a tolerance to cold unimaginable to Westerners – and to native Sherpas too, for that matter. They are mostly Buddhist monks who have quite deliberately trained themselves to withstand cold by the practice of *gtum-mo* (pronounced 'tumo' and meaning 'psychic heat') in which they meditate on the theme of a great fire within the body; but the purpose of such exercises is to achieve higher states of awareness rather than prodigious feats of endurance.[12] And in fairness to Westerners, there are conspicuous examples of tolerance to cold from the 'heroic' age of polar exploration. Shackleton and his *Endurance* party are notable in this respect, living as they did in lightweight tents or under upturned boats for a year and a half, with quite unsuitable clothing, which anyway was in rags by the time they were rescued. They had a high calorie diet of seal meat and inspired leadership, and the only lasting injury among twenty-eight men was the loss of five toes by frostbite.

Heat [5,7,13,14]

Going into a very hot room is stimulating, and efficiency may increase. However, once the core temperature has risen by 1–1.5°C (1.8–2.7°F) a person will feel uncomfortably hot and aroused. This psychological arousal may improve the performance of simple tasks (such as vigilance) but the efficiency in more complex tasks (calculations) will deteriorate. General deterioration in performance occurs with rising core temperature until the individual collapses with heatstroke by 40°C (105°F).

There are three main forms of adverse reaction to heat. *Heat cramps* are unpleasant cramps in the limbs and trunk due to loss of salt by sweating. They are rapidly relieved by salt and then prevented by taking salt tablets regularly. *Heat exhaustion* usually occurs when unacclimatised people in a hot country are too energetic. It is due to excessive loss of water and salt, and leads to headache, dizziness, drowsiness and general collapse, the skin becoming cool, pale and moist. But there is a good response to treatment with salt and water. In both these states the body temperature remains normal. In *heat stroke*, on the other hand, the body's cooling mechanisms have failed and the body temperature rises uncontrolled, so that the body must be cooled by any means if death is to be avoided.

When the air temperature rises significantly, people are liable to become irritable and tempers can run short, especially if conditions are humid and people are confined. The violence of the 'long hot summers' in the United States testifies to this, in particular the homicide rate in New York City, which seems to vary with the summer temperature.

The body loses heat only by evaporation, which is why dry heat is more tolerable than moist heat. Acclimatisation to heat occurs by increasing the blood flow to the skin and by the consequent production of large quantities of sweat which is low in salt. This is a very effective process, but it takes up to two weeks – too slow, for example, to permit large armies to be airlifted into tropical countries ready for instant action.

Sleep loss

After one night with only two hours' sleep, or after two consecutive nights with only five hours each, deterioration in the performance of tests can be reliably demonstrated. When one whole night has been spent without any sleep at all the impairment is much more marked, and even one good night's sleep is not sufficient to restore the subject to full efficiency.[15] These findings were based on inevitably dull tests of vigilance, so if people are engaged in activities which are interesting or vitally important, their performance will be impaired relatively less[16] – but impairment will always be more than the person thinks it is.

After long periods of sleep deprivation the deterioration in efficiency will be greater, but individual variations are considerable.[17] Some stalwart people may keep going effectively for up to forty-eight hours, but many after thirty hours awake report burning or itching eyes, or blurred or double vision. Later on, spots on the floor may be seen to undulate, and even something as familiar as a chair may appear to change size.

Sleep deprivation is not just a simple matter of deprivation of rest. The body rhythms are disrupted so that the individual is trying to function at a time when his physiological and psychological processes are adjusted for sleep. This aggravates the problem, and by the time someone has been kept awake for fifty hours, frank hallucinations and paranoid delusions can be expected, and a complete loss of sense of time.[18]

Many of the features of prolonged sleep loss have been demonstrated by a New York disc jockey, Peter Tripp, who stayed awake under public gaze for eight days as part of a fund-raising exercise.[19] During this time he was watched continuously by doctors and psychologists as well as by hundreds of onlookers, and he continued his radio broadcasts. When he had been awake for about fifty hours he saw cobwebs in his shoes and was having difficulty remembering things, and soon after that the psychologists who were following his progress gave up trying to test him – it was probably as painful for them to see him struggling as it was for him to make the effort. After 120 hours without sleep he ran from a room in terror when he thought he saw flames leaping from the drawers of a desk, believing it was a plot on the part of the doctors to test him. After 150 hours he repeatedly saw a 'Dracula' face on the clock and by now he was becoming thoroughly disorientated, not knowing where, or even who, he was. On the final day he thought the doctor examining him was an undertaker come to bury him alive, and tried to escape naked into the street. Despite all this, he put out his radio show from 5 to 8 p.m. each evening, handling the stress of records, chat and advertisements with ease so that no one listening would ever guess the state he was in for the rest of the day. At the end of eight days he had thirteen hours' sleep, nothing like the amount he had lost, but he awoke completely restored to normal, although a mild depression continued for three months afterwards.

It is easy to see why interrogators of all kinds use enforced sleep deprivation to break down their victims, since it is effective, simple to administer, and leaves nothing to show afterwards.

Because of the way they organise their lives, doctors can quite easily find themselves working round the clock. For others, a whole night's sleep will be missed only under unusual conditions. A sleep-deprived person is not like a mechanical toy which gradually goes slower as it runs down (although this may be true of the earlier stages of sleep deprivation), nor like a car engine which continues satisfactorily until its fuel runs out and then stops dead. Such a person is much more like a motor which after much use misfires, runs normally for a while, then falters again, and so on.[20] It is during these faltering periods that severe errors of judgement may occur, so that the weary doctor who sets off for home feeling just ordinarily very tired then crashes his car during a brief but fatal lapse.

David Blagden, sailing the Atlantic in a 19-foot (5.8 m) boat, was chronically short of sleep even when conditions were reasonable as the motion of such a small craft was appalling. On the thirty-second day conditions were bad, and he was suffering from painful salt-water sores as well. He has described something like faltering, but fortunately without disastrous results, and he called the state 'sleep-wake':

> My body continued to function normally, changing sail, checking the course, keeping up the log, cooking, even making elementary decisions. But for long periods my mind was fast asleep. It would be hooked on to half a pop tune which would go round and round in my head without beginning or end, or it might be a single word ... Then suddenly I would 'wake up'. It would dawn on me that I hadn't had a sensible thought for a long time. My mind had been switched off, yet everything was in order, all the routine tasks had been carried out. I usually came to feeling somewhat refreshed or at least no more tired than before, although I was averaging less than three hours' 'proper' sleep per night during the period between 17 and 27 July.[21]

After a prolonged period of wakefulness, a person will fall quickly into a deep sleep. If that person is then roused during this 'recovery sleep', recall of conversations during that rousing or of decisions taken then is likely to be impaired.[22] There is also good reason to avoid making decisions or doing anything that requires skill of any kind, certainly within four minutes, and possibly within twenty minutes of waking. For this reason flight crews are not supposed to sleep while on standby duty,[23] although the same restrictions are not placed on doctors.

Time zones and body rhythms[24]

Flying from the United States to Europe leaves most people slightly 'jet-lagged', with varying degrees of lassitude and weakness, broken sleep, poor appetite, headaches, and possibly blurred vision and some depression. These are liable to last two to five days. They are slightly less of a problem on westerly flights, as that conforms with the apparent movement of the sun, and scarcely any problem at all on north-south flights. The effects may be mitigated by early daytime departure from the United States, thereby arriving in Europe late evening local time, and by eating and drinking in moderation before, during and immediately after the flight. Whether the flight is outward or homeward may make a difference, according to the significance of the direction for the individual.

Body temperature and body levels of steroids, sodium, potassium and other elements vary in a cyclical manner throughout twenty-four hours; so also do a variety of psychological functions, such as the quality of performance in tests of visual and auditory vigilance, reaction time and motor skills, as well as subjective states of well-being.[17] People function with measurably lower efficiency between two-o'clock and five o'clock in the morning, when all the physical and psychological processes mentioned are at their lowest ebb — which is why raids and arrests are sometimes carried out at such times.

The regular appearance of night, and of social events such as meals, keeps the 'biological clock' running to a twenty-four-hour cycle. By crossing time zones so that the night comes several hours later (or earlier) the individual's activities fall out of step with his rhythms, so that the cyclical processes may be at their lowest point just when peak efficiency is required. Adjustment takes a week or so for most people, and that is certainly too long for political leaders on world tours or for troops on long-range combat missions, and probably also too long for actors, musicians, chess players, athletes, and all those who dominate the world's headlines. Yet, among the attributes of the more successful of these may be the ability to withstand body rhythm desynchronisation.

The circadian (*circa* — about, *dies* — day) cycles can also lead to problems amongst night-shift workers and for those who may have to be roused from sleep in emergencies, since they are being expected to function effectively when their body rhythms are synchronised for sleep. Because of the generous off-duty arrangements for night-shift workers they are unlikely to spend long enough continuously in their night routine to allow their systems to adjust to the different rhythm, and so they remain most of the time in a desynchronised state.

The nature of these body or circadian rhythms remains elusive despite all the research (the empirical evidence of their existence),[17] and the fact that rhythms, as manifested also in the seasons, tides and menstrual cycles, are an integral part of nature. There is also a larger concept, usually referred to as 'biorhythm', which claims that there are cycles of from twenty-three to thirty-three days which govern physical, emotional and intellectual activity. It is a beguiling idea that there are times when we function with maximum efficiency and feel at our best, and other times when we are altogether less effective, less happy and more likely to have accidents and fall ill,[25,26] but it is an idea that has to be handled with some caution.

Reports about reducing industrial accidents by warning employees of their critical days are interesting, but they do not allow for the inescapable fact that after such warnings people are liable simply to be more careful. Nevertheless, they have stimulated some statistical work on the matter. Four thousand and eight general aviation accidents listed in the National Transportation Safety Board accident briefs for US civil aviation in 1972, for which date and time of accident, accident cause and pilot birth date were available, were analysed, and the 'critical days' calculated.[27] These critical days were then related to accident dates but the correlation turned out to be random; in other words, they could demonstrate no statistical association between a series of four thousand odd accidents and critical days in the biorhythm cycles. This must not be taken as a dismissal of the concept of biorhythms, but simply that if such rhythms do govern our overall level of function they are likely to be a good deal more subtle than the enthusiasts would have us believe.

Hunger and thirst[28,29,30]

Hunger

The hungry man thinks of virtually nothing but food, except, if he is so addicted, of tobacco and alcohol. Long-term goals, the progress of an expedition and the welfare of his companions become irrelevant. In more extreme cases, food may be stolen from these companions (and from family members too) or they may be murdered for the food they are supposed to possess, or their corpses will be consumed to keep the others alive.

After about two days without any food at all, intense, gnawing pangs of hunger will be experienced, but these will tend to disappear after another three days or so. Weight will begin to fall as body fat is being used to supply the body's energy requirements. In practice, food is usually short rather than totally absent, so the process will be gentler and more extended.

During the early stages of hunger, physical activity and reactions to emergencies become slowed so that the hungry man may fail to avoid common dangers. Concentration, short-term memory and efficiency in all mental activity decline, and the mood is depressed. There should be no impairment of vision and hearing in the short term, and in the longer term only if specific nutritional deficiencies occur. (Some writers[31,32] maintain that the visions of religious ascetics are partly induced by their self-imposed fasting.) Gradually apathy and lethargy prevail, with most of the time spent lying wrapped in whatever coverings are available, to keep warm and to pad the body now deprived of its cushioning layer of fat. The victim lies in a torpor that can only be disturbed effectively by news of food. Food is the sole preoccupation, and only ceases to be so when death is near, but by this time there is no more will to search for food or to make even the simplest effort to obtain it.

Water and salt lack

Thirst is a more immediate and pressing problem than hunger, as under unfavourable conditions survival may not be much more than a day with no water at all. Under favourable conditions a person may last up to fourteen days. The body requires about 500 ml (0.9 pint) of water per twenty-four hours if sedentary in a life-raft at sea, rising possibly to around 15 l (26 pints) per twenty-four hours for troops on a desert exercise.[29]

Thirsty people become agitated and may talk incessantly until the mouth becomes too dry for speech. Irrational behaviour, visual hallucinations (especially of pleasant places) and delusional ideas are commonly described, but these are due as much to the disturbances of salt metabolism (through diminished intake and/or excessive sweating) as to simple loss of body water.

The hunger and thirst described in this section are different from the *chronic starvation* which afflicts a large proportion of the world's population, and which is associated with specific deficiency states plus a vulnerability to a variety of chronic diseases. The victims of the more 'acute' hunger should start off in good physical shape but may have to endure greater extremes of heat and cold, and are likely to have their resistance further reduced by painful skin ulcers and infections and by any of the diseases endemic in the particular part of the world in which they find themselves. In addition they may become caught up in the panic and conflict which can overtake any group that fears its food and water supply is in jeopardy.

Cannibalism

Cannibalism always makes headlines, and never more so than when the full story broke about the Andes survivors. By setting out in grisly detail exactly what happened, Piers Paul Read[33] has perhaps reduced the morbid fascination that anthropophagy has so far held for the modern public. He has shown it to be a form of human behaviour appropriate to certain extreme conditions, but one resorted to only after deep heart-searching and after overcoming some pretty intense revulsion.

The Andes survivors related their growing realisation that the only hope for them would be to eat the flesh of their dead fellow passengers, and in some cases team mates. All twenty-seven survivors came together to debate the issue. Some shrank from it, at any rate so long as there was a scrap of alternative food remaining. Others argued that they had a moral duty to stay alive, that 'the souls have left their bodies and are in heaven with God. All that is left here are the carcases, which are no more human beings than the dead flesh of the cattle we eat at home.' (The people concerned here were normally very heavy meat eaters, if that might have anything to do with their attitudes.) There was also the feeling that God had spared them and had provided them with the means of survival. In the end, everyone ate the flesh, but those who hesitated longest weakened rapidly until they changed their minds. Although the corpses of certain people were not eaten by some because of particular associations they had with them, those that were eaten were consumed quite thoroughly, including a number of organs not normally regarded as edible. This was in order to obtain as balanced a diet as possible, and in that the survivors were successful, as none suffered any serious deficiency although all of them were thin. It was not a comfortable diet, though, as there was too little of the dietary bulk that comes from eating vegetable products.

An influential factor in the decision of some to eat the flesh was the likening of it, by one of the group, to Holy Communion. 'When Christ died he gave up his body to us so that we could have spiritual life. My friend has given us his body so that we can have physical life.'

After the rescue, a number of the survivors had considerable difficulty over the morality of what they had done. The Roman Catholic Church, however, was unequivocal in its response in support of their action – not only locally but even in *L'Osservatore Romano*: 'We justify on an ethical basis the fact the survivors of the crash of the Uruguayan airplane fed themselves with the only food available to avoid a sure death. It is legitimate to resort to lifeless human bodies in order to survive.'[33] I only hope that the taboo does not become so eroded that the weaker and younger members of survival groups will feel that their comrades may have greedy eyes upon them.

Cannibalism is probably quite common where survival is concerned, and three examples will be described later on in connection with a breakdown of leadership;[28] but anthropophagy for ritual reasons, although cherished in folklore, may perhaps be something of an illusion.[34]

Noise and vibration[1,5]

Noise[35,36,37]

Noise can be the source of the greatest distress to some, while others feel uncomfortable without a pretty high level of noise in the background; others again can exist in a noisy environment but manage to 'tune out' all but the sounds they want to hear.

Intermittent noise or noises can impair performance mainly by distraction, so that fifteen to thirty seconds may elapse before concentration is regained – a problem for those whose work involves constant vigilance, such as pilots, drivers of any vehicle or air traffic controllers. Continuous noise, provided the intensity is not too great, is much less distracting.

The intense annoyance and domestic disruption that occur around international airports have been claimed to lead to an increase in mental illness, but although this seems likely the association has not clearly been established.[38]

Vibration

Sitting in a moving car trying to write is difficult and unsatisfactory because the eyes, the hands and the piece of paper are all moving with their own slightly different frequencies. Experimental work confirms that visual perception is impaired with even moderate vibration, but when the whole body is vibrated at 25 cycles per second, generating forces of 10 g, internal bleeding can follow (and laboratory animals can be killed by severe vibration). Frequencies of one cycle per second or lower (sometimes called infrasound) can lead to motion sickness. *Acceleration* and *deceleration* forces can also lead to decrements in perception and performance.

Drugs and alcohol

People buy their own alcohol, but there are a great many other drugs, prescribed by doctors, that can impair efficiency by interfering with perception, judgement and motor ability, and a great many motorists[39] and flight crews of aircraft[23] are at risk without even knowing it.

The effects of *alcohol* are directly proportional to the dose. At low levels of blood alcohol perceptual judgement – for example, estimation of speed and distance – is impaired. At slightly higher levels decison-making ability – based on these erroneous perceptions – is liable to be faulty, and at higher levels still there will be motor incoordination. There can also be a narrowing of the visual fields known as 'tunnel vision', which further aggravates the problem, and all these impairments are more pronounced at night, which is when most people drink.[39] There is no evidence that alcohol ever improves performance or, to comment on another myth, that people can judge accurately the strength of alcoholic drinks.

A great deal is known about the effects of alcohol on performance because it is rapidly absorbed, its action on the central nervous system is predictable, and a proportion of it is excreted unchanged in the breath and urine, so that it can be measured easily. Despite this and the fierce legislation, alcohol is still the most important single preventable factor in road accidents, accounting in the United States for up to 50 per cent of highway fatalities.[39]

A high proportion of all drugs prescribed by doctors are capable of affecting performance either through their main action, such as excessive sedation from tranquillisers, or through a side effect, such as the blurring of vision caused by some anti-depressant drugs.

Here are some of the drugs in common use. Most important are those affecting mental state, and these include sedatives, tranquillisers, anti-depressants, sleeping pills and stimulants. In 1975 there were fifty-one million prescriptions for these in England and Wales – or one sixth of all the prescriptions written by doctors in that year.[40] There are also anti-convulsants, anti-hypertensives and ganglion blockers (for high blood pressure), digitalis-like drugs and beta blockers (for heart conditions), anti-spasmodics (for intestinal cramps), anti-motion-sickness drugs, anti-diabetic agents, diuretics (for improving urinary output), anaesthetic drugs and cough suppressants.[39] There are doubtless others, but this list represents a fair cross-section of the prescriptions of any general practitioner on a routine morning. Their undesired effects are variously general sedation of the system and drowsiness, excessively reduced blood pressure, dizziness or fainting, muscular weakness and difficulties in focusing.

While there is no doubt that alcohol degrades performance, the same cannot always be said about these drugs, and it is clearly desirable that someone prone to convulsions should take something which will suppress them, or that blood pressure is not allowed to rise to the level where it might cause a stroke, and so on. The whole issue is further complicated by the fact that the people involved are generally physically impaired to start with. Thus it is a matter of fine judgement whether a given person with a particular condition is better with the drug or without it.

The naive reader might suppose that people with serious physical or psychological ailments possibly ought not to drive at all, but such a large proportion of the population drives (seventeen million licence-holders in Great Britain[40]) and so many drugs are consumed (303 million prescriptions in England and Wales alone in 1975, excluding those for hospital outpatients), that a huge and unidentifiable number must be taking drugs and driving. Anyone trying to investigate the problem has a frankly impossible task. Unlike alcohol, the response is not directly related to the dose. Some of the drugs are hardly excreted at all and others are excreted only after chemical breakdown, so that measurement of the quantity of a given drug in the body would be difficult.

For these reasons it is hard to judge the size of the 'drugs and driving' problem. In the United States there are estimates that 'up to 20 per cent of the driving population is under the influence of some prescription or nonprescription drugs at any time',[39] and in a survey in Britain in 1969, 14 per cent were found to have taken 'pills or medicine' in the previous twenty-four hours.[41]

Surveys in various countries have shown that drugs other than alcohol have been a factor in up to 14 per cent of road accidents,[41] but accurate figures are difficult to obtain for the reasons given. When it comes to illegal drugs known to affect performance, notably cannabis,[42] the matter becomes even more complicated. Nevertheless, it is quite clear that very large numbers of people are driving, professionally or for pleasure, who are regularly taking drugs known to impair performance. It is only fair to make it clear that most drivers have adequate driving skills to compensate for a mild degree of drug and alcohol intoxication. The real problem is not with the motor skill but with the quality of perception and the interpretaton of what is seen.

If the story seems rather grim on the roads, let us see how things are in the air. What are the immaculate flight crew actually doing when we are not looking? Much the same as drivers on the roads.

Flight crews suffer from the time zone disturbances already mentioned, and a good many take alcohol and other drugs to deal with the disruptive effects, although the same people are not normally habitual drinkers *and* drug users. Captain Frank Hawkins, who for years has been studying these and related problems, carried out a survey on 348 flight crews of a 'large international airline'.[23] Of the eighty-one cockpit crew, 30 per cent 'sometimes' or 'frequently' used sleeping drugs (predominantly nitrazepan/mogadon), usually between six and eight hours before take-off, sometimes as close as four hours but not more than ten hours before. Only 4 per cent of the same group used sleeping drugs 'sometimes' or 'frequently' outside the working environment. The drugs were usually obtained over the counter in the many countries where they are freely available, and the crews seemed to have little idea of their action, in particular that performance decrements could be demonstrated over nineteen hours after ingestion of nitrazepan. They believed they were better off flying drugged than excessively tired.

Sleeping on arrival at foreign stations is difficult, as body rhythms are desynchronised, and 90 per cent 'never' or 'rarely and only with difficulty' managed to sleep in aircraft when off duty and travelling in the passenger area, as they commonly have to do on international routes.

Alcohol was used 'sometimes' or 'frequently' by 50 per cent of the cockpit crews interviewed, and usually as an aid to sleep *after* a flight, as opposed to drug usage, which was predominantly *before* flight and not connected with social drinking habits.

Multiple factors and the person

The sailor is wet, cold, hungry, seasick, desperately tired and frightened because he is lost. The pilot is behind schedule on a charter flight (in danger of incurring heavy extra costs), he is having difficulty communicating in English with the air traffic controller whose English is not very good either, he has just crossed five time zones, and visibility is bad. He is also chronically worried about his heart, but he feels he cannot consult a doctor for fear of being taken off flying duty, with a consequent drop in salary. The motorist also is late for an appointment, is frustrated by the heavy traffic, cannot see well because of the driving rain ... and so on.

Although the environmental and personal factors are not simply additional, it stands to reason that the more adverse physical factors a person has to cope with the more his performance is likely to be impaired. Therefore those engaged in interrogation and thought reform impose as many kinds of ordeal as they can and vary them continuously: isolation, haranguing from a crowd, cold, excessive heat, shortage of food, deprivation of sleep, repeated interrogation alternately aggressive and sympathetic; and always a state of anxiety is maintained.

PART III

Reactions

7

The People

The personal attributes of adventurers

What kinds of people embark on great adventures or seek out demanding occupations?

Among the thirty-four sailors I studied in the 1972 Singlehanded Transatlantic Race, nineteen were British, five American, three French, two Australian, two Polish, two West German and one Italian. They ranged in age from twenty-six to fifty-seven (average forty), twenty-five were married or had been married, and nine were single. Two were grandfathers. There were seven serving or retired officers from the armed forces, seven in various branches of engineering, three journalists, four professionally concerned with yachting, a newspaper publisher, a dentist, a bank manager, a shop proprietor, a pharmacist, an architect, a farmer, a croupier, a lawyer, an editor, a bandleader, an actor and director, and a freelance photographer.

No formal study of the personalities of these people was made because no available test would have been very illuminating. Personality inventories and the like have a certain value in research and can measure such factors as 'introversion' and 'neuroticism' (as defined by the compilers of the tests), but this tells us nothing about the person as a whole. Judging from the range of occupations, these men were clearly a diverse bunch, and even on board their boats they adopted totally different styles of behaviour. Some were gregarious to an extreme and never missed an opportunity for a party, and the only reason they sailed singlehanded was that it was one of the rules of the race. Others tended to avoid company, especially that of non-nautical types. One thing they all had in common was an enthusiasm for sailing their boats across the Atlantic. They were all highly competent individuals who had either made the money to pay for their boats or had had the energy and imagination to find commercial sponsors. They were also all able, mostly with limited means, to equip a boat to withstand the Atlantic weather; they had mastered celestial navigation, meteorology, something of ocean currents and the movements of icebergs, radio-telephony, general seamanship, and the provisioning of a boat for up to five weeks on the ocean.

There are some sailors who only come into their own at sea. On land they are inclined to be moody and restless, at sea they are alert and energetic. Some are inclined to be authoritarian and obsessional – but a measure of obsessiveness is a good thing on board a small boat.

Mountaineers have been subjected to personality investigation,[1,2] but I find the results unilluminating because either they are expressed in terms of personality factors which have no generally agreed meaning, or else they are simply reports of pencil-and-paper psychological tests. James Lester[3] has tried to get beyond this in his study of the 1963 American Mount Everest Expedition. All the same his findings refer principally to the personality attributes which make for good interpersonal relations. Those in his group who did well were open, considerate, cheerful, inviting, free from anxiety and spontaneous: those less successful were inclined to be closed, untactful, non-inviting, irritable, moody, worrying, methodical and precise, or painstaking.

It is altogether more productive to consider how people react to hardships and crises than to inquire into the kind of personality they have, since it is their reactions which matter: reactions to personal danger, isolation, irritating companions, extremes of physical discomfort, lack of food or water, and so on. Although basic personality patterns are likely to affect these, the only really reliable way to judge an individual or group in this respect is to observe them in genuine adverse situations.

Expectations

Most people embarking on an adventure have some idea of it leading somewhere. A few may go 'just for the ride' or because they were at a loose end when the opportunity offered, but for most people an adventure into the natural environment is something which seizes their imaginations and absorbs most of their physical and mental energy for months or years before the event. It is thus an idea which dominates life, for a while at any rate.

It may also be or become an event which in some way is going to transform their lives. Certainly the lives of Sir Francis Chichester and Robin Knox-Johnston were transformed by their heroic circumnavigations of the world. Their achievements made large numbers of people realise that great adventure does not necessarily require a large team on a huge budget, and that one man with a boat, properly prepared, can find abundant fulfilment – provided it is possible for his expectations to be met by such an adventure. And this is the crucial factor: the extent to which the expectations can be met by the attainment of the goal. There is an inner need which lies behind the outer action, and it is important – perhaps crucial – that the outer action should fulfil the inner need if the enterprise is to succeed. In ordinary life it is commonplace for people to project these inner needs on to outside events: 'If only I could have this new car (or new job, or new house or new wife), then everything would come right.' When the outer object is attained the person still feels and is the same person; the inner needs are less easily resolved, as they are inevitably complex and elusive.

There is a moment in all enterprises when the immediate reality shatters the fantasies: the first hard gale at sea, or a mishap on a cliff face which forces the individual to realise the constant danger involved in rock climbing. In ordinary life the actuality of a new job or a new house sharply challenges the buoyant expectations which may have accompanied such changes. Likewise, the reality of the marriage ceremony or the birth of a baby may be joyful, but fanciful expectations are likely to be shattered, and if such expectations predominate then disappointment will follow.

Would-be adventurers should examine their armchair fantasies and expectations, to see to what extent they can realistically be met, and then to what extent their vehicle or equipment, or their own skills and personal qualities, are up to the challenge. If they can debate these issues with partner and critical friends, then at least they will lessen the chances of a disastrous trip. I say this with some feeling as I was in exactly that position myself with regard to the 1976 Singlehanded Transatlantic Race. My experience in my researches with the competitors in the 1972 race had encouraged me to try my own chances. In many ways it was a perfectly natural thing to do, as I felt I had sufficient sailing experience and knowledge of the issues involved, and could have procured a suitable boat.

My plans developed up to the point where I began to consider precisely what I was looking for in such an enterprise and what might be expected to flow from it. Did I feel it would bring me some kind of fulfilment, compensate for some lack, provide a new and desired sense of identity, resolve personal problems? I shall never know, but I do know that as soon as I began to confront these questions I realised that sailing the Atlantic singlehanded was not for me.[4]

The enchantress

Expectations are about what will happen during and after an event, and what good and new things will flow from it. There is also, in the case of sailing, the matter of being on the ocean, and what actually happens 'out there'.

The sailor seems to have a relationship with the sea that has a dominating effect on his life. As a simple statement on the page this does not, of course, make much sense, because how on earth do you relate to a stretch of water? It is not a literal statement but a figurative, psychological, or even poetic one, and as such the relationship can be described in terms of a lifelong love affair with the sea. Sailors seek, and maybe occasionally find, in this relationship something which never seems accessible to them on land. It is hard to say precisely what it is they seek or experience out at sea, but clearly it is an attraction powerful enough to draw them time and again back to the apparently lonely expanses of the ocean. This fascination can make them restless on land, and many sailors lead unfulfilled lives ashore because they put little energy into anything not directed towards the next journey over the horizon. It is almost as though there were an irresistibly alluring woman beckoning to them from somewhere beyond the reach of land.

There is an obsessional attention to detail which affects everything to do with the boat; there is complete subordination of the interests of job, family and domestic arrangements, to the demands of the sea; irritability when plans to get to sea are frustrated; a total transformation of personality when on the water; and then a sense of anticlimax on returning home: all these have a good deal in common with the behaviour of someone in love.

The comparison can be taken further. The sea is a great symbol of the mother and of the feminine principle in general. All life comes from the sea, and, perhaps, ultimately all life returns to it. The mother gives life, and also offers the possibility of the perfect relationship in which the infant is uniquely special, is accepted and loved unconditionally, and is cared for completely. No subsequent relationship in life can ever equal this, but fortunately most people as they grow up do not actually desire it: they seek relationships based on partnership rather than dependence. Nevertheless, most people from time to time have a need to be weak and dependent, and for some, who have not enjoyed this unconditional acceptance in their earlier years, there may be a lifelong yearning and searching for something they sense they have missed.

Jung describes this process in his psychology in terms of what he called the *anima*.[5] This is, as it were, an image of the perfect woman that a man holds inside himself. It is an ideal that man may imagine he finds in an actual woman, although in reality the woman concerned may be either quite unattainable or else totally unsuitable. In addition, or alternatively, the man can seek this ideal by journeying into unknown areas. I have referred to the sea because the process applies especially to those who sail, and because of the symbolic significance of the sea, but probably all remote parts – the polar regions, mountains, deserts – can draw particular men for the same kinds of reasons.

Flying can also be an adventure into the unknown, and here the earth and its attendant problems quite literally can be transcended. The same issues broadly apply here, but there is an important difference in that flying is an occupation that can employ many people, and a very demanding one at that. Certain young men are attracted to flying as a way of dealing with their problems of maturing, breaking away from parents and learning to make adult-type relationships. These men can become effective aviators and display great feats of daring – where this is still possible in modern highly controlled flying conditions.

It is risky when flyers become so enamoured of flying that it dominates their lives. A classic, indeed heroic, example is Antoine de Saint-Exupéry, who was active in opening up air routes in Africa and to South America in the 1920s and 1930s, as well as flying as a test pilot. During the Second World War he became engaged in a variety of dangerous reconnaissance and rescue missions, and was eventually killed in 1944, at the age of forty-four, when his plane was shot down over the Mediterranean. He was also a writer and a poet, and he glorified flying as a way to self-transcendence. By contrast, his life on the ground and his marriage brought him little satisfaction. In the words of one commentator:

> When he was not allowed to fly he always became depressed and irritable and would walk up and down in his flat from morning till evening, desperate and irritated, but when he could fly he became his normal self again and felt all right. When he had to stay on the ground and be with his wife, or remain in some other situation, he fell back into these bad moods, so he always tried to get back into flying.[6]

Some adventurers will be drawn to their deaths pursuing their irresistible yet ultimately unattainable goals. Others draw back in time. If they happen to belong to the group for whom adventure into the unknown is a way of dealing with personal conflicts, they may find resolution of these conflicts *while* they are making their intrepid journeys, although not necessarily *because* of these journeys. In that case, around the age of thirty, they will opt for a more regular life in which they are able to manage longer-term relationships with people, especially with the opposite sex.

This is a satisfactory outcome from the psychological point of view, but it became a source of concern to Swissair, who were troubled about the number of highly trained pilots who were leaving them around the age of thirty, after expensive training and just when they were really becoming useful. These people ceased to want to fly and became anxious when pressed to do so, so much so that it seemed possible that they would crash eventually if forced to continue flying. The Swissair authorities accordingly consulted the C. G. Jung Institute in Zurich to see if they could help them select men for training as pilots who were not using flying as a means of dealing with their developmental problems – especially in relation to their mothers.[6] Swissair now seem to be able to identify those who have these personality characteristics and who therefore are liable to drop out of flying in mid-career, and so they turn down even more local applicants than before.

It is as though these young pilots, as well as the sailors, have a lifelong yearning to be special, to find the perfect partner and perfect occupation, to be uniquely successful in whatever they do because merely ordinary success would not be good enough for them. Such people, therefore, are unlikely to find much satisfaction in everyday life, work and relationships, and so they go off into the unknown where perfection may be imagined to exist. This describes a personality pattern known as the *puer aeternus* – the eternal boy – in which certain kinds of men, dissatisfied with the routine and the ordinary,[6] are forever seeking the unattainable. As a concept it is broadly related to that of the *anima*, mentioned earlier, since both concern the relationship of men to feminine figures.

People who have accidents

The people most likely to have accidents on the road tend to be more aggressive and prestige-seeking than those who do not, and less well able to tolerate tensions and feelings of hostility; to have worse employment records, drink more, have less stable personal relationships, and a greater likelihood of having a record of delinquency and childhood accidents and deprivations. At the risk of over-generalisation, this summarises a great deal of the research carried out into the question of who has accidents,[7,8] and can be epitomised by the remark of one of the early researchers: 'A man drives as he lives.'[9]

This leads on to the idea of 'accident-proneness': that is, the idea that certain types of people are more likely than others to have accidents. It is an empirical fact that accidents − like physical and mental illnesses in general[10] − are not distributed evenly throughout the population, nor are they distributed evenly in time. Certain people have more accidents and illnesses than others; and for everybody there are periods in which accidents and illnesses will cluster, and these will almost certainly relate to difficult periods in a person's life. For example, a study in the State of Washington showed that there was a substantial rise in the number of accidents between six months before and six months after filing for divorce, but the greatest rise (which included traffic violations as well) occurred in the' three months between the filing and the granting of the divorce.[8]

The motorbike is the perfect contemporary symbol for masculine, or macho, assertiveness.[11] It is powerful, flashy, fast and great fun. It challenges father's advice to play safe, and travels faster than father's car anyway; and there is always the excitement of being on the edge of danger. It augments the possibly insecure feeling of masculinity in a teenager, so that we have the synthesis of boy + bike = successful man. To a lesser extent the same applies to car driving, and in each case the subject is likely to be quite unaware of the role he may be acting out.[12] He may be getting a harmless boost to his ego or some quasi-sexual lift, as some writers would have it; or there may be quite profound personal problems and feelings of inadequacy which cannot be resolved by fast riding or driving, and so are liable to lead to really reckless behaviour on the roads.

Perceiving the world

Good decisions and purposeful action are based on accurate information. The quality of this information depends on the efficiency of the apparatus for observing, recording and interpreting what goes on in the world outside, and a great many of the mistakes people make derive from faults in the way they perceive their surroundings. We are mainly concerned with visual perception because that is the sense that we, as humans, mainly rely on when dealing with our surroundings. It will form the basis for discussion, and most of the examples will relate to things seen or not seen; but, of course, the other senses are all simultaneously apprehending the same world, and on occasions will be equally if not more important.

There are three main components of perception (using vision as the model): an object or other visual stimulus; an eye to register the signal, and a brain to process it; and some knowledge and theories about what is being observed.

Object, stimulus or signal

The object of attention ideally should be familiar and clearly visible. If the object is familiar but poorly illuminated, such as a cat creeping through the bushes on a dark night, or else completely new and unexpected, however well illuminated, such as a novel system of traffic lights or a strange object in the sky, then mistakes can occur, particularly if the observer is anxious.

Sometimes the signal is ambiguous because it is poorly illuminated – the cat is thought to be a malevolent human. Or a signal may be inherently ambiguous – for example, when a motorist flashes his headlamps at another car he is either communicating: 'Get out of my way!' or 'Please go ahead. I'll make way for you.'

Eye and brain – receiver and information-processor[13,14]

The eye is an outgrowth of the brain, and is an integral part of it rather than a separate organ. The eye converts visual information into electrical impulses which the brain then organises into a meaningful account of the outside world. For this process to work well, the eye and brain must be free of disease, injury or the effects of drugs or ageing, and the person should be rested and not excessively anxious.

Knowledge and theories about what we observe

It is impossible simply to 'observe'. There is so much information contained in almost every view that it would be impossible to describe it all. Some limitation must therefore be imposed to prevent all this input overloading our sensory apparatus, and to help us organise the incoming information. This is done by constructing hypotheses or sets of assumptions about what we see.

First of all we suspect that 'there may be something there'. Then we 'know that there is something'. Then it becomes clear that the object is becoming larger, although it is not yet evident what it is. Soon there is enough information to guess that it might be an aeroplane, and then it plainly *is* an aeroplane, and in a short time it will be apparent what kind of aircraft it is and even what course it is on.

Simple as it may appear, quite a complex sequence of informed guesses is being made, each of which is tested against all the available information – what is actually seen, what is heard, the location, the likelihood of an aircraft being in the vicinity, and so on. An analysis like this could not be made without a good deal of background knowledge, and the more one knows about the object under scrutiny the more useful will be the observations.

The observer needs to be able to take in the information as a whole, which means observing everything and giving appropriate (but not excessive) weight to each part. For example, the sound of the conjectured aircraft will immediately make it clear that it is not a balloon or a large bird up there, but someone who was concentrating on what could be seen at the expense of what could be heard could easily make such a mistake. This kind of selective attention is very important with regard to errors that can be made in perception, and will be taken up further in Chapters 8 and 9.

Sad to say, no matter how hard we try we can never make totally accurate observations of the world about us, and the more observers present the more different versions will be offered.[15]

Perceptual style

Apart from knowledge, experience, and possibly cultural factors as well, people vary in how they perceive their surroundings. Some people are better than others at picking out objects from their surroundings, such as finding the hidden head embedded in a child's puzzle picture. Those who do this easily can be called field-independent; those who have difficulty identifying the object from its surroundings can be called field-dependent, in that they cannot easily fix on the essential item in a complex scene.

Transposed to the roads, the field-independent drivers will pick out the road signs, and the vehicle some distance ahead which is about to change lanes, more easily than the field-dependent driver, who is less able to identify rapidly the immediately relevant items amongst the mass of visual information all around. There is some evidence that field-dependent drivers have higher rates for road accidents than do field-independent drivers.[8,16]

Personal threat and anxiety

Personal threat refers to most of the unpleasant things that can happen to someone. There is the obvious threat of injury, death or personal loss, but the possibility of failure can be threatening, and so can being at odds with the crowd.

The common denominator amongst the numerous examples of threats that have been given is that they all raise the level of arousal within the body, that is, the general level of alertness and preparedness for activity. Heart rate and blood pressure increase, the muscles tone up, and the adrenal cortex becomes more active.

A moderate increase in the level of arousal improves the quality of performance; if it is increased beyond a certain limit then efficiency falls off. The class will be stimulated to do better work by the presence of the school inspector, but if he remains there too long, or if he stands brandishing a cane, then the quality of the pupils' work may deteriorate because they are too highly aroused.

Anxiety includes all the feelings and responses associated with personal threat, and a good deal more besides. It is a state of tension, of anticipating that something unpleasant is about to happen, and may be a response not only to immediate threats and issues but to all kinds of distant problems as well. These may concern previous experiences relating to the present time, or matters – such as difficulties in a relationship – which have no direct connection with the current activity but which nonetheless preoccupy the individual, thus raising the general level of anxiety.

Anxiety and performance[17,18,19]

In practice, raised anxiety, as opposed to a modest rise in the level of arousal, leads to a deterioration in the quality of performance. Individual experience shows this, and so do a number of ingenious experiments in which anxiety and fear are generated. For example, a situation is set up in which one of the subjects is led to believe that through an error of his someone else has been seriously injured. He is then given clear instructions about what to do to help the injured person, but is subsequently frustrated in his attempts to deliver this help; all the while he is being monitored for his bodily responses to the anxiety he hears he has caused.[20] Similarly, a subject may be connected to monitoring equipment in a laboratory, ostensibly, say to record his heart function. Then a technician bursts in in a state of alarm, imploring the subject not to move a muscle lest he gives himself a fatal electric shock. The subject lies motionless and the (mean) experimenters make their recordings of physiological responses to fear.

The effects of anxiety on perception, thinking and reaction patterns, and performance will feature prominently in the succeeding chapters, but some of the main tendencies can be summarised here.

Perception may be impaired in states of raised anxiety by disturbing the process of forming assumptions or hypotheses about what is being observed. Instead of waiting until the object under scrutiny is clear enough to make an informed guess about what it is, the anxious person guesses too soon and then revises these guesses (or hypotheses) repeatedly, with the result that perception is inconsistent, which precludes the formation of any realistic course of action.

Attention may also be narrowed from a balanced comprehension of the whole to a preoccupation with details, often in themselves irrelevant; and there is also a tendency for the anxious person to become easily distracted from the main task. There is some evidence that peripheral vision becomes limited in anxious subjects,[21] but this is probably part of the process of concentrating attention on what are perceived (quite possibly wrongly) as the central issues and disregarding the rest.

Thinking and reaction patterns are liable to become rigid and stereotyped. The anxious person sticks to practices which are familiar and which have worked well in the past, even though they may not match the present needs. He is liable to become suspicious about the motives of others, who come to be seen as responsible for the current difficulties, and there is also a tendency at times of great crisis for the anxious person to become uncharacteristically superstitious, reading meanings into coincidences and events such as thunderstorms, which in the ordinary way would have passed unnoticed.

Anxious people become extra-suggestible, which makes consistent action in a crisis more difficult. This tendency is of course made use of by interrogators, who can manipulate their victims better if they have first raised their anxiety level.

For the *performance* of simple repetitive tasks, the optimum level of anxiety or arousal is higher than that for accurate and intellectually demanding work. Thus a level of anxiety which would rouse a group of fruit-pickers to record production would paralyse the same group if they had instead to solve a difficult mathematical problem.

Recently learned skills and patterns of behaviour can be forgotten when the individual is under pressure, with a reversion to more firmly established and primitive patterns. With pilots this may show as a breakdown of the more complex tasks such as instrument flying. When learning to fly by instruments, the pilot is trained to ignore the bodily sensations indicating movement and orientation in space, because they can at times be dangerously confusing. However, when anxiety mounts, there is a tendency to fall back on these basic bodily sensations, even to the extent of being unable to interpret the cockpit instruments, so that just at the time when a calm, rational response is needed, the pilot tends to regress and act in a cruder, more emotional way. Air crews on operational missions during the Second World War made more errors in navigation, for example, on account of raised anxiety than they did from the effects of prolonged activity and physical discomfort.

Navigation of aircraft in the 1940s was much the same in principle as that for small boats, except that the processes of observation and plotting were almost continuous, on account of the much greater speed of aircraft. The numbers of navigational errors made on non-operational flights were relatively small, and indeed fell slightly towards the end of each flight. On operational bombing missions, however, the rate of errors increased fourfold. It was highest during and immediately after combat, and there was a smaller peak while flying over the enemy air defences on the coast of France. Towards the end of these flights the error rate fell markedly.[22] There was a very clear relationship here between obvious anxiety and the clusters of navigational errors.

Amongst some of the singlehanded sailors, however, clusters of errors could occur when environmental conditions were good and no anxiety or sense of threat or danger was consciously felt. This happened to Bill Howell in the 1972 Singlehanded Transatlantic Race while sailing through the nine islands that make up the Azores. It was a perfectly familiar route for him, and weather conditions were fair and he was in apparently good spirits, but during the five days from approaching the islands to leaving them well behind he made five navigational errors. He was at sea for twenty-five days altogether, making excellent progress until his catamaran collided in fog with a Russian trawler a hundred miles from the finish at Newport, Rhode Island. In the whole of the rest of the voyage he made only five other errors, one of them occurring on the day he wrote: 'Have just had the first full gale of race. Difficult sailing conditions under working jib only. Motion appalling.'

Another sailor made five navigational errors in the six days before arrival in Newport. Conditions were good, but he gave evidence of some psychological tension in the daily record of subjective state he had been keeping. During the rest of the thirty-eight-day trip he made only five further errors. The contrasts between the periods of error and the error-free periods in each of these two examples are highly significant statistically, and I would infer that, in the absence of obvious physical hardship or lack of sleep, such a clustering of errors was evidence of raised anxiety, even if it was not consciously perceived as such.

Fear and motivation[22,23,24]

Fear is intense anxiety in the face of some immediate threat of injury, death or severe personal loss. It is motivation that keeps people going in dangerous conditions, and so motivation becomes an important factor in any consideration of fear.

Fear involves the subjective experience of feeling afraid; the associated bodily changes such as sweating, heart-pounding, and desire to empty bladder and bowels; and the physical response in terms of action taken to overcome the threat or to seek safety.

In war the primary fear is about injury or death; there is also anxiety about how one will behave when conditions become tough, whether one will act honourably and not let down one's mates. However, with actual combat experience, the fear of cowardice diminishes and the fear of being wounded or killed increases.[23]

Reducing and controlling fear

Armed forces of various countries have tried hard to devise means of selecting those who will continue to function effectively under dangerous and other adverse conditions, and in this they have all been singularly unsuccessful. This is largely because they have tried to answer the question: what kind of person will stand up best to fear? Rather more productive has been a study of the factors which appear to reduce fear and keep people functioning effectively. Here are some important factors.

Training, experience and technical skills The sailor who has survived a tropical hurricane will not be as afraid in the same boat in a North Atlantic gale. The soldiers who are well trained and know it will experience less fear and perform more effectively than men from units accepting a lower standard of preparedness. Special units such as the American Green Berets, British Special Air Service and Commandos, or the Waffen SS, exemplify this, with the high morale that comes from being part of an elite group (even though they may suffer greater casualties). The greater the technical mastery, the greater the feeling of being able to do something about one's circumstances. However, along with this can go a sense of invulnerability which, while good for morale, can easily lead to unnecessary risks being taken.

Control of circumstances The more control a person has over his circumstances the better he feels – and the less afraid. Special troops are, of course, self-selected; they tend to be highly individualistic and it is hard to generalise from them, but the opportunities for personally directed action are a necessary condition of their engaging in their highly skilled and dangerous activities. The same goes for secret agents and certain terrorists.

Fighter pilots with a casualty rate of 48 per cent have reported experiencing less fear than bomber pilots whose casualty rate was 22 per cent,[23] and furthermore their morale was generally higher. There are temperamental differences, of course, but within broad limits the fighter pilots made their own decisions and did not have to fly remorselessly along a prearranged course. Most pity goes to the rear gunner of a Second World War bomber, who had to sit cold and isolated at the back of an aircraft over which he certainly had no control at all, simply waiting to be shot at by enemy fighters.

Active participation in events is a step in the direction of control over one's fate, and any degree of participation is better than none.

Information   In conditions of danger, anxiety can provoke all kinds of terrifying fantasies. Factual information, even if it is disagreeable, reduces uncertainty and hence the overall level of fear and anxiety. A total lack of awareness of danger, either from ignorance of the situation or from an ostrich-like denial of realities, similarly will maintain anxiety at a low level, but such lack of conscious awareness will not necessarily aid a person's ability to cope or to survive. How much information is appropriate really depends on how much individual initiative is required in the particular dangerous or threatening situation. After a heart attack, a lack of awareness of the closeness of death may, according to some authorities, improve a person's chance of survival.[25] On the other hand, information about what may be expected after a surgical operation in terms of pain, together with instructions on how to move so as to minimise the pain and how to relax and exercise the muscles involved, reduces not only the pain (as measured by the amount of pain-killing medication given) but also the length of the stay in hospital.[26]

A research psychiatrist, Peter G. Bourne,[24] joined a group of Green Berets in an isolated forward position in Vietnam to study their anxiety levels (by means of steroid excretion levels). He obtained results from one of the two officers and six of the ten enlisted men, over a period before and after an attack. Before the attack, the officer showed a high level of anxiety, since he was receiving a great deal of information about troop movements and the like. The enlisted men enjoyed a relatively low level of anxiety, because, although they knew an attack was a possibility (it was always a possibility for isolated groups of special troops), they were intensively occupied laying mines, reinforcing barbed wire defences, checking ammunition stores and even preparing the medical bunker for casualties, so that there was little time for reflection and rumination. An exception was the radio operator who was in close contact with the officer and was, of course, party to all the radio messages.

The attack, as it happened, never materialised, so complete readings could be obtained in the days following. The anxiety levels of the officer and the radio operator dropped, and the levels for the enlisted men rose to normal. In other words, the enlisted men had maintained a level of emotional calm by throwing themselves into activity, which was acceptable because there was someone there who could carry the anxiety for them – someone in whom they had confidence.

The question of how much information and knowledge helps in combating anxiety or frightening reality comes up regularly and sharply in relation to life-threatening illness. In the numerous studies made about 'what to tell', the overwhelming majority of sick people report that they want to be told the truth,[15] and the reason is usually so that they can cooperate better with their care. This does not mean that people will react straight away to the fateful truth with calm and resignation: they may become depressed, angry or resentful, and why not? But with sympathetic guidance, these feelings can be worked through constructively until there is a placid acceptance in the full awareness of the realities.[27]

In war and other physically dangerous predicaments the possession of accurate information is a necessary prerequisite to effective action, so that at least the sense of panic at the prospect of unknown forces can be replaced by a simple terror at what can be clearly identified.

Motivation   If the drive to achieve the objective is strong enough, then any amount of fear will be overcome. Amongst the troops of both sides in the Second World War, the overriding motivation was to support the group – one's immediate comrades must not be let down. Equally important was the desire to get the war over and return home. Ideologies of any kind were of minimal importance, 'a belief in war aims' being the most important factor in overcoming fear in only 6 per cent of a sample of regular US troops. By contrast, 77 per cent of a comparable group of volunteers in the Spanish Civil War were there for ideological reasons.[23] The same probably applies to terrorist and guerrilla groups dedicated to achieving political change by any means, and all the more so if their religion and culture approve of sacrificing one's life for a cause.

Danger

Someone may be said to be 'in danger' when, in the view of ordinary people, there is a real and immediate risk of injury or death. Many of the issues relating to danger have already been discussed in connection with anxiety and fear, but there remain issues that apply to two other kinds of people: those who evidently seek out danger quite deliberately, and those who apparently deny the danger inherent in certain activities and situations.

Seeking danger

A little risk enhances enjoyment: a horse race becomes more exciting if money is at stake. There is a special exhilaration sailing a boat hard to windward with the maximum sail area that the boat will carry; skiing down a precipitous slope where the smallest misjudgement will lead to falling several hundred feet through the snow; cornering fast on a motorcycle where the line of the turn must be judged precisely because no correction is possible once the turn has been commenced. All these are exciting acts, and the closer one is to disaster, the better the performance. Ocean sailing and high altitude climbing are also activities where danger can be expected, but careful preparations are made and a high level of risk is not the norm. By contrast, free fall parachuting and motor racing are sports where high risk is the essence of the activity.

'I really like to get the adrenalin running before I pull the rip cord.' This is a characteristic statement of someone who thrives on the stimulus that comes from taking risks, and this man always delays pulling the rip cord until the last possible moment. It caused him little anxiety to be parachuted into the mid-Atlantic close to the *Queen Elizabeth II* to investigate a bomb scare on the ship, but a short time later when sailing in the English Channel he admitted to being intensely frightened while sitting becalmed in his small boat in fog and hearing all around him the hooters of big ships – which of course could have pulverised his small boat without even knowing they had hit anything.

It is unwise to make general statements about exceptional people, but there certainly are those who seek and apparently thrive upon the stimulus of danger. Sometimes they speak of themselves as 'adrenalin addicts', which is just as well because it shows that at least they recognise consciously what they are doing. I am more concerned about those who clearly are stimulated by danger but who are quite unaware of the fact.

Another group comprises those who are trying to demonstrate

something by exposing themselves to danger. An act of bravery (which is only so regarded because it involves danger) has from earliest times in certain communities been required of boys before they could make the transition to manhood. Although such a *rite de passage* is no longer required in our more controlled society, where indeed individual adventure or stepping even temporarily off the ladder can be frowned upon, it is nonetheless important for young people to make the transitions from adolescence to adulthood in their own way.

Nowadays we speak of identity formation, which is a rather more flexible concept than simple transition to manhood and better suited to our more complex society, where, apart from anything else, young women as well have identities to develop. The sense of identity, which is really the awareness of who one is and what one can do, is intimately bound up with questions of meaning. You find out who you are and how you can satisfactorily relate to society.

For some young people the approach of adulthood brings with it feelings of futility. 'If I am really *meant* to live, and if life really has any meaning,' go the young man's thoughts, 'then I can take a risk with my life and I will be preserved.' This apparently bizarre idea can totally dominate the thinking of a person beset with feelings of meaninglessness. Unfortunately it can lead to risky and potentially self-destructive acts – varieties of 'Russian roulette' – which sometimes do end in death. Whether surviving the dangerous acts leads on to a sense of meaning in life, I do not know: I have certainly never witnessed such a transition. People may discover a sense of meaning and richness in living after having come close to death by accident or illness, but that is different from danger deliberately sought in order to find meaning. Donald Crowhurst's life would have taken on a new meaning if he had actually succeeded in sailing around the world (as opposed to getting away with a faked voyage), but although I do not believe there was a self-destructive element in the planning of the trip, there was a potentially fatal gulf between the idea of circumnavigating the world and the reality of getting the boat through the ocean.

Two people not so far mentioned are David Johnstone and John Hoare. In May 1966 they endeavoured to row the Atlantic from west to east, but after 106 days at sea their 15 ft. 6 in. (4.7 m) boat was overturned, probably in a hurricane, and the two men were lost.[28] To include their story at this point is to suggest that it was an adventure to prove something, and that is what I think it was. To use Johnstone's own words: 'I began to think of a two-man trip as a desirable purity of idea: go the penance way.' The trip was well planned, but inadequate sea trials were allowed, as with Donald Crowhurst, in order to meet a deadline for departure. In this case it was a self-imposed deadline, as they wanted to leave before Chay Blyth and John Ridgway who were also rowing the Atlantic from west to east.[29]

After eighty-three days at sea and barely half-way across, Johnstone and Hoare had encountered the US coastguard vessel *Duane*. They had received supplies and confirmation of their position, and Hoare had gone on board. Johnstone had preferred to remain on board their own boat, *Puffin*. This would have been a reasonable moment to give up, on account of serious inadequacies in the boat and in their preparations, which would make a successful outcome unlikely. They would have emerged with credit, and from their mistakes and miscalculations they could have planned a successful voyage the following year. But that is to take a detached and logical view of the matter. For Johnstone, his moment was *now*, and there was probably never any serious thought of abandoning the trip. How it would have affected Johnstone's life if he had succeeded is hard to say. Blyth and Ridgway succeeded and each went on to further adventures because adventure was a way of life for them, and I suspect that when they finally look back, they will regard their transatlantic row as the supreme adventure of their lives. Johnstone was not such a natural adventurer. This enterprise was quite out of the ordinary for him, and I fear that the high expectations he had may have blinded him to some of the harsh realities involved in trying to row a small boat across three thousand miles of ocean, and during the hurricane season at that.

Denying danger

In every hilly and coastal area, scores of people inadequately clad with little idea of what they are doing are rescued each year from slippery crags and upturned dinghies – cases of *simple ignorance*. Danger simply does not occur to them. More of a menace are those who *deny the reality* of the risks. They almost proudly disregard advice, sometimes from the very people who will subsequently have to rescue them. They may be showing off to their friends or perhaps be caught up in a fantasy about adventure which they have picked up from the media, without any proper understanding of the practicalities or any realisation of how quickly conditions in the natural environment can change.

Even experienced adventurers can temporarily deny – or fail to acknowledge – risks, when fatigued or tremendously keen to attain some objective, such as reaching the summit of a mountain before the weather closes in, or making it into harbour in deteriorating conditions; in both instances the prudent course would have been to hold back.

A *sense of invulnerability* has led countless brilliant and redoubtable people to their doom. Elite troops may feel they are so well equipped and trained that they can overcome or evade any enemy, but they can withstand the impact of a bullet no better than anyone else. In the same way a superlative climber may be swept away in an avalanche or a superlative sailor simply sail away over the horizon and never be seen again. Modern materials and equipment – and weapons for that matter – enable people to attempt what might have been quite unrealistic a decade before, but this can easily lead the unwary into imagining that technology can be a substitute for technical skill and physical and psychological resourcefulness.

8
Simple Errors, Poor Concentration and Forgetfulness

The term fatigue refers to the deterioration of performance with the passage of time. The onset of fatigue is insidious, with the person unaware that his efficiency is beginning to deteriorate. I have seen doctors, weary from hours on duty, talk in a ponderous manner and move like old men. They seem to get through their work, but at a much reduced rate. Looking back on the numerous occasions when I worked throughout a night after a full normal day, and spent as long as twenty-eight hours on end in the operating theatre, I can recollect only a kind of dreamy euphoria, and even a sense of pride at keeping going on the job when the rest of the world was sleeping.

A group at the Presbyterian Hospital in New York City[1] have investigated doctors who work long hours. Fourteen interns (thirteen men and one woman) were tested when well rested and again when deprived of sleep in the course of night-time duties. On each occasion they completed rating scales dealing with mood and bodily sensations. They also had to read an electrocardiograph tracing and indicate the episodes showing abnormalities of rhythm.

In their rested state they had on average seven hours of sleep, when fatigued on average 1.8 hours (range 0.3–8 hours). When rested they made an average of 5.2 errors in interpreting the electrocardiograph tracing, and when sleep-deprived 9.6 (prizes of 50 and 25 dollars were offered for the fewest errors made in the reporting when tired). The mood scale showed significantly less 'vigor, elation and social affection', and significantly more 'fatigue and sadness'. They also made significantly more complaints such as feeling weak or nauseated or having difficulty in focusing their eyes.

Four of the fourteen stopped the electrocardiograph during the experimental and control trials, and three of these four took on average 7.3 minutes longer to complete their study of the record when fatigued than when rested, although this extra time did not seem to improve their performance.

Familiar routines, such as performing standard operations, driving a car or piloting an aircraft, may be managed satisfactorily even when an individual is deprived of sleep (whether or not he feels tired). The danger lies mainly in one's ability to cope with new situations.

Brian Cooke, then aged fifty-one, was a most experienced sailor who for years had been in the habit of waking himself every hour to check that the boat was on course and in good order. He was making a routine check at 10.15 p.m. on the seventh day of the 1972 Transatlantic Race when he found a lower shroud (steel cable supporting the mast) lying loosely on the deck of his yacht *British Steel*. It was dark, and there was a heavy swell at the end of a gale. Without this shroud the mast was inadequately supported for heavy conditions or hard sailing, and it had to be repaired. Aware of the dangers of precipitate or poorly thought out action, he decided to consider the problem for at least two hours before doing anything, and he 'discussed everything out loud'. Eventually, when he was ready to act, he set the boat on a point of sailing that would lessen the appalling oscillation, and climbed 30 feet (9 m) up the mast to the point where the shroud had broken. It took him two hours, with five trips up and down that mast, to secure the heavy steel cable back on to the mast. By that time it was five o'clock in the morning on day 8.

The next day, according to his log entry, he 'found it extremely difficult to think clearly due to tiredness and apprehension regarding the shroud breaking – it was a difficult enough exercise for anyone fresh'. He found it hard to remember simple things. He would go below to fetch something and then forget what he had gone for. He also recorded in his log: 'I thought I heard voices.' He had not slept at all that night, but had rewarded himself with three tins of lobster soup. The subjective record (dealing with his general state of well-being or otherwise), which he completed each day, showed an uncharacteristic tension and lack of confidence in the boat.

On day 10 he 'tried to put saucepan away in cutlery drawer'. He had a total of four hours' sleep the previous night and was still apprehensive about the integrity of the boat. Day 11: 'Made a pot of tea this morning which I had been looking forward to – left it for 15 minutes to draw, having promptly forgotten about it (not distracted by any other important duty).' Apart from this, his function was virtually back to normal; sailing conditions were good and he went on to make a creditable fourth place in the race.

Navigation is easily the sailor's most complex task, from the psychological point of view. Out on the ocean the angle of the sun must be recorded with a sextant (a good one can measure the angle to an accuracy of ten seconds of the arc) and the time of measuring the angle noted to within four seconds of time. Working out one's position then involves looking up several figures in nautical tables which have large pages densely packed with numbers, and making a series of simple calculations. There is great scope for error, bearing in mind that the calculations are being done on an unstable platform, sometimes on scraps of paper on the person's lap and often in poor light. It was for this reason that special attention was paid to navigational accuracy in my study of the transatlantic sailors.

In the vicinity of land, there is much more information available to guide the sailor and, equally, to confuse him. There are radio beacons, lighthouses with individual flashing patterns, landmarks, shoals and other hazards in the sea itself, tidal stream atlases and navigation buoys.

Mike McMullen was seasick for the first four and a half days of the 1972 race, and during that time ate nothing but two boiled eggs and a cup of oxtail soup. Although he had adequate sleep he regularly misread the scale on his chart. Later when he was feeling better and there was at last sun for a sun sight, he found he was two hundred miles east of where he had thought he was. Sir Francis Chichester reported a similar experience:

> When I came to plot the night's doings on the chart I found I had made a most stupid blunder the night before in my plotting. There were two charts on the chart table. The top one on which I was plotting had its left-hand margin turned down to make it fit on the chart table. The edge of the chart below was showing on the left and I had measured my distance off the coast from its latitude scale which was less than half the scale of the chart above. (This was all by candlelight.) Therefore instead of being 20 miles from land I must have been only 8 off, and when I tacked only 3. Therefore, had I gone into a deep sleep for two hours I might have had a rude awakening.[2]

In other words he would have run on to the treacherous rocky coast of Nova Scotia, and in fog too.

Falling asleep at the helm of a sailing boat is a common experience and generally does not matter too much, as one is wakened quickly by the boat yawing off course: there is less latitude for the motorist.

In a study of drivers who had been driving for nine hours continuously and had gone without sleep for the previous twenty-four hours, eye movements were slower, and the drivers tended to fix their gaze almost compulsively on the edge of the road rather than scanning ahead and around for road signs and other traffic. In another similar study, the sleep-deprived drivers were able to maintain a steady speed but were unable simultaneously to keep the vehicle in a constant position in the lane: they could manage either task separately but not both at the same time.[3]

Before actual nodding, or falling asleep, occurs, a number of changes can be observed by interested passengers: more body movements, fidgeting and stretching, rubbing and screwing up the eyes; slower responses to traffic signals and other events on the road; delayed braking and probably less steering correction.

It is a wise precaution to take seriously every absent-minded act, and to assume that it is indicative of overall impairment of function until proved otherwise. Soon after the onset of the Antarctic winter in 1934, Richard Byrd in his solitary hut wrote: 'Last night I put sugar in the soup, and tonight I plunked a spoonful of cornmeal mush on the table where the plate should have been.'[4] Byrd was getting over a period of depression but otherwise there was nothing particular going on, so it did not matter too much if his function was slightly impaired. For others, like an ill-fated bomb-disposal sergeant in Northern Ireland, there was no latitude at all.

The sergeant had his hands down inside a milk churn trying to neutralise a bomb there. On the intercom he said to his assistant: 'Oh, Christ, what've I got here...?' Then there was a bang. Lt.-Col. Derrick Patrick, trying to understand why things had gone so badly wrong, noted:

He was a self-assured young man – confident and liked by his team. He was also impatient. Normally these are not traits which would kill an operator. Unfortunately a collection of circumstances were against him.

First, he had been back from rest and recreation leave only one full day before he went out on the clearance operation. So he had not had time to get himself back into the frame of mind necessary for the [bomb disposal] operator's tasks. Don't forget, he was a confident young man.

Second, he had made some very successful clearances. Unknown to us at the time this included one when he had knocked the lid off a milk-churn bomb with a hammer.

Third, he did not go to bed early the night before the clearance.

Fourth, the inexplicable had intervened. As someone said later:

'What the hell was he doing putting his hands inside the milk churn full of explosives?' A drawing of the booby-trapped milk-churn I had neutralised beside the tanker on the border on Christmas Eve was actually on the wall of his office in Omagh!

Furthermore, he had been asked by the [police] Special Branch to visit them before he started the clearance. They had some information for him on the bomb . . . which he did not call to receive.

Finally, the owner of the shop, who had found the bomb behind the counter, had advised him to blow it up *in situ*. It was good advice. But he did not take it.

He had not even worn his bomb suit.[5]

In November 1979 a DC-10 crashed into Mount Erebus in Antarctica. This was a very peculiar place for such an aircraft to be, but it later turned out to be an Air New Zealand tourist flight offering a ten-hour round trip to get a glimpse of the Antarctic continent. What went wrong?

To begin with, the computerised routing fed into the aircraft's inertial navigation system was changed *after* the crew had been briefed for the flight. They therefore flew a course that was incorrect by over 2° of longitude, which meant that by the time they had reached McMurdo Sound some 2,500 nautical miles (4,600 km) away, they were twenty-seven miles east of where they thought they were. In fact they were on a collision course with Mount Erebus which is 12,500 feet (3,800 m) high. By then they had no precise idea where they were, and, being almost all new to Antarctic flying, they seem to have been perplexed by the white-out conditions in which the boundary between land and sky becomes blurred. The cockpit voice-recorder revealed that there were six or seven people on the flight deck and evident disagreement among them about what should be done. The disagreement did not last long. The ground proximity warning system began to sound, and within a few seconds they crashed at 260 knots at an altitude of 1,500 feet (460 m) into the mountain they had gone to see, killing all 257 people on board.[6,7]

The (locally) inexperienced crew, through no fault of their own, set off on an erroneous course, but they did not check their course later on nor did they manage to make contact with the US air base at McMurdo Sound which might have given them their true position. Instead, various people in the cockpit looked out, making guesses about what they thought they could see through the murky conditions. The pilot, who was flying far below the recommended height, was doubtless feeling uncomfortable in this predicament, but he could not disregard the fact that he had on board 237 passengers who had paid 350 dollars apiece to get a view of the Antarctic continent, and it was up to him to give them their money's worth. It was a terrible accident, but it seems to be tempting fate to take a pleasure trip into regions which should only be approached with the greatest respect and caution.

Even established tourist regions can be hazardous when they are in mountainous terrain, as when a Dan-Air Boeing 727 on a charter flight from Manchester, England, crashed in April 1980, killing 138 holiday-makers and the eight crew. Conditions were bad at Los Rodeos airport on Tenerife, and since there was no radar there it was not clear to the air traffic controller that the Dan-Air Boeing was slightly off course or that it was overtaking a smaller Iberian Airways aircraft. When the air traffic controller did realise there were two aircraft close together, he put the Dan-Air into a holding pattern (a circuit in the air) to await clearance to land, but this was not a recognised, or published, holding pattern.

The air traffic controller radioed to the Dan-Air pilot, 'Turn to the left', which is a specific instruction. What he meant to say was 'Turns to the left', that is, all turns should be to the left instead of, as is usually the case in such circumstances, to the right. The Dan-Air pilots were puzzled by this instruction, which would take them over high ground where the safe clearance is 14,500 feet (4,400 m). They did what they were told, but they certainly would not have done so if they had had any idea where they were. The air traffic controller had no idea where they were either – he may have thought they were out over the sea, as he brought them down to a height of 5,000 feet (1,500 m). A few seconds after that while the crew were still debating what to do, the ground proximity warning system broke in and they crashed into the mountainside at 5,450 feet (1,660 m).

The Spanish and British interpretations of the events vary, the Spanish primarily blaming the aircrew, and the British primarily blaming the air traffic controller.[8] The BBC 'Panorama' team have claimed that the thirty-four-year-old air traffic controller had just learned that his mother was dying of cancer, with the implication that this may have affected his concentration and judgement.[9] This could be a fair deduction, but we know nothing of the pressures prevailing on the British pilots. All that is clear from the complete transcripts of the communications between ground and the various aircraft in the vicinity at the time is that there were misunderstandings which led to the fatal errors. In fairness to the air traffic controller, it must be said that Los Rodeos is a dangerous airport, being located at 2,000 feet (600 m) on a mountainous island and without radar, and over a thousand people had already been killed there, including the 562 who died in a collision in fog three years before. It is, however, by no means the most dangerous of the popular 'holiday' airports.

Five examples have been given in this chapter. The doctors were short of sleep but not under any other kind of pressure, and certainly in no personal danger. They merely slowed down and were less reliable, and in the future these doctors will probably be more aware of the possibility of impairment of the quality of their observation, judgement and manual dexterity after long hours on duty, when short of sleep or when roused from sleep.

Brian Cooke was fully aware of these factors: he took adequate precautions and so managed a difficult, exhausting and dangerous repair job. The unfortunate bomb-disposal sergeant acted as though he was quite unaware not only of the importance of being well rested but also of being in the right frame of mind when approaching a challenging task. It also seems that he suppressed from his consciousness technical data and specific warnings given to him in connection with this particular bomb.

On the Air New Zealand sightseeing flight the plane was not where it should have been on reaching the Antarctic continent, on account of a navigation error. Conditions were not good, but they were not exceptionally bad for those regions. Although there were six or seven people on the flight deck (which may or may not have been an advantage), they continued flying at between 1,500 and 2,000 feet (460–600 m) searching for a mountain of 12,500 feet (3,800 m). At Tenerife, the Dan-Air pilots similarly did not know where they were, but they were in contact with an air traffic controller who thought he did know where they were and so they acted on his instructions, even though they were irregular and perplexing. Errors were made on both sides, but who made the greater or more crucial error?

9

Faulty Judgements and Perceptions

A subject is shown a picture of a five-bar gate with an unreadable notice behind it. At first the picture is so poorly illuminated that nothing about it can be identified with certainty. As the level of illumination and/or the length of time the subject looks at the picture is increased, guesses of varying degrees of accuracy will be offered. To begin with the outline of the gate might be perceived as a house, later as a factory building, and so on. Once the gate has been correctly identified, the notice will be recognised as such, but some people may go so far as to make assumptions about what might be written on it, for example, 'Trespassers will be prosecuted'. Only later will these people realise that nothing was written on it. All along hypotheses are being made about the content of the picture, and are constantly revised in the light of the increasing information.

This process of forming and correcting hypotheses may be disturbed in two principal ways. First, hypotheses may change so rapidly that none is held long enough to plan useful action. In an experiment,[1] healthy relaxed subjects may make six or seven guesses before giving the correct answer. When the same test is applied to highly anxious people, because of their high level of arousal or their inability to tolerate the uncertainty of the ill-defined visual image, they impose an interpretation on the visual image prematurely, and they switch rapidly to alternative interpretations as the level of illumination increases. The result is that these anxious subjects may make fifteen to twenty or more guesses before reaching the correct answer.

If such a person is trying to navigate a small boat into harbour at night, the multiplicity of lights which can be observed could form the basis of a series of rapidly changing (and all false) hypotheses which would render a consistent plan impossible.

The second abnormal reaction is to stick rigidly to the first (and false) hypothesis. Although not manifestly or measurably anxious, the person is rendered uncomfortable by the presence of ambiguity in his environment. He therefore seizes on an explanation for the poorly illuminated picture at the outset and refuses to modify it even though his interpretation becomes progressively more inappropriate as the level of illumination increases.

This is a pattern of reaction seen in ordinary life when someone develops a delusion idea (that is, a conviction that cannot be altered by rational explanation). For example, there is a knock on the door early in the morning. It is a rather aggressive knock and the person assumes that the police have come for him – that is his false hypothesis. Later on, when the postman returns, he explains that it was he who made the earlier knock, but the explanation is not accepted; indeed it may occur to the person that not only was the earlier knock the police but that the second caller is really a policeman in disguise. This is a classic paranoid reaction, which has the effect of fulfilling the individual's need for an explanation that will reduce uncertainties or that will provide him with an acceptable explanation for events which he cannot handle directly. Such a reaction is more likely to occur in someone who is in an anxious state, and also in someone ordinarily of a rigid temperament who has a smaller tolerance than usual for uncertainty or ambiguous situations.

False expectations: seeing what you want and expect to see

Stand at a crossroads when there are tired and frustrated motorists about. The driver wants to go straight ahead, the light for him shines red but a green arrow allowing traffic to filter off to one side lights up. The driver moves forward in the direction he wants to go even though 'his' light is still red. He pulls up in a greater or a shorter time according to how weary or tense he is. He is responding to the signals as he would like them to be as opposed to how they actually are.

Every year an appreciable number of train drivers pass signals set at danger. At the inquiry which always follows, a common reply is to the effect that: 'That light is always at green.' Leaving south London for the Kent coast on a foggy December afternoon in 1957, the driver, on the left-hand side of the train, could not see the signals from a distance. His fireman, who under such circumstances would read the signals which were placed to the right of the train, was otherwise occupied, and the driver failed to cross over to see them for himself. The first signal he missed was set at double yellow (proceed with some caution), the second at yellow (proceed with caution). He therefore did not check his speed, and by the time the fireman had returned to his lookout post and noticed the next signal, which was at red, it was too late to stop, and the express ran into a stationary train at St John's Station, Lewisham, killing ninety people and injuring many more.[2]

When the driver was asked at his trial (for manslaughter) why he had ignored the warning signals, he said he was expecting a green signal at St John's 'because I have never been stopped there in the whole time I have been travelling'. Even months afterwards, he still refused absolutely to believe that the light had been set at red. Conditions were foggy but the journey was routine, and there was no other reason known which might have impaired the driver's performance.[3]

In addition to hazards encountered on the journey, a driver may have other things on his mind which have nothing at all to do with the running of a train – problems with family, friends, work, money – but which may impair his concentration and thus his overall efficiency.

The Cornish express left London just before ten o'clock in the evening, just as the sirens were sounding the all clear to mark the end of another night's bombing in the London blitz in 1940. Because of rain, strong winds and difficult blackout conditions this large train lost time, and so it was diverted on to a relief line at Norton Fitzwarren in Somerset to leave the main line clear for a rapidly gaining smaller newspaper train. This relief line was parallel to the main line, but the signals for the relief line were to the left of it while the signals for the main line were on the right. Unfortunately, though further over to the right than normal, these main-line signals were clearly visible from the relief line, and the driver of the express, now on the relief line, looked to the right as he had been accustomed to do at that point when on the main line, and saw the signals set at green. He did not appreciate that they were further across than they should have been, merely that they gave him the kind of signal he wanted. He increased speed sharply, and at that moment the newspaper train roared past at full speed. He instantly realised his terrible mistake – that he had read and responded to the signal intended for the newspaper train – but it was now too late to brake effectively, and a few seconds later the train with its nine hundred passengers ploughed off the track into soft ground. Twenty-seven of them and the fireman were killed, and ninety-five were injured, while the newspaper train continued on its way unaware that anything unusual had happened. The driver of the express had a miraculous escape, and was able to get to a nearby signal box to give warning of the blocked line.

It later transpired that the driver, who was experienced and had a good record, was suffering much hardship and distress from having had his house in west London bombed. Because of this and the difficult conditions of the run, he was treated leniently by the investigating team, but he never forgave himself and died a year or so later without apparent cause.[4]

Another feature of this accident was the automatic warning system, which was found afterwards to be in perfect working order. A siren would have sounded in the cab when the driver of the Cornish express passed the signal on the relief line which was undoubtedly set at danger, and he would also have felt the application of the automatic vacuum brake. The driver denied any recollection of hearing the warning siren, and the investigators assumed that he must have cancelled the warning subconsciously. A similar overriding of safety devices (which would have averted the accident) occurred before the Trident air disaster of 1972.

Sailors, too, can misread lights so as to fulfil their expectations. Adrian Hayter, a New Zealand army officer who had already made two singlehanded passages between England and New Zealand, was trying to enter harbour at three o'clock one morning after a difficult approach in the dark.

> ... I eventually got myself lined up off the entrance lights and to my relief and surprise picked up the leading lights almost at once, two lights one above the other which in line led straight along the true bearing given on the chart and through the centre of the breakwaters.
>
> The lights kept moving off the line, but I was tired and put that difficulty down to bad steering and the strong cross currents off the entrance. I clung to the line of lights, continually correcting *Valkyr*'s helm, grateful that they were visible at all through the rain that was falling, and afraid of losing them at that critical time so close to the breakwaters.
>
> A sudden gust of wind cleared the visibility, and for a moment faint red and green lights showed below and to either side of the leading lights. I was lined up on the yellow masthead lights of a huge tanker.[5]

Tiredness, rain and poor visibility contributed to his mistaking masthead lights which appear one on top of the other when a ship is heading straight for you, for harbour lights which also appear one on top of the other when you are exactly on course for the harbour entrance.

One of the most experienced and intrepid singlehanded sailors of all, Lt.-Col. 'Blondie' Hasler, who originated the idea of a singlehanded transatlantic race, relates with characteristic coolness and modesty a near-fatal accident while on a singlehanded Atlantic crossing in the early 1960s:

> I started on a Saturday morning after staying awake the whole of the previous night trying to get the boat ready. After three days and nights of beating to windward in a seasick condition I was only just north of the Scilly Isles, heading north west on the port tack. The next day I took my first sun sight, which told me that I would pass at least 50 miles [80 km] clear of the south west of Ireland. That night it was thick fog and several times I heard a gun, but I simply dismissed it from my mind as I caught up on some sleep. Next morning I was still on the port tack in a light breeze with visibility down to half a mile when the boat put herself about while I was lying on my bunk. Putting my head out, I saw rocks at the base of Mizzen Head [south west tip of Ireland] which I would have hit if she hadn't tacked. My sun sight must have been wrong, but I had believed it because it was encouraging. The gun would have been the Fastnet [lighthouse] fog signal, and I think I passed inside it.

No one would ever choose to sail between the Fastnet Rock and the cliffs of the mainland in foggy conditions.

The risk of such errors is reduced by the presence of other people, but it is not eliminated. A party of four including a doctor were sailing a 27-foot (8.2 m) chartered yacht back to England from Guernsey. They started late because one of the party had been lingering over shopping, and so they missed the tide which would help them clear the Channel Islands. However, they made a fast crossing on account of a freshening wind, and sighted the south coast of England sooner than they had expected. They picked out three lights which they identified as the lighthouses on Anvil Point, the Needles and St Catherine's Point (see over), although they were further west than they had expected. By heading just to the west of the Needles light they would find the Needles Channel, which would bring them to their destination in the Solent. Three-quarters of an hour later the skipper checked the flashing patterns of the lights and found that they were in fact Portland, Anvil Point and the Needles, so their present course would have them pass close to the west of Anvil Point, eventually to pile up on the rocky coast there. They immediately changed course to east, but by this time they had missed the tide which would carry them up the Needles Channel. The wind had steadily strengthened from the south-west and so they could no longer stand off in that exposed position and wait for the tide to turn. Instead, they quite sensibly kept well clear of the coast and tried

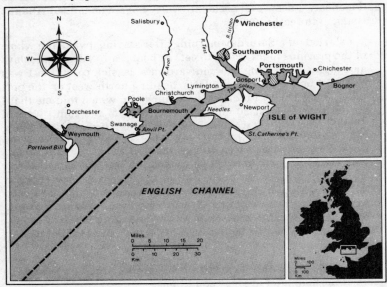

Expectations and Realities

The broken line indicates the hoped-for track and the solid line the actual track. After an arduous sail back from the Channel Islands, the crew were wearying and the left-hand three lights were wrongly assumed to be the right-hand three with the result that they would have piled up on the rocks of St Alban's Head.

simply to avoid being blown right up to Dover in what now had become a gale. Inevitably they wearied, and two of them became totally incapacitated with seasickness.

So here was a group of only moderately experienced sailors who started off badly by missing their departure tide, and somehow never regained their equilibrium. They recognised they had misread the lights, but it was too late to sustain the original plan. Then came the gale, which reduced them all to a point where they were incapable of any effective physical or mental activity. 'We had abjured decision,' said the skipper. It was in this setting that they evolved the 'plan' to run the boat up on the beach on the south coast near Bognor in Sussex, where they hoped they would then be able to jump through

the waves and scramble ashore. In the event they were saved by the
gale abating, but their plan if executed would almost certainly have
drowned the lot of them.

A good many sailing boats disappear at sea or are wrecked on the
coasts, and not many of the sailors are around to describe exactly
what happened and why. One who did survive was Peter Pye,
another doctor, who spent much of his life sailing the oceans of the
world. He has related in his book *Red Mains'l* his experiences while
sailing in the Bahamas:

> With our ship looking smart in a new coat of paint, we left
> Hatchet Bay the next morning, but for unavoidable reasons we
> were two hours late. I was furious, because it meant that instead of
> going through Current Cut we should have to go round by the
> Fleeming Channel, twenty-five miles out of our way, and spend the
> night behind a rock if we could find one. Current Cut is a narrow
> channel between Northern Eleuthera and Current Island. The *Pilot
> Book* says of it '... a narrow channel through which the tidal
> streams rush with the force of a rapid, but which is used by small
> craft with local knowledge at slack water'. As we had missed slack
> water by two hours and had no local knowledge, anyway, we were
> hardly justified in attempting it. We shaped our course for the
> Fleeming Channel, but it was galling to see the Cut across the way,
> looking so simple at this distance.

The temptation was too great for them. They changed course and
headed for the cut, and battled their way through against the tide.

> Pleased that we had made the Cut despite all the *Pilot Book* said
> about it, I was relaxed and off my guard. I had studied the entrance
> to Royal Island Harbour; it was narrow and there were two rocks,
> one big, the other small; both of them, I thought, above the water.
> As we drew near, I saw two rocks. They looked closer to each other
> than they appeared on the chart, but I was not particularly
> concerned as we should be coming in close to the eastern side,
> away from both of them. As we sailed in, the wind came more off
> the land and I paid-off to keep way on her to bring her to an anchor.
> Anne and Bob took in the headsails. There was a sudden cry from
> Anne as she glanced over the side, then a grinding jarring sound as
> *Moonraker* struck the reef, listing over to port, her stern nearly two
> feet above its normal level. For a moment time stood still. I saw
> *Moonraker* wrecked on this lonely island and our venture ended in
> ignominy, and all for lack of that extra care. I never knew till then
> how much I loved our ship. It was easy to see what had happened:
> the two rocks I had seen were one, separated by a few feet of water

at high tide. The second reef, which we were now on, had its ugly head just hidden below our starboard bilge. If we had come in at any time except high water, the mistake wouldn't have been made.[6]

Faulty judgements and irrational plans

The party of four referred to in the last section, who misread the lights on the English coast after sailing home from Guernsey, provide an example of irrational planning in their decision to beach their boat. They were of course in a pretty bad state, but somehow they agreed to head for a stretch of sandy beach near Bognor. The idea was to set the yacht square on to the beach and sail hard to it. As soon as they touched bottom they would jump into the breaking waves and scramble ashore. Even in a relatively calm sea and in good physical conditions this would be a difficult operation: in the gale that was blowing and with the crew exhausted from seasickness and lack of sleep it would have been suicidal. Yet at the time to those on board it seemed the best way out of their difficulties. In the event they were saved by the gale abating sufficiently for them to run to shelter round the east side of the Isle of Wight.

Although groups of people are generally likely to make fewer errors than people on their own, the factor of suggestibility may have had an influence here. One person floats the idea of beaching the boat, and the others clutch at it as a solution to their predicament, without any real understanding of what would actually be involved. Their enthusiasm further encourages the person who put forward the plan in the first place, and so on until gradually they have convinced one another that there is a real alternative to wallowing helplessly in the gale.

Suggestibility is always enhanced by distress and anxiety; indeed, as I have already described, such states are deliberately generated by political and religious indoctrinators to soften up those whose ideas and values they seek to change. Recently bereaved people, too, are extra-suggestible and quite often fall victim to unscrupulous salesmen; similarly, the stunned survivors of a natural disaster will be almost totally passive and docile, showing virtually no will of their own.

In prison, a preliminary period of isolation can render someone more vulnerable to subsequent indoctrination, and already while isolated the individual is more vulnerable than he would otherwise be to his own irrational thought processes.

Donald Crowhurst was two weeks out from Teignmouth in Devon on his ill-fated circumnavigation of the world when he made this appraisal of his boat and its equipment in his log entry for 15 November 1968 (in summary):

No electrics; no radio communications; no masthead buoyancy; no time signals, and my chronometer is useless; no light – not essential I suppose. Leaky hatches: the port forward float hatch let in something like 120 gallons in 5 days, though I think I've cured that; the cockpit hatch has leaked 75 gallons overnight. Incorrectly cut sails.

No method of pumping out the saloon, forward and aft float hatches, forward main hatch, or aft main hatch without lifting hatches, which is potentially highly dangerous. The after collision bulkhead is leaking. The evidence for this is in the brown water in the saloon.

The Hasler [self-steering] gear needs attention to screws every few hours, and they still drop out.

He goes on then to debate how various people would be affected if he were to drop out of the race, especially Stanley Best who had invested so much money in the venture. He sets out the course of action open to him (again summarised):

1 Go on to Australia. It would be quite an achievement and there might be a market for the Navicator [his navigational device].
2 Save face by going to Capetown.
3 Return to UK. Not feasible, because it involves Clare [his wife] in 14 days or so of unnecessary worry.
4 Put in locally, then communicate with Mr Best.
5 Get the necessary work done then go on to America, Australia, South Africa or back to UK.

Two days later he made a second assessment of his situation. He was by now level with southern Portugal; he drew up a table of daily distances he would have to sail if he were to reach Cape Horn before the winter there, and he realised clearly that he could not do it. This second assessment was made in preparation for radio-telephone conversations he had booked for the following day, 18 November, with his wife and with Stanley Best. He was presumably going to put his plight to them, but when he actually spoke to them he minimised his difficulties and gave no hint of retiring from the race. Again on 21 November he spoke to Best, and they had a technical discussion about some of the problems of bailing, but he did mention that he was having difficulty with the generator and that there might be radio silence in the future.[7]

After such a devastating appraisal there was only one rational course of action, which was to put in to harbour for repairs as soon as possible. But Crowhurst's solution was quite different. He evolved a plan (which may have occurred to him even before he left England) to fake a voyage round the world. While cruising slowly around in the South Atlantic he would record weather bulletins for those parts of the Southern Ocean he was supposed to be traversing at the time, and at the same time maintain the radio silence he warned of in his log entry of 15 November, since radio transmissions would give away his approximate true position.

His logs contained some thirty pages of pencilled notes of the weather conditions for the areas he should have been in, but the conjectured fake log-book containing the supposed route through the Southern Ocean was never found. Eventually on 9 April 1969, Crowhurst broke his radio silence with a cryptic message indicating he was approaching Cape Horn, while actually sailing somewhere off Buenos Aires.

When Crowhurst's abandoned trimaran was found floating intact in mid-Atlantic on 10 July 1969, the three log-books were retrieved. They were examined by Captain Craig Rich, an expert in navigation. After two or three minutes' perusal he suspected a fraud; after twenty minutes he said he was certain. Sir Francis Chichester, incidentally, had suspected a fraud from quite an early date in the voyage because of the peculiar quality of the messages.

Sailors and navigation experts have since discussed on many occasions whether it would be possible to construct *in absentia* a plausible log based solely upon radio weather forecasts, a log which would give distances travelled consistent with the weather conditions. Even if such consistency could be achieved, the retrograde calculations of the sun's altitude would be exceedingly awkward. In short, no one in full possession of his powers of reasoning would seriously imagine that such a fraud could succeed, and I would argue that this was evidence of impaired judgement on Crowhurst's part, and of his inappropriate response to a situation (his inadequate boat) which he was unable to deal with effectively.

A much more experienced ocean sailor, Frank Mulville, was sailing singlehanded from Cuba to the island of Faial in the Azores where he was expecting his wife, Celia, to be waiting for him.

> I became convinced that I wasn't really wanted at home – that it wouldn't matter to anyone if I never got home and at the same time I wanted to get to England and have done with the voyage as soon as possible ...
>
> I began to weave for myself a completely new life, independent

from and quite different to anything that I had experienced before. It would be a fine thing to start life all over again – to form a new set of associations, a new pattern of living, a clean sweep away from everything that had gone before. I would go off into some wilderness in pursuit of ideas – break away from the humdrum for ever.

It may have been a series of Freudian errors which put my DR [Dead Reckoning] positions far north of my actual position in the three days of gale when I was approaching the Azores. The plotting of a DR position is a very subjective business – especially when one is alone ...

After three days of racing before the wind I had convinced myself that the Azores were far to the southward of me, assuming, quite without rational foundation, that I would never fetch them. I altered course to the north and irrevocably made the decision to carry straight on for England. This I now realise I had subconsciously wanted to do ever since leaving Bermuda ...

The moment of truth came to me when I telephoned home from Spain, where I fetched up 29 days out of Bermuda. My son, Adrian, told me on the 'phone 'Celia's in Faial ...' 'Christ,' I said.[8]

These two examples are of men on the ocean in reasonably good weather conditions, but alone. It is almost inconceivable that such faulty judgements could have prevailed if there had been anyone else on board. Mulville was brought back to rationality by a single telephone conversation. Crowhurst was probably more conscious of and deliberate about what he was doing, although no more rational in the long run, and would not at the stage of writing his appraisal of the boat's condition have been influenced by contact from outside.

Preoccupation and distraction

One night in December 1972 an Eastern Airlines L-1011 wide-body jet was approaching Miami airport but could not land, as it was unclear if the nose landing gear was locked in the down position. With air traffic control clearance, the pilot climbed to 2,000 feet (600 m) to investigate the problem, and to reduce the workload in the cockpit the autopilot was engaged. While the crew were occupied with the landing gear, they failed to detect a gradual and unexpected descent of the aircraft which was occurring because the autopilot had accidently become disengaged. The Miami approach controller also failed to notice it, and as a result ninety-four of the 163 passengers and five of the thirteen crew were killed, the remainder being injured. Both the aircraft and the ground control had sophisticated equipment, with the result perhaps that undue reliance was placed on it, instead of on human vigilance.[9]

When tired or anxious, an individual tends to concentrate on one aspect of the task in hand instead of maintaining the usual balanced view of the whole.

In the ordinary way, someone performing a familiar task under good conditions responds to all the stimuli from the surroundings in a coordinated manner, so that all the information is integrated and viewed as a whole. To give a simple example – someone walking along the street moves at a suitable pace to reach his destination on time, allowing for the state of the road surface, the presence of other people, and the traffic. At a more complex level, the pilot of a commercial aircraft integrates all the information about the external conditions and the state of the machine to give him a complete picture of its effective state.

When the outcome of such an activity seems to be in doubt for any reason at all, the person involved, if highly motivated, will become anxious. This anxiety, although possibly stimulating in a mild degree, is eventually liable to cause this well-coordinated behaviour to fragment. That is, instead of seeing his physical surroundings and instruments as giving him an integrated picture of his situation, he concentrates upon a detail and neglects the whole. He tends to respond briefly to each new stimulus and to forget his main task. For example, at the official inquiry into the crash of an Argonaut aircraft near Idris in Libya, it was observed that '... having made three unsuccessful attempts to line up and land on runway 11, the pilot (on his fourth attempt) allowed his desire to keep the runway lights in view to affect his judgement, in that during a visual approach to the runway he failed to make adequate reference to his flight instruments. Unknowingly he permitted the aircraft to descend below its correct approach path.'[3] Similarly, the man hurrying along the street to an important interview is so preoccupied with his thoughts that he steps out in front of a bus.

These processes of preoccupation and distraction lend themselves to experimental investigation. They were first identified in the Cambridge 'cockpit experiments' conducted in the Second World War to investigate the problem of pilot error.[10] When subjects in the training cockpits were stressed by tasks which were designed to frustrate them, a common reaction was to become preoccupied with a detail, for example, the altimeter. A change in the 'altitude' of the training cockpit would become the stimulus for correcting this fault, with the consequent neglect of the other elements necessary for the safe handling of the aircraft.[3]

In the early days of cardiac resuscitation I once saw a junior doctor so unnerved by a cardiac arrest that he threw himself into the business of getting blood transfusion going, which he insisted was an essential preliminary to cardiac massage, despite the obvious uselessness of such a course and the objections of the rest of us. He was preoccupying himself not only with a detail to the neglect of the whole, but with an irrelevant detail at that. Faced with a problem which was beyond him, he was concentrating on an activity which he could understand, but, more importantly and dangerously, he had re-interpreted the problem of cardiac arrest to suit his limitations, and nothing anyone could do at the time could shift him in his beliefs.

Another kind of preoccupation was demonstrated by Donald Crowhurst during the preparations for his voyage around the world. Because of various delays, he was left with only three weeks to equip the boat for its 30,000-mile (48,000-km) voyage before the deadline for departure on 31 October 1968. There was little evidence of any systematic planning, and so all kinds of vital equipment such as rigid tubing for pumping out the floats was ordered late and then did not arrive. Amidst the confusion and under the continuous scrutiny of the television cameras, Crowhurst busied himself with the minutiae of electronic equipment. True, he was an electronics engineer and would be expected to be well equipped, but the profusion of radio components and spare parts was quite irrelevant when such fundamentals as bailing gear were missing. Yet these details which he understood well diverted his attention from the unacceptable reality that his boat was inadequate for the task. Perhaps if he had not fallen victim to his preoccupation he would have been compelled to face this very reality while there was still time to pull back and abandon the voyage.

Combinations of false expectations, preoccupation and distraction can occur, of which the Norton Fitzwarren crash is a good example. Very similar but occurring over thirty years later was the response of a train driver who was involved in a collision near Haywards Heath in Sussex. He was driving a local 'loopline' train when he saw the signals on the main line change to green as he approached. He mistook these for his own signals and proceeded on to the main line. Moments later he was struck from behind by an express train travelling at between 70 and 80 miles per hour (120 kph). Amazingly, no one was killed and only eleven injured. At the inquiry the driver revealed that he was going through a divorce at the time with the attendant financial troubles, and that he had had an operation for a stomach ulcer and was living alone and caring for himself.[11]

In November 1981 the driver of a commuter train collided with

another train during the morning rush hour. The light he thought was
yellow was in fact red, but he realised his mistake too late. The driver
had been dosing himself with pain-killing drugs for a headache and
an aching wisdom tooth. Six days earlier his wife had given birth to
their first child after a difficult delivery, and his mother was suffering
from cancer.[12]

These are further examples of preoccupation with matters remote
from the task in hand, which raised the drivers' anxiety level and
made them more vulnerable to false expectations regarding the
signals.

Relaxation after stress
One of the worst accidents in railway history occurred in 1952 near
the end of the four-hour journey from Crewe to London. It had been a
difficult run through darkness and fog, with visibility often down to
fifty yards. The driver had lost time all the way, but as he approached
London shortly after 8 a.m. the sun began to shine and it must have
looked as though they would have a clear run home. But it was not
to be. Ahead of him a light signal was set at yellow (proceed with
caution) and two semaphore signals were set at danger, but somehow
he missed or disregarded all three of them. He applied his brakes
eventually but much too late, and ran at 60 miles per hour (96 kph)
into the back of a commuter train standing in Harrow station and full
of morning travellers. A few minutes later the London to Liverpool
express came in the opposite direction along the adjacent track and
plunged into the wreckage of the first collision. A hundred and twelve
people were killed and almost as many injured. The inquiry
concluded that '... an engineman of considerable experience and
mature age with a good record ... must have relaxed his concentration on the signals for some unexplained reason'.[3,13]

Merchant seamen talk of 'Channel fever', the seductive sense of
actually having arrived home as soon as they enter the English
Channel, which puts them in danger of taking less trouble in
handling the ship just when they should be concentrating most.

On passing the finishing point of the 1972 Singlehanded Transatlantic Race after a magnificent crossing in a 26-foot (7.9-m) yacht
never designed for ocean sailing, one man – who was to be the winner
on handicap – became totally incapable of any purposeful action for
at least an hour. He simply drifted around in the entrance to
Narragansett Bay (Newport, Rhode Island) until he was taken in tow
by a launch. He had achieved his objective, and for a while, at any
rate, his reserves were exhausted.

Most of the competitors during the course of this race experienced periods of anxiety or had to grapple with crises in which extra effort was required, such as gales, emergency repairs (possibly calling for a trip up the mast), or close shaves such as being nearly washed out of the cockpit. Afterwards the competitors usually tried to rest, and generally rewarded themselves with a special item of food or an extra can of beer. The next day, however, and sometimes for several days, a number of them gave evidence in their records that they were by no means functioning at full efficiency – forgetfulness for two days after a difficult repair job up the mast, navigation errors on the day after a gale. Phil Weld (who came twenty-seventh in the 1972 race and went on to win the 1980 race) anticipated such failing in himself. His port backstay had frayed and the jib furling gear had stopped functioning, so he hoisted himself up his 48-foot (14.6m) mast on a special seat he had rigged. Then, having effected the necessary repairs, he found he was stuck. He wrote: 'Up the mast solo in a seaway is hard work at fifty-seven years, especially as for half an hour I was trapped up there not knowing how to get down.' Eventually he had to extricate himself from the chair and slither down the mast. On the next two nights he slept six and seven hours, when his usual longest continuous sleep was three hours. He gave no evidence of errors in performance but he assumed that his judgement was liable to be impaired and so took extra care: 'Because of general lethargy from cold and up-mast bruises, I'm babying myself and boat by going to windward at an old man's 7 knots instead of, with more sail, going 9 knots.'

Anyone nearing the end of a tiring journey or after a close shave of any kind is extra-liable to make mistakes. The motorist after a near miss or on reaching the outskirts of his home town needs to take extra care. The surgeon, after completing the main operation, still has a long way to go until the patient is ready to leave the operating table: there are plenty of opportunities for error which could prove fatal for the patient.

10

Illusions and Misinterpretations

Because of our assumptions and expectations about how we feel things ought to be in the world, conditions can exist in which we are almost certain to perceive inaccurately. There are other circumstances where misperceptions depend mainly on the physical and psychological state of the observer. In this chapter both forms of misperception will be described, separately and also as they occur together.

Ordinary anomalies of perception

The eye functions according to strict mechanical principles. Seeing, however, is a conscious activity which involves the interpretation of visual signals according to the subject's knowledge, previous experience, expectations and overall mental state. Thus we have the familiar optical illusions where, for example, parallel lines can be drawn so as to appear askew or lines the same length to appear unequal, and perspectives can be deliberately distorted so that a photograph of two people of the same size in a room can have one of them looking twice the size of the other.[1]

Perceptions of size and distance and of movement can easily become distorted even under good conditions, let alone under bad ones, and so will be described here under variations of the normal; so also will some of the special problems encountered by pilots. These disturbances can afflict well rested, relaxed and undrugged people, but are all the more likely to occur when a person is fatigued and anxious.

Size and distance
Distant objects and features ordinarily appear hazier and bluer because of the intervening atmosphere, and this gives landscapes

their sense of depth and distance. In very clear regions this important cue can be missing. Richard Gregory[1] has described an experience in the New Mexico desert when he was looking from a mountain viewpoint to mountains which appeared to him to be some twenty to thirty kilometres away: if he had set off to walk with a day's food and water he would probably never have been seen again, as the mountains across the desert were in fact a hundred kilometres distant.

The moon normally appears larger when on the horizon than when at its zenith. It also appears redder. Just before dawn on the first morning after a hurried and illegal departure from an English port in an old sailing boat called *Reliance*, Ann Davison was at the helm, and in her own words, feeling 'extremely happy'. Then 'suddenly out of the corner of my eye I glimpsed something huge and red. Anything as big as that would have to be near. I pulled the wheel over and ducked. Then I looked out again. At the moon grinning redly through the morning mist ... Wide awake, I pulled myself together, thankful there was no witness of my humiliation.'[2]

Also on the horizon, mountains can appear to be higher than they are, and slopes may seem steeper or flatter.

Wherever visibility is bad distance is liable to be overestimated, and the murkier the conditions the more marked this tendency. The same applies to the sea and to polar regions where the lack of features deprives the observer of the normal cues for estimating distance – again, particularly when visibility is bad.[3,4]

Along with the tendency to overestimate distance is the tendency to overestimate size. Objects, such as a man or an aeroplane, are assumed to remain constant in size but to appear smaller the further away they go. A man seen at a distance of thirty feet (9 m) under ordinary conditions is perceived as being of a size compatible with that distance. If, however, there is fog or a snowstorm, the thirty-foot distance may appear as sixty but the man's size is still perceived as appropriate to half that distance. Therefore he is seen as being much larger than normal. Early on in his Antarctic experience, at the beginning of the long polar darkness, Admiral Byrd wrote:

> The morning may be compounded of an unfathomable, tantalizing fog in which you stumble over sastrugi [hard snow ridges], you can't see, and detour past obstructions that don't exist, and take your bearings from tiny bamboo markers that loom as big as telegraph poles and hang suspended in space. On such a day, I could swear that the instrument shelter was as big as an ocean liner.[5]

Byrd's circumstances and isolation were rather special, but more than thirty years later a group of men on a Sno-cat in an Antarctic white-out could describe the same kind of experience:

> The men in one vehicle radioed to the others that a large container had dropped off their sled and asked those following to pick it up. When sighted, the object appeared to be about 3 to 4 ft. long and 1 or 2 ft. in width. On approaching to within 3 or 4 ft. it was perceived in its actual size which was a small food tin, about 6 in. long and 3 in. wide. Standing several feet away and looking at the tin, it appeared at first to be large and then to reduce to its actual size and then to be large once more.[6]

This fluctuation in perception is similar to that experienced when one looks at an ambiguous picture which can alternately represent a young girl or an old lady, or a drawing of a hexagon which can equally well be regarded as a hollow cube.

In white-out conditions there is almost complete reflection of light from the snow, so that irregularities on the snow surface and the horizon cannot be defined and objects cast no shadows. Similar disturbances can occur when one is merely looking downwards from a height.

From an aircraft or other high vantage point, the ground may appear further away than it actually is, presumably because of the same lack of intervening objects to give cues to distance. Cars and houses down on the ground may also appear smaller, as they are not intermediate objects like the bamboo poles, the instrument shelter or the container mentioned in the examples, but part of the background itself. In mountains there are high vantage points which may be enjoyed under conditions of great clarity when everything appears close, as is the case at other times when visibility is bad or when there is moonlight, another great falsifier of perceptions. The climber, therefore, is vulnerable to all kinds of distortions when trying to make sense of his surroundings.

Walter Bonatti has described his winter ascent with Carlo Mauri of the north face of Lavaredo in the Dolomites in February 1953. They spent a night in sub-zero temperatures, held on to a narrow ledge by five unreliable pitons:

> To fall asleep would probably mean to freeze and even more to let our weight fall on to the ropes, with a resultant headlong dive to the foot of the rock face a thousand feet below, after tearing away our few weak anchorages. To prevent ourselves from sleeping, we forced ourselves to talk, to sing, to tell any sort of story, merely to

keep our eyes open ... I yelled at Mauri, clutching his arm, when, with disconnected words, he made a sudden movement. He then told me of his hallucination: 'There was one moment when the snowfield below us, lit up by the moonlight, seemed as if it had risen to where we were and that all I had to do was to stretch out a leg and reach it and at last be able to go to sleep.'[7]

That snowfield was at least one thousand feet (300 m) down.

In winter 1966 Chris Bonington and Mick Burke, during the direct assault of the north face of the Eiger in which they were participating as climbing photographers, had an opposite experience. They had just come from identifying the body of a comrade, John Harlin, who had the day before fallen 4,000 feet (1,200 m) to his death, when they engaged a light helicopter to lift them up to a high point on the mountain so as to be able to photograph the climbers as they neared the summit. The slope was far too steep for a landing so the only way out was to jump, which they did without any knowledge of what was underneath that snow covering (to make matters more difficult, it was getting dark). They saw a snowfield below them – about two hundred feet down. Bonington abseiled down and hit the snowfield after only forty feet: they had overestimated the distance fivefold.[8]

Towards the end of his singlehanded sail from England to Sydney, and the evening after discovering that two of his four forestays had broken (although conditions were reasonably light at the time), Sir Francis Chichester wrote:

I was at the stem, taking the starboard navigation light to pieces, when I suddenly felt that I was close to the water; and that it was almost within reach, whereas the stem should be 5 ft above the water. I looked aft, and the boat seemed to have settled in the water. It must be sinking. I scurried aft, and went below to lift the hatch in the cabin above the bilge. I expected to find it full up with water coming in from some unknown hole with a tremendous rush; I was amazed to find no water at all in the bilge. There was nothing at all the matter.[9]

As every motorist knows, the shape or geometry of road curves can be misleading, as there is a general tendency to underestimate the degree of curvature of roads which are clearly visible throughout the length of the curve. David Shinar, who has written an important book on the psychology of driving,[10] showed drivers photographs of a number of pairs of road curves, in which one of each pair had been associated with at least three daytime accidents in the previous three years and the other with no accidents at all. Although the pair of curves were identical in their geometry, the subjects perceived high-accident curves as 'closer, wider, and more visible than the low-accident curves'. They did not regard them as more dangerous and did not indicate that they would slow down for these high-accident curves any more than they would for the low-accident ones.

Movement

Even under optimum conditions there are many ways in which the perception of movement can be inaccurate. Distant objects will project a smaller image on to the retina and will move more slowly across it than if the same object was closer and so projecting a large image. This can lead to a number of illusions: a fast-moving light (such as an aircraft at night) can appear closer than it is, slower-moving lights may appear larger than fast-moving lights, and large lights may appear to move more slowly than small lights.

In foggy conditions, where distances appear greater than they are, an approaching object can seem to be moving faster than it is, a source of possible danger for motorists.

When you look out of the side of a moving vehicle, even in good visibility, the foreground seems to rush past; the point of fixation of gaze is more or less stationary but the further distance may appear to be moving in the direction of the vehicle. Similarly, when looking forward, the foreground rushes towards the vehicle, the fixation point is stationary but the further distance may even recede. More pronounced distortions can occur when acceleration and rotational forces are acting on the subject, especially at night when there are fewer visual cues.

Small distant objects may appear to be moving, so that rocks can look like climbers. This is probably a factor in the claim by Odell that he had sighted Mallory and Irvine in 1924 some 1,200 feet (360 m) below the summit of Everest. On the 1933 Everest expedition, and at around the same place on the mountain, Eric Shipton and Frank Smythe had a very similar experience.

Shipton suddenly stopped and pointed. 'There go Wyn and Waggers on the second step,' he exclaimed. Sure enough, there were two little dots on a steep snow-slope at the foot of the cliff. We stared hard at them and could have sworn they moved. Then, simultaneously, we realised that they were rocks. And, strangely enough, there were two more rocks perched on a snow-slope immediately above the step; these again looked like men and appeared to move when stared at.[11]

This occurred at about 27,400 feet (8,350 m), and Frank Smythe, who wrote this account, was well aware that altitude and fatigue may have played a part. However, similar experiences have been reported at heights of around 4,000 feet (1,200 m) in Scotland:

> When we started on the last rise to Cairn Toul there came a wider clearance than usual. Suddenly Mortimer gripped my arm and pointed uphill through the misty charm. 'Look!' he exclaimed, 'Two men crossing to Glen Einich.' Upon looking up at the slope I was duly surprised to see two climbers a long way ahead of us ... I watched them traverse a full fifty feet from the east to west across the snow-slope, one about ten yards in front of the other ... We advanced and saw them halt, apparently to wait for us. At a hundred yards' range they turned out to be two black boulders. So great was our astonishment that we failed even to laugh at ourselves. It was a perfect illustration of the eye's absolute need of some framework before it can distinguish a moving object from a stationary.[12]

John and Gordon Stainforth, who are twins, were desperately tired after having climbed the east face of the 5,900-foot (1,800 m) Store Trolltind in the Romsdal region of Norway, during which they had had a fall which they had expected would be fatal. Walking gently downhill after thirty-six hours without sleep, they were hearing the sounds of pitons being banged in, when ahead of them they both saw two people standing in their path. They were some distance off, but the boys (they were nineteen at the time) were thankful to make some human contact after their ordeal, and most of all to discover that they were on a track which would lead them to safety. They approached the people with mounting excitement, and it was not until they were within a few feet of them that they both simultaneously realised that all along they had been looking at two boulders streaked with water. They were shattered by their discovery, which brought home to them what a perilously fatigued state they were really in. Whether being identical twins had anything to do with their (apparently) identical misperceptions is hard to say, but their very close empathy certainly helped them on the treacherous lower part of their descent, when they seemed to work in perfect harmony with scarcely any need for verbal communication.

Disorientation among pilots[13]
Pilots are something of a special case, for although they normally work in comfortable surroundings, they are regularly subjected to quite exceptional physical forces. The sources of difficulty may lie in

the external environment leading to what may be called 'input' errors (corresponding to the first category in Chapter 7, p. 100), or they may lie within the pilot himself, leading to 'central' errors (corresponding to the second and third categories).

External environment and input errors   At high altitude, above the weather, pilots may feel in something of a 'goldfish bowl', with a dark sky above merging imperceptibly into the uniform cloud cover below. Lower down there can be cloud, haze, fog, snow, rain, smoke, dust, and of course darkness. Vibration, especially in helicopters, can render instruments impossible to read;[14] and any breakdown in heating or pressurisation can put the pilot fairly rapidly out of action.

It is during approach and landing that the pilot is most dependent on external visual cues, as all landings require the use of these cues at some stage to judge distance, angle of approach, altitude and height above ground. The glide path has to be accurate to within $2\frac{1}{2}$–$3°$, and distance is judged mainly by the relative size of familiar objects, a process which is prone to error. For the pilot travelling at over a hundred miles per hour (160 kph) the issue becomes much more pressing. The climatic hazards mentioned tend to cause distances to be overestimated, as they are when landings are made over watery or other featureless approaches, when the runway slopes upwards, or when it is narrower than usual.[4] This is because runways at commercial airports tend to be of fairly standard dimensions, and a narrow one may mislead the pilot into believing he is further from it than in fact he is. Conversely, distances can be underestimated in conditions of very good visibility such as at airports at high altitude. Also, landing at night where the runway lights are unusually bright can cause the pilot to imagine that he is closer to them than he is.

Pilot and central errors   During take-off and landing – which is when most accidents occur – the pilot is subject to tremendous and sustained acceleration and deceleration forces. Similar forces are endured when turning or otherwise changing direction in the air, especially if at the same time the pilot moves his head. This is a somewhat complex subject but essentially these external forces confuse the pilot's perception of gravity. Sustained acceleration or turning at speed can lead the pilot to imagine that gravity is pulling in a direction other than vertically downwards. This is due to the unusual forces acting on the vestibular balance and orientation mechanisms in the inner ear. What may happen during the powerful acceleration and climbing at take-off, is that the inertial forces cause the pilot to perceive gravity somewhere behind the vertical, so that he feels he is climbing at a steeper angle than he really is and may be afraid of stalling. He therefore 'levels off' a little – still accelerating and thus maintaining the illusion of steepness. Although he now may feel that he has reduced the angle of climb, he is in fact pointing downwards – still accelerating – and if he continues to fail to recognise the true orientation he could crash his aircraft.

These problems can occur equally during the sustained deceleration during descent and during turns and spins – especially coming out of a spin, when there is a risk of turning the aircraft the wrong way and back into the spin. With good visibility the horizon is a great help in orientating the pilot, but it does not abolish the danger.

Orientation errors are common. Sixty per cent of 321 pilots questioned in 1970 had experienced the sensation of one wing being low even though the plane was in level flight. After levelling off in a bank, 45 per cent had on some occasion tended to bank in the opposite direction. Thirty-nine per cent felt themselves to be straight and level when in a turn, and 29 per cent to be turning in the opposite direction on recovery from a steep climb. Twelve per cent were so intent on their 'target' – for example, an airstrip before landing – that they came in too close to the ground. Some 10 per cent of civil and military accidents in recent years have been associated with orientation errors.[13]

The pilot receives information about his orientation and speed through his perception of his surroundings and from his instruments. Of the two sources of information, his own perceptions will seem the more real, if only because he actually experiences them. This is known as flying 'by the seat of the pants', and a deliberate conscious effort is required to pay attention to impersonal instruments when they are giving a different message from one's own body.

In winter 1980 a cargo-carrying Lockheed Electra four-engined turboprop was five minutes out after a night-time take-off from Salt Lake City, under instrument-flying condition, when there was a partial failure of the electrical system. Some of the navigation instruments had failed and some were working, and communications with departure control were maintained. There was confusion in the cockpit about their heading, and they requested departure control to guide them back to Salt Lake City. The aircraft was descending (and the increase in airspeed could be heard on the cockpit recording) but the captain was convinced he was climbing and was on climb power. He went into a full right turn, accelerated to 320 knots, and the aircraft disintegrated in mid-air. The captain had had his aircraft in a spiral dive at climb power, descending at a rate of 12,000 feet

(3,660 m) per minute and the g loads exceeded 5.5.[15] This means that a force greater than five and a half times the pull of gravity was being applied – more than the aircraft could stand.

Part of the captain's problem lay in the *partial* electrical failure, so that he did not know whether any given instrument was working or not. He was probably more flustered than he would have been by a total failure. In fact, it is likely that it was mainly the co-pilot's instruments that had failed rather than the captain's and that the captain had adequate information available to him if only he had been able to use it. Although he was flying on instruments, there was audible evidence of descent from the increase of airspeed, and there was a dialogue going with departure control about the descent; but this was insufficient to overcome the captain's presumed bodily sensation that he was still climbing, even though they were by then a good ten minutes into the flight.

With the increasing sophistication of computer control, some flight crews may wonder what useful function they perform (the same applies even more to train drivers), but only human ingenuity can deal with the totally novel and critical situation, as was shown dramatically during the Apollo 13 crisis out in space. Humans can still hold much more information in terms of experience gathered over years than any current computer, even though humans will err more often than a computer will.

Misinterpretations

An *illusion* is simply a mistake in perception – a shrub at night is mistaken for a man on the side of the road – but the mistake can be corrected easily by a rational explanation. A *misinterpretation* is similar but the experience may carry a greater sense of reality and be adhered to with greater conviction, so that in the short term at any rate a rational explanation would not satisfy.

Visual experiences
Ten days out on the 1972 Singlehanded Transatlantic Race, David Blagden, a big man sailing in a 19-foot (5.8 m) sloop which was the smallest boat ever to sail in this race, was feeling anxious and physically uncomfortable although he was sleeping adequately at this point. He reported '. . . spots before my eyes when looking at the sky. I feel my tactics in staying south and east so long have backfired with this weather and more or less put me out of the competitive race.' On day 26 he wrote: 'Spots before my eyes again. Not serious and only occasional . . . I think I've been spoiled by all that calm weather.

Conditions have not been all that rough but I'm really exhausted.' The daily record he was keeping of how he was feeling showed him to have been unusually tense.

He struck heavy conditions in the region of the Gulf Stream, which carried him in the wrong direction, and on day 35 wrote: ' Usual spots before my eyes when tired. Three days of gales and storms. Very miserable. Poor progress.' Sleep was virtually impossible in his tiny boat in these conditions, where he was permanently saturated and suffering from salt water sores as well. He made a number of errors in navigation and sail handling around this time, and recorded on tape his distress and despair in a most poignant fashion.

Another man described a rather more differentiated perception after twenty-six days at sea: 'While at the helm last night I saw what looked like the reflection of a window moving down the portside, say 20 feet below the surface. It was very faint and passed three or four times. There were a few stars but no moon. It did not worry me.' This occurred just after leaving the iceberg area where there had been fog and calms, and he was now approaching the coast of Newfoundland and the shipping lanes. He made one navigation error that day.

On the thirty-third day out on a fine and clear day, another sailor less experienced than the last two was setting foresails for the first time when he saw an object in the water. 'A baby elephant,' he thought, 'a funny place to put a baby elephant.' A little later, looking at the same object, 'A funny place to put a Ford Popular.' He accepted his initial observation without question, but on closer inspection he realised the object was a whale. This experience occurred three days before arrival in Newport under good conditions and with the sailor fully alert. The only unusual feature was that he was carrying out a manoeuvre for the first time which could have presented problems if the wind had got up suddenly.

A much more complex series of visual experiences was reported by one of the competitors, actually from his qualifying trip, not from the race itself. He had been at the helm continuously without sleep for fifty-six hours because of bad conditions, and was making do with only occasional snacks. He saw his father-in-law at the top of the mast. They were aware of one another's presence, and the experience was in no way alarming. At the top of the mast there is a metal radar reflector, a box-like structure 12 in. (30 cm.) or so across. A short time later the same evening he looked down into the cabin and saw his wife, then his mother, then his daughter lying on the bunk where a sleeping-bag was stretched out. Later again he was up at the bows changing a sail and saw in the water by the bows a large flat fish like a ray – very unlikely off the east coast of England – which was probably a misinterpretation of the boat's bow wave, just as the other experiences were misinterpretations of the radar reflector and the sleeping-bag.

There is a kind of hierarchy of misperceptions here, ranging from ill-formed spots before the eyes at one end to an elaborate misinterpretation of the radar reflector as an actual person at the other. All these misperceptions have been associated with fatigue in its widest sense, and the greater the fatigue, and the anxiety as well, then the more complex and differentiated the perceptual disturbances are likely to be.

Quite a common form of illusion amongst climbers and hill walkers has come to be known as the spectre of the Brocken, after a peak of that name in the Harz mountains in Germany. The climber stands with his back to the sun and sees a greatly enlarged image of himself projected on to the clouds, or if you prefer it a giant spectre in the sky. The projected image may in fact be quite close but is thought to be distant, and it is this erroneous assumption on the part of the subject that may lead to the figure appearing larger than life.[3]

While climbing alone on Everest at 27,600 feet (8,400 m) Frank Smythe reported a similar visual experience.

Chancing to look over the north-east shoulder, now directly in front of me, I saw two dark objects in the sky. In shape they resembled kite balloons, and my first reaction was to wonder what on earth kite balloons could be doing near Everest, a certain proof that lack of oxygen had impaired my mental faculties; but a moment later I recognised this as an absurd thought. At the same time I was very puzzled. The objects were black and silhouetted sharply against the sky, or possibly a background of cloud; my memory is not clear on this point. They were bulbous in shape and one possessed what looked like squat, under-developed wings, whilst the other had a beak-like protuberance like the spout of a tea kettle. But what was most weird about them was that they distinctly pulsated with an in-and-out motion as though they possessed some horrible quality of life. One interesting point is that these pulsations were much slower than my own heart-beats; of this, I am certain, and I mention it in view of a suggestion put forward afterwards that it was an optical illusion and that the apparent pulsations synchronised with my pulse-rate.

After my first reaction of 'kite balloons' my brain seemed to function normally, and so interested was I that, believing them to be fantasies of my imagination, I deliberately put myself through a series of mental tests. First of all I looked away. The objects did not follow my vision, but when my gaze returned to the north-east shoulder they were still hovering there. I looked away again, and by way of a more exacting mental test identified by name a number of peaks, valleys and glaciers. I found no difficulty in Chö-oyu, Gya-chung Kang, Pumori and the Rongbuk glacier, but when I again looked back the objects were in precisely the same position.

Nothing was to be gained by further examination and, tired as I was with the apparently endless succession of slabs, I decided to carry on to Camp 6. I was just starting off when a mist, forming suddenly, began to drift across the north-east shoulder. Gradually the objects disappeared behind it. Soon they were vague shadows, then, as the mist thickened, they disappeared altogether. The mist only lasted a few seconds, then melted away. I expected to see the objects again, but they were no longer there; they had disappeared as mysteriously as they came.[16]

Auditory and other experiences

Not long after Ann Davison had recounted her experience with the moon, she became aware of the sounds on board – the Davisons were at the time enduring their first gale. 'All wooden ships talk,' she wrote. '*Reliance* spoke in a multitude of tiny voices that came from behind bulkheads, under floorboards, everywhere all round, chattering, gossiping, gabbling incessantly and shrieking with gnomish laughter.'[17] In addition, sails flap, hulls groan, the sea splashes and gurgles around and below, the rigging rattles and the wind whistles past it. On the second day out from Plymouth in the 1972 Singlehanded Race, after a gale, Bill Howell wrote: 'Usual voices in the rigging – calling "Bill, Bill", rather high pitched. Dreams of people and boats. Neglected cleaning up in the cabin and cooking supper last night because of motion of yacht and queasiness.' Another singlehander after the same gale said: 'Someone knocked on the side deck as if asking to come in – I was petrified. I found a stanchion [support for the guard rail round the deck] loose. Seasickness almost gone. Starting to clear up and dry out after the gale.'

One man mistakenly heard his radio on four occasions. The first two were when he had been short of sleep, was feeling lethargic, and had complained of the uncomfortable motion of the boat. The others were while he was negotiating the iceberg areas in light variable winds and fog.

One of the singlehanders, nineteen days out, described 'a strong smell of coffee coming from the west. Clear visibility and no ship in sight.' He said it was like the smell outside a shop where coffee is being roasted. At the time he was approaching the iceberg area, having just had some calms and fog. The next day the same smell returned and lasted about half an hour. He did not drink coffee on the trip.

Another singlehander several times had 'this strong feeling of locality – in this case for where I have been becalmed for close on 24 hours. I keep thinking of it as a place I have been to before and can almost picture it.' Sometimes he felt 'as though I had just left somewhere familiar'. A few days later he wrote, 'I still have this preoccupation with place, to the extent that if I did not have a compass it would be very easy to become unbalanced about it.' It is as though the time and weather conditions constituted a locality: 'I did not like that place last night ...' These feelings tended to be associated with calms and the consequent frustration.

David Lewis, one of the five competitors in the first Singlehanded Transatlantic Race in 1960, experienced another kind of spatial illusion when '... for a whole day in fog the sea appeared to slope uphill; during a foggy night I had seemed to be sailing on a height with the lights of two passing steamers on a plain far below.'[18] This occurred at the end of more than a week of fog and frequent calms off Newfoundland, while listening to the foghorns of large ships which could easily have run him down. Sir Francis Chichester, who was the winner of this first race, had an experience similar to David Lewis' except that conditions were good for him at the time, and he was crossing the equator on his homeward journey during his round-the-world singlehanded sail:

> Just before crossing the Line [the equator] the boat appeared to be sailing up a gently sloping sea surface, in other words, uphill. At the time I was a little worried, but when I was 240 miles north of the Line I noticed the same thing again. This time the sea appeared uphill in every direction, as if I were sailing in a shallow saucer.[19]

Part of the explanation of the last two examples probably lies in the tendency, observed in mountains, of distant peaks viewed approximately horizontally to appear higher than they really are, in these circumstances the sea horizon being perceived in the same way.

Robert Manry, a modestly experienced sailor, was fulfilling a dream in sailing his $13\frac{1}{2}$-foot (4.1 m) boat across the Atlantic. He had been awake for thirty hours (with the aid of amphetamines) because of heavy conditions, and had shortly before had his tiny boat knocked flat by a wave. He felt he was accompanied by other people in other boats, and

... eventually we got to a part of the ocean called the Place of the Sea Mountains, an aptly named spot, for the waves there were as lofty as snow-capped Alpine peaks ... We all seemed to be trapped in a maze, unable to find the way out. That's what the trouble was: the Place of the Sea Mountains was a maze-like ocean realm, set entirely apart from the regular ocean we had been on the day before.[20]

Manry also encountered various 'people' there who will be mentioned later on in the section on the 'other person'.

In his masochistic voyage around the Antarctic continent, referred to at the beginning of Chapter 2, David Lewis explained that when conditions became too awful even for him

... present reality became illusory. In my exhausted state the wild irregular seas that were tossing us around like a cork were only half apprehended. I jotted down in the log that everything was an effort; there were constant mistakes of every kind in my sight workings; I could no longer grasp simple concepts. Twice, I recorded with scientific detachment that I had heard ill-defined imaginary shouts. I drifted out of reality altogether ... The whole sea was white now. Sheets of foam, acres in extent, were continually being churned anew by fresh cataracts. These are not seas, I thought: they are the Snowy Mountains of Australia – and they are rolling right over me. I was very much afraid.

Some time later – I had no idea how long – my terror receded into some remote corner of my mind. I must have shrunk from a reality I could no longer face into a world of happier memories for I began living in the past again, just as I had in my exhaustion in the gale two days earlier. It is hard to explain the sensation. I did not move over from a present world into an illusory one but temporarily inhabited both at once and was fully aware of doing so, without feeling this to be in any way strange or alarming. My handling of the tiller was quite automatic.

Mounts Kosciusko, Townsend, the broken crest of Jagungal; sculptured summits, sweeping snow slopes streaked with naked rock; all this mighty snow panorama rolled past like a cinema film. It was moving because those snow mountains were simultaneously the too-fearful-to-contemplate watery mountains of paralysing reality.

But why are those snow mountains rolling onward? Where are they going? I have drifted away even further from the present and my tired brain baulks at the effort of solving the conundrum.

The intolerable present became too intrusive to be ignored; the past faded into the background. Veritable cascades of white water were now thundering past on either side, more like breakers monstrously enlarged to perhaps forty-five feet, crashing down on a surf beach. Sooner or later one must burst fairly over us. What then?

I wedged myself more securely on the lee bunk, clutching the tiller lines, my stomach hollow with fear. The short sub-Antarctic night was over; it was now about 2 a.m.[21]

Seconds later, David Lewis' boat was picked up and rolled over through 360°, snapping off the mast in the process and bringing him back suddenly to his terrible reality.

Endurance being crushed by ice in the Weddell Sea in the Antarctic stranding Sir Ernest Shackleton and his twenty-seven men 1,400 miles (2,240 km) from their base and without any prospect of rescue. Shackleton brought his men through a year and a half of continuously appalling conditions and the only lasting injury was to one man who lost five toes from frostbite. Without Shackleton's supreme qualities as a leader, none of the men would have survived at all. (*See p. 205.*) (*Scott Polar Research Institute*)

Sir Ernest Shackleton with five companions launching their 22-foot (6.7 m) boat in which they sailed 800 miles (1,280 km) over the roughest seas in the world. It was a desperate attempt to seek rescue for the twenty-eight men marooned on Elephant Island in the Antarctic. In an unparalleled feat of seamanship and navigation, after sixteen days exposed to the Southern Ocean, they managed to hit South Georgia, an island a mere 25 miles (40 km) across. (*See p. 206.*) (*Royal Geographical Society*)

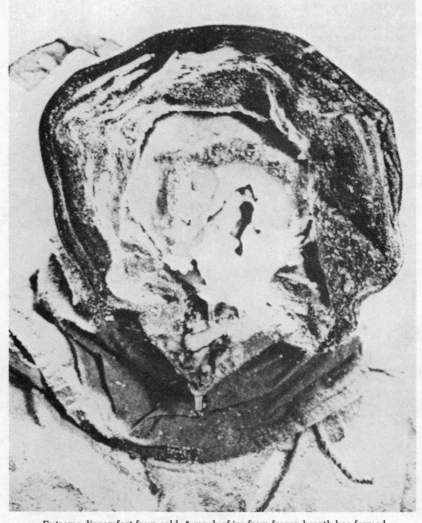

Extreme discomfort from cold. A mask of ice from frozen breath has formed over the face of this unknown meteorologist on Sir Douglas Mawson's Antarctic expedition of 1912–13. (*See p. 215.*)

Three faces of August Courtauld: (*left*) before his expedition to the Arctic; (*bottom left*) immediately on rescue after five months' total isolation in winter, in a snow-covered tent where the last month was spent in darkness as his lighting fuel had run out (*Iliffe Cozens*); and (*bottom right*) ten years later as a naval officer in World War II. He has a softness of expression after his rescue, 'like an egg without a shell'. Without any other person about he had no need of that protective exterior (persona) which most people present to the outside world. (*See pp. 57 and 201.*)

Trident 1 Flight Deck, similar to the ill-fated Papa India, which crashed 2¼ minutes after take-off. Among the complex array of dials and controls, the automatic safety devices are indicated which came into operation three times because of the inadequate airspeed, and three times were manually overridden until a fatal stall was inevitable. 1 Droop lever; 2 Flap lever; 3 Thrust levers; 4 Stick-push 'dump' (stall recovery override); 5 Droop position indicator; 6 'Stall recovery low pressure' and 'droop out of position' warning lights. (*See pp. 11 and 221.*) (*Department of Trade and Industry*)

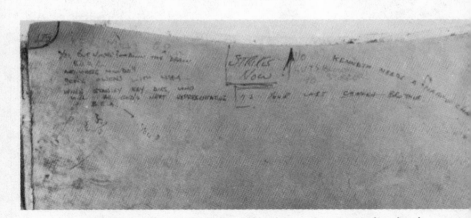

Graffiti found on the third pilot's table of the Trident, Papa India, after the crash. Referring to the aircraft's captain, was written: 'KEY MUST GO'. 'STRIKE NOW'. 'WHEN STANLEY KEY DIES, WHO WILL BE GOD'S NEXT REPRESENTATIVE IN BEA'. The industrial and personal conflicts lying behind these remarks were not judged by the commission of inquiry to be worthy of further investigation. (*See pp. 11 and 222.*) (*Daily Telegraph*)

11

Hallucinations and 'The Other Person'

Hallucinations

A hallucination is a perception that has no origin in external reality and is not triggered by some outside event. In practice, especially out in the natural environment, it can be extremely difficult to establish that there has been no external stimulus, so the distinction between illusions and misinterpretations on one hand and hallucinations on the other should be more a matter of degree than kind. Furthermore, it does not matter much whether the experience is totally spontaneous or not; it is the meaning that the experience has for the individual that is important.

The hallucinatory states to be described here have all come from people in arduous conditions. Hallucinations can also occur in experimental isolation; as a part of religious exercise; following the ingestion of lysergic acid diethylamide (LSD), amphetamines and a variety of other drugs – medicinal and otherwise; as a result of clinical states affecting brain function such as fevers, delirium tremens, starvation and organic brain disease; and as part of so-called schizophrenic disorders – but in this latter group the hallucinations are most likely to be auditory while in the other groups they are usually visual.

With such a variety of possible causes, ranging on the one hand from the clearly psychological (as in experimental isolation) to specific brain disease on the other, a single underlying process is difficult to elucidate and is at present still a matter of speculation;[1] but since we are mainly concerned here with the phenomena and the factors which predispose to them, the question of underlying mechanisms is not so crucial.

Here is an example of the kind of event which can occur. A thirty-eight-year-old sailor of some experience was approaching the Dutch coast, having set out singlehanded from the Thames estuary the day before in a 20-foot (6-m) sloop. The normal thirteen-hour crossing had already lasted forty hours on account of bad weather and the loss of his mainsail, and he could not leave the helm to eat properly or to rest. 'There was quite a gale blowing,' he wrote.

> The lights of Vlissingen are complicated at the best of times, but they are impossible when you are alone, and half past three on Monday morning I was ready to give it up as a bad job. The waves were as high as a small building by then and for the first time in my life I felt sick at sea. The lights, as far as I was concerned, had gone haywire. Following a green light I almost beached the boat, and then I realised it was a red one. Then I saw two men in yellow oilskins on a jetty with a lamp post, waving lights to attract my attention. When I had almost reached the jetty I suddenly realised there were no men there, neither was there a jetty, only a breakwater of horribly sharp looking sticks. At that time I decided to let come what was to come, and in a last effort threw the anchor overboard with about 80 feet of nylon cable attached to a leading chain, and went into the cabin ... Strangely enough, during these last few hours I was under the impression that my wife was on board, and when I took radio bearings I handed the tiller to her. When I almost beached the boat following the imaginary green light, she shouted a warning to me.

A short time later he woke and got directions from a passing boat to the harbour which was quite close by. Looking back on events, he recalled that it had taken him an hour to gather the fallen mainsail in after its halyard had broken (which happened after twenty-six hours at sea), and that 'I kept seeing at this stage other sailing boats and the Belgian coast, but I found that if I turned my head away and looked again they were gone.' This early and relatively minor hallucinatory experience was an indicator to the sailor of his overall psychological state, and a warning not to extend himself too much. He recognised that the sailing conditions were 'awful' but not excessively so. He also recognised that he 'was depressed due to difficulties regarding two children by an earlier marriage, and decided that a cruise on my own would enable me to sort things out'.

Lt.-Col. 'Blondie' Hasler had a similar, though less complicated, experience as a young Royal Marines officer. He had been sailing a small dinghy along the south coast of England from Devon to the Solent, and heaving the boat ashore each night so that he could sleep.

The winds had been very light and I was having to do a lot of pulling with the oars, and cut down on my sleep, in order to make something of my limited leave. I was very frightened of Portland Bill [with its fierce tide races], and finally approached it under oars, very tired, just as it was getting dark and the tide was turning foul. The wind then filled in from the East, giving me a dead beat against the tide, short-tacking between the rocks and the race but making no headway and feeling increasingly desperate. I remember shouts from the rocks telling me to turn back; I imagined that several of my friends were there shouting at me, although next day I realised that they weren't, and that this might have been the coastguard. Then I remembered nothing until I woke up with the sun shining, lying in the bottom of the boat which was anchored with jib lowered but mainsail set, close in under the cliffs on the west side of the end of the Bill – a really hideous anchorage which I would never have contemplated if I had been conscious.

I think it is highly unlikely that there was anyone there, least of all a coastguard, as the sight of a small boat in such a dangerous place would have led to some kind of rescue attempt.

Vito Dumas, an Argentinian, was one of the early solitary ocean sailors. In 1931 he was on a passage from Arcachon, in western France, to South America:

I was two days from Arcachon when one night, off Bilbao [northern Spain], the silence was broken by a conversation which I heard distinctly; it was almost monosyllabic. Two people appeared to be speaking. I was astounded. I asked myself how they could have come aboard, for I had not left the boat for 24 hours previous to sailing.

They could only be hidden forward in a locker that I never used, with a small door which separated it completely from the rest of *Lehg I.*

'Listen,' said a voice with a strong Spanish accent, 'I'm going to look for something to eat.'

'Shut up; he'll hear you.'

'No, he won't.'

It was nearly 30 feet from the tiller to that point, which was also hidden by the mast; the fore hatch might well have been open.

At the moment I did not dare to speak, but sought for a logical explanation of the presence of these individuals. One of them frequently asked for cigarettes. I also heard a number of unusual sounds that satisfied me that there were strangers on board.[2]

Dumas had been forced to remain at the helm for hours – it was before the days of reliable self-steering gear – and so was unable to investigate the problem. When eventually he searched the boat he found no one, and indeed no one really could have been there hidden on that particular boat. Nevertheless, he remained certain that others had been on board and assumed that they had simply swum ashore – even though he was several miles from land at the time.

'The other person'

Examples of hallucinations have so far all involved other people, and in two of them the other persons were friendly. Such friendly visitations have been reported by many venturers at times of grave danger or anxiety. The presence may be vivid and the companion identifiable, or it may be a shadowy, unrecognisable personage.

After Sir Ernest Shackleton's ship *Endurance* was crushed in the ice in the Weddell Sea in Antarctica in 1915, he retreated with all his men to Elephant Island. Then, with five companions he made his incredible 800-mile (1,500 m) journey across the Southern Ocean to South Georgia to seek rescue. They eventually landed safely but on the opposite side of the island to the base, so that the only way was for them to tramp – with the aid, incidentally, of a carpenter's adze and fifty feet of rope – over the unexplored mountains, rising in places to 9,000 feet (2,700 m).

> When I look back at those days I have no doubt that Providence guided us, not only across those snowfields, but across the stormy white sea which separated Elephant Island from our landing place on South Georgia. I know that during that long march of thirty-six hours over the un-named mountains and glaciers of South Georgia it often seemed to me that we were four, not three. And Worsley and Crean [Shackleton's companions on this last stage] had the same idea. One feels 'the dearth of human words, the roughness of mortal speech' in trying to describe things intangible, but a record of our journeys would be imcomplete without a reference to a subject very near to our hearts.[3]

When Frank Worsley came to write his memoirs of what Shackleton called a 'march' but which anyone else would call a feat of mountaineering, he found that:

> While writing after seven years ... each step of that journey comes back clearly, and even now I again find myself counting our party – Shackleton, Crean, and I and – who was the other? Of

course, there were only three, but it is strange that in mentally reviewing the crossing we should always think of a fourth, and then correct ourselves.[4]

On the 1933 Everest expedition, Frank Smythe and Eric Shipton had established a camp at 27,700 feet (8,440 m). On account of Shipton's illness, Smythe decided to climb on alone and without oxygen. Although he probably got to within 1,000 feet (300 m) of the summit, he felt 'separated from it by an aeon of weariness'.

After leaving Eric a strange feeling possessed me that I was accompanied by another. I have already mentioned a feeling of detachment in which it seemed as though I stood aside and watched myself. Once before, during a fall in the Dolomites, I had the same feeling, and it is not an uncommon experience with mountaineers who have a long fall. It may be that the feeling that I was accompanied was due to this, which in its turn, was due to lack of oxygen and the mental and physical stress of climbing alone at a great altitude. I do not offer this as an explanation, but merely as a suggestion.

This 'presence' was strong and friendly. In its company I could not feel lonely, neither could I come to any harm. It was always there to sustain me on my solitary climb up the snow-covered slabs. Now, as I halted and extracted some mint cake from my pocket, it was so near and so strong that instinctively I divided the mint into two halves and turned round with one half in my hand to offer it to my 'companion'.[5]

It was shortly after this that Smythe saw the 'kite balloons' already described.

Twenty years later, a German climber, Herman Buhl, found himself climbing alone at high altitude in the Himalayas. On the final assault on the summit of Nanga Parbat his companion had dropped out so he had to go on alone. He reached the summit of 26,670 feet (8,125 m) by early evening after having climbed since 2.30 that morning. By the time he had descended 450 feet (140 m), he had lost a crampon and darkness had fallen. He was therefore forced to stay where he was on a 50 degree slope, without food and unable to move adequately to keep himself warm. It was not until 4 a.m. the next morning that it was light enough to continue his descent. He later wrote:

Throughout this day I had the feeling that I was not alone, that someone was accompanying me. Many times I found myself in the act of turning round to address my companion, and when I was looking for my gloves he told me that I had lost them. It was only when I looked round that I realised that I was alone.[6]

Buhl was clearly in an extreme state, but he managed to reach his rucksack where he found some food 'and after a prolonged rest began to feel better again'. Far away on the Silver Saddle he wrote: 'I saw two specks. Oh, the joy of it! Someone was coming! I heard voices too, calling my name ... But what was wrong? The two specks remained static. There was no movement in them. Then I realised that they were rocks. How bitter, how painful was this disillusion!'

By contrast, Nick Estcourt, on the 1975 Everest expedition, experienced 'another person' under good conditions. He was making a routine climb up fixed ropes at around 24,000 feet (7,300 m) between camps 4 and 5. In his words:

I was about two hundred feet above the camp when I turned round. I can't remember why, but perhaps I had a feeling that someone was following me. Anyway, I turned round and saw this figure behind me. He looked like an ordinary climber, far enough behind so that I could not feel him moving up the fixed rope, but not all that far below. I could see his arms and legs and assumed that it was someone trying to catch me up.

I stopped and waited for him. He then seemed to stop or to be moving very, very slowly; he made no effort to signal or wave; I shouted down, but got no reply, and so in the end I thought, 'Sod it, I might as well press on.' I wondered if perhaps it was Ang Phurba coming through from Camp 2, hoping to surprise us all by being at Camp 5 when we arrived that morning.

I carried on and turned round three or four times between there and the old site of Camp 4 (the one used by the previous expedition) and this figure was still behind me. It was definitely a human figure with arms and legs, and at one stage I can remember seeing him behind a slight undulation in the slope, from the waist upwards as you would expect, with the lower part of his body hidden in the slight dip.

I turned round again as I reached the old site of Camp 4, and there was no one there at all. It seemed very eerie; I wasn't sure if anyone had fallen off or what; he couldn't possibly have had time to have turned back and drop back down the ropes out of sight, since I could see almost all the way back to Camp 4. The whole thing seemed very peculiar.[7]

Explanations in terms of oxygen lack, fatigue or anxiety are hard to advance here. Chris Bonington was inclined to regard it as something of a psychic phenomenon, linked possibly to the death of Mike Burke which was to occur later that day during his solo bid for the summit, or to a tragedy in the past. In 1973, a Sherpa who had worked very closely with Nick Estcourt the previous year was killed while climbing with a Japanese party, only a short way below the point where the 'other person' had been seen.

So far, the experiences of another person have been friendly and reassuring but not much more. Perhaps there is not much that the presence can actually do on the mountainside compared with in light aircraft or small boats.

While on his famous solo flight across the Atlantic in *Spirit of St Louis*, Charles Lindberg experienced:

... vaguely outlined forms, transparent, moving, riding weightless with me in the plane. I feel no surprise at their coming. There's no suddenness to their appearance. Without turning my head, I see them as clearly as though in my normal field of vision. There's no limit to my sight – my skull is one great eye, seeing everywhere at once.

These phantoms speak with human voices – friendly, vapor-like shapes, without substance, able to vanish or appear at will, to pass in and out through the walls of the fuselage as though no walls were there. Now, many are crowded behind me. Now, only a few remain. First one and then another presses forward to my shoulder to speak above the engine's noise, and then draws back among the group behind. At times, voices come out of the air itself, clear yet far away, travelling through distances that can't be measured by the scale of human miles; familiar voices, conversing and advising on my flight, discussing problems of my navigation, reasuring me, giving me messages of importance unattainable in ordinary life.[8]

One of the 1972 singlehanders, in the qualifying trip, was sailing his 52-foot (15.85 m) trimaran up from the Bay of Biscay around Ushant. He could not put into any harbour west of St Malo, and because of the treacherous rocky coast there, with fast tides and congested shipping lanes, he could get little rest. Furthermore, he had only one day's food to last, as it turned out, for six days. He was lying on his bunk when he heard someone up on deck putting the boat about on to the other tack. He stirred himself to go up and investigate, but as he went up on deck an unidentified man passed him coming down into the cabin. On deck he found that the boat had indeed been put about properly and that everything was in order. The process was repeated several times – as the sailor went up the man came down, and as the sailor came down the man went up, but the man was in no way recognisable.

Ann Davison, during the prelude to her solo crossing of the Atlantic Ocean in 1954, described how she felt:

> ... dizzy with fatigue, having been at the helm without sleep or respite for forty-eight hours; and there had been little enough sleep or respite before then either. Life now simply resolved itself into one of imperative urges, and the most imperative urge of all was sleep. I wanted oblivion with every fibre of my being. And here we were right at the entrance to the Straits [of Gibraltar] where ships were crowding through like sheep at a gate. One might as well pull up in the middle of Broadway for a quiet nap.
>
> Extreme fatigue does strange things. As in a dream I became aware of two other people aboard, and as in a dream it seemed perfectly natural that they should be there. One of them sat on the coachroof and the other came aft holding on to the boom, quiescent in its gallows. 'O.K.,' he said, 'You kip down. We'll keep watch.' Obediently I went below and slept till morning.
>
> Stretching and yawning and still weary, I climbed into the cockpit in the light of day. 'Thank you,' I said. 'That was good ... ' but they had gone. Never had the cockpit looked so empty.[9]

Identifiable companions

The most famous phantom companion at sea is the pilot of Columbus' boat *Pinta*, who appeared to and aided Joshua Slocum on his round-the-world sail in the 1890s. Slocum had been stricken with fever and was delirious when this bewhiskered figure appeared and guided his yacht for him. Unlike those already described, this man was readily identifiable from the remarks Slocum ascribed to him: 'I am the pilot of the *Pinta* come to aid you. Lie quiet, señor captain ... and I will guide your ship tonight.'[10]

During Robert Manry's spatial hallucination of 'the Place of the Sea Mountains', he encountered the ruler of this sea kingdom: 'a crusty old Scotsman named MacGregor, a man with scraggy white sideburns, plaid tam-o'-shanter, knobbly knees showing beneath his kilt ... And for some unknown reason he was determined to do me in.'[11] He appeared as a malevolent figure, which is uncharacteristic, but this may be due to the fact that Manry was under the influence of amphetamines at the time.

On 4 March 1973 Maurice and Maralyn Bailey had their yacht holed and sunk by a killer whale in the Eastern Pacific near the

Galapagos Islands. After an incredible 118 days in an ordinary life-raft with an inflatable dinghy in tow, Maurice Bailey said:

> For a long time I could not rid myself of the feeling that there were three people in the raft, an impression I had frequently had before. In my half-sleep I imagined clearly Maralyn and myself and an American yachtsman called Wayne, whom we had met briefly in Cristóbal [Panama].
>
> Someone was shaking me, a disembodied voice was calling, 'Maurice,' and again 'Maurice ...' I thought, 'For pity's sake leave me alone and wake Wayne.'[12]

Maralyn was at that moment trying to rouse Maurice to tell him to signal at a ship she had sighted, the seventh they had seen, as it happened, but this was the one which rescued them.

The year before, the Robertson family were cast adrift in the Pacific in similar circumstances. Six of them spent thirty-seven days in a 9-foot (2.75 m) fibreglass dinghy and life-raft, and in the dinghy alone after the life-raft sank. On the twenty-third day Dougal Robertson wrote: 'Lyn [his wife] told us she had counted seven people in *Ednamair* [the dinghy] in the night, that she had had a vision of a presence rather than a person behind me, helping us fight the storm.'[13]

Out-of-body experiences

Sometimes the other person turns out to be oneself or part of oneself. David Lewis described it this way:

> ... after several days at sea, particularly when very tired in the hours before dawn, there came a distinct feeling of having been divided into two personalities, one of which would speak to the other, and sometimes would advise. At times it appeared that another person was at the helm, while the other 'part personality' was critically observing his actions and problems.[14]

Frank Smythe on Everest had exactly this feeling earlier on in his 1933 climb, 'a feeling of detachment in which it seemed as though I stood aside and watched myself', and he felt that his sense of being accompanied arose from this. Forty-two years later another Everest climber, Doug Scott, who with Dougal Haston reached the summit by the previously unclimbed south-west face, describes a remarkably similar experience on the final climb towards the top:

> It was whilst trail-breaking on this last section that I noticed my mind seemed to be operating in two parts, one external to my head.

In my head I referred to the external part somewhere over my left shoulder. I rationalised the situation with it, making reference to it about not going too far right in the area of the cornice, and it would urge me to keep well to the left.[15]

People who are seriously ill and close to death and people in trance-like states have often described the sensation of being separated from their own bodies, which remain in their original position in some other part of the room. Arthur Koestler experienced this 'splitting' while a prisoner during the Spanish Civil War and expecting to be shot:

> There had been three occasions when I believed that my execution was imminent ... The third time ... after [Captain] Bolín had told me that I would be shot at night, they took me out of the police station at nightfall and put me into a lorry, with five men behind me, their rifles across their knees; so that I thought we were being driven to the cemetery ...
>
> On all three occasions I had benefited from the well-known phenomenon of a split consciousness, a dream-like, dazed self-estrangement which separated the conscious self from the acting self − the former becoming a detached observer, the latter an automaton, while the air hums in one's ears as in the hollow of a seashell. It is not bad at all; the unpleasant part is the subsequent reunion of the split halves, bringing the full impact of reality in its wake.[16]

A woman has described her cardiac arrest. She experienced in hospital the cessation of breathing and heart-beat, and then the ensuing emergency action:

> I could feel myself moving out of my body and sliding down between the mattress and the rail on the side of the bed − actually it seemed as if I went through the rail − on down to the floor. Then, I started rising upward, slowly. On my way up, I saw more nurses come running into the room − there must have been a dozen of them. I drifted on up past the light fixture and then I stopped, floating right below the ceiling, looking down. I felt almost as though I were a piece of paper that someone had blown up to the ceiling.
>
> I watched them reviving me from up there! My body was lying down there stretched out on the bed, in plain view, and they were all standing around it. I heard one nurse say, 'Oh, my God! She's gone!', while another one leaned down to give me mouth-to-mouth

resuscitation. I was looking at the back of her head while she did this. I'll never forget the way her hair looked; it was cut kind of short. Just then, I saw them roll this machine in there, and they put the shocks on my chest. When they did, I saw my whole body just jump right up off the bed, and I heard every bone in my body crack and pop. It was the most awful thing!

As I saw them below beating on my chest and rubbing my arms and legs, I thought, 'Why are they going to so much trouble? I'm just fine now.'[17]

The double

The experience of meeting one's double, or coming face to face with oneself, is generally regarded in our society as a sign of mental illness.[18,19] There is no essential reason why this should be so, but I know of no example of an adventurer into the natural environment who encountered 'himself' walking to meet him on a mountainside.

The double is a popular theme in literature, where the device can be used to present other aspects of the hero's personality.[20] In the tales *William Wilson* by Edgar Allan Poe and *The Double* by Dostoievsky, the double appears as a conscience whenever the hero has committed or is about to commit some unscrupulous act. In *The Picture of Dorian Gray* by Oscar Wilde and also in *The Secret Sharer* by Conrad, the process is reversed, and the double, the figure which reflects the hero, carries his darker, evil side. Dostoievsky was epileptic and may have had some hallucinatory experiences of himself as a result of this – certainly he has described states of 'bliss ... the moment before a seizure'.[21]

Personalisation of objects

Objects (such as rocks) can be misperceived as people, and all kinds of sounds can be heard as human voices, but sometimes the process can go further. David Lewis has described a self-steering gear which he put together at sea. He consistently regarded it as of 'feminine construction', and when it went wrong cursed himself heartily for allowing a 'woman' to meddle with his ship.[14]

Doug Scott, after reaching the summit of Everest in 1975, was forced to spend that night with his partner, Dougal Haston, in a snow hole at 28,700 feet (8,750 m). This pair had neither equipment nor extra clothing for this unplanned bivouac – the highest ever attempted – and they had not eaten for eighteen hours. They forced themselves to stay awake as, in a temperature of around minus 30° centigrade, they would almost certainly have died if they had fallen asleep; they warmed their hands and feet against each other's bodies. Doug Scott said:

> I found myself talking to my feet. I personalised them to such an extent that they were two separate beings needing help. The left one was very slow to warm up and, after a conversation with the right one, we decided I had better concentrate on rubbing it hard. All the time my external mind was putting its spoke in as well.[15]

Dougal Haston found that Doug Scott's incoherent speech helped to keep them both awake – otherwise, he said:

> I was locked in suffering silence except for the occasional quiet conversation with Dave Clarke [another climber, actually in a camp much lower down the mountain]. Hallucination or dream? It seemed comforting and occasionally.directed my mind away from the cold ... I don't think anything we did or said that night was very rational or planned. Suffering from lack of oxygen, cold, tiredness but with a terrible will to get through the night, all our survival instincts came right up front. These and our wills saw the night to a successful end.[15]

Neither of them sustained any frostbite, which was quite remarkable in the circumstances.

Any consideration of the meaning of 'other person' experiences leads one to that uncertain borderland between life and death. People who have to all intents died – such as after a cardiac arrest – and then have been brought back to life, frequently refer to the presence of a friendly other person. As Elisabeth Kübler-Ross has put it: 'These people have experienced a floating out of their physical bodies, associated with a great sense of peace and wholeness. Most were aware of another person who helped them in their transition to another plane of existence.'[22] This was such a powerful and wonderful experience for many people that coming back to earthly life was often something of a disappointment.[17]

The adventurers described here were nearly all at the very limits of their abilities to cope. They could easily have died without anyone ever knowing of their experience, and that seems to justify aligning them with those who have come close to death in domestic or medical environments.

The significance of the other person depends on the beliefs of the people involved. For Shackleton it was clearly religious, and his account inspired T. S. Eliot's lines in *The Waste Land*:

Who is the third who walks always beside you?
When I count, there are only you and I together
But when I look ahead up the white road
There is always another one walking beside you.

Eliot probably also had in mind the image of the risen Christ who appeared to the two travellers on the road to Emmaus.

Those without a religious attitude to life will tend to accept the friendly and supportive nature of these visitations and leave it at that.

Physical factors

Certain brain disorders, when the parietal and temporal lobes are affected, can lead to hallucinations and experiences of another person. Macdonald Critchley in his book *The Parietal Lobes* gives this account of a woman with brain atrophy:

> She would wake in the night with the very intense feeling that someone was in the room – a person she knew; indeed, with whom she was very familiar. Sometimes, she was at a loss to decide who this could be, but on many occasions, it would dawn on her that this person was none other than herself ... The impression was so vivid that she would leave her bed and go from room to room on tiptoe trying to surprise this familiar interloper.[23]

Hallucinations can be produced when the brain is stimulated in certain operations done under local anaesthesia for epilepsy,[1] and they can be caused by drugs such as LSD,[24] amphetamines and L-dopa (a drug used in the treatment of Parkinson's disease).[25] Deliberately induced hunger and thirst as part of religious exercise may so disorder the body chemistry and water balance that hallucinations – referred to here as visions – may result. Similarly, mortification of the flesh and self-flagellation may lead to toxic infective states of the skin, and hallucinations may occur in the subsequent toxic delirium.[26,27] I do not believe that the visions of ascetics can be explained away in terms of bodily disturbance or that some such physical disturbance is even necessary, but it does seem to have been a factor for a good many. Where generally healthy people are concerned, cold, hunger, high altitude, lack of sleep and toxicity from rotten food all contribute to a state where hallucinations and the other person may appear; the psychological factors of anxiety and isolation may be contributory as well, but they are not in themselves sufficient to bring on these states. Sleep loss can lead to illusions and hallucinations, but these are usually of a fragmented and bizarre

nature,[28] and nothing like a companion has appeared in any
deliberate study of it. The nearest thing to have been observed in any
controlled setting was in the first sensory deprivation experiment
(p. 56) when two of the twenty-two subjects, confined alone for three
to four days in a dim soundproofed room, reported a sensation that
there was another body lying beside them on the bed.[29] Apart from
this isolated instance, the other person and, to a lesser extent,
hallucinations in general in natural environments, are phenomena
which occur almost exclusively where people are not only deprived of
basic physical necessities but are in danger of losing their lives as
well.

12

Ecstasy to Black Despair

Just as weather conditions out in the harsh environment can vary rapidly from the blissful to the foul, so can the adventurer's mood. There are moments of sublime contentment and mastery which can alternate with the deepest depression, frustration and sense of futility. On the whole the good spells predominate, certainly in retrospect, and the profound emotions experienced at moments of triumph or during many of the little episodes along the way, can help in trying to answer the questions about 'why they go'.

The sense of oneness and the oceanic feeling
Geoffrey Williams was sailing his yacht *Sir Thomas Lipton*, eventually to win the 1968 Singlehanded Transatlantic Race, but ten days out of Plymouth he could write:

> I was no longer *Lipton*'s helmsman. I became part of the ship. I was a limb of *Lipton*, another sail, another tiller; the ship and I were one. But *Lipton* was part of the scene so I became part of the scene, no longer outside looking in, but inside looking out. I was part of the chorus, neither conductor nor spectator but singing as part of the environment.[1]

Admiral Byrd, isolated on the Antarctic continent at the coming of the polar night (i.e. winter), said:

> My frozen breath hung like a cloud overhead. The day was dying, the night being born – but with great peace. Here were the imponderable processes and forces of the cosmos, harmonious and soundless ... It was enough to catch that rhythm, momentarily to be myself part of it. In that instant I could feel no doubt of man's

oneness with the universe ... It was a feeling that transcended reason; that went to the heart of man's despair and found it groundless. The universe was a cosmos, not a chaos; man as rightfully part of that cosmos as were the day and night.[2]

After the first and successful all-American assault on Everest in 1963, which was in fact a traverse up the west ridge and down the south-east ridge, four men were reported to have had to bivouac at 28,000 feet (8,500 m) without oxygen. A year after the event, one of them wrote:

> When we bivouacked that night I was much clearer in the things that counted to me, than in recalling time, temperature, etc. ... I could see my body lying on that rock and snow, but that didn't matter ... I knew that we would survive, anyway I felt like I could peek into the other side of life and understand death. Physical space, distance, time, etc., completely vanished ... Everything was gone and I was alone. Yet in that strange singleness I was part of everything in the universe ... I reached a void where everything became one, and I knew that I could never turn back to normal life without destroying whatever I was capable of doing. I knew that I would have to go on alone in life. That most of my relatives would scorn me, that my children meant as little to me as everything in the world. It seemed to me that I understood so many things that I was dangerous. I was quite sure that I was not emotionally strong enough to bear looking at myself that critically.[3]

This experience seems to have crystallised this man's ambivalent feelings towards his family, as after returning to the United States he divorced and remarried.

Sportsmen may transcend themselves at supreme moments in competition. David Hemery has described feelings of unity with his opponents, so that he was no longer engaged in a contest with others but somehow united with them in some higher activity. Similar experiences of sportsmen have been gathered together by Michael Murphy and Rhea White in their book *The Psychic Side of Sports*.[4] For example, in judo:

> There will be no curtain to separate you from your opponent. You will become one with him. You and your opponent will no longer be two bodies separated physically from each other but a single entity, physically, mentally and spiritually inseparable. Therefore the motion of your opponent may be considered your motion. And you can lure him to any posture you like and

effectively apply a large force on him. You can throw him as easily as you can yourself.

And just as sailors in small boats feel a sense of unity with their boats, so the racing driver can regard his car: 'I don't drive a car, really. The car happens to be under me and I'm controlling it, but it's as much part of me as I am of it.'[4]

Pilots of single-seat aircraft can become quite ecstatic at high altitude. There is just the deep blue sky above and the clouds below, so they can feel totally separated from the material world down there but at the same time connected with everything. Amongst aviators this is called the 'break-off' phenomenon, and it may be associated with a degree of anxiety, which is a good thing for the pilot of a passenger jet flying at 30,000 feet (10,000 m) or so. The real danger used to be for pilots of open-cockpit aircraft who would become so intoxicated by their surroundings that – like divers in a similar state of mind – they would remove their oxygen masks so as better to enjoy the experience.

So far the experiences described have been generally positive and memorable for the people who have had them. They have been elevated briefly to another plane of awareness and they have brought something back from it, but such new and intense awareness is not without its hazards. Once you embark on this journey, intentionally or otherwise, there is no knowing where it will lead. The experience might be terrifying or it might be seductively dangerous.

Christiane Ritter was living over one winter with her husband and a hunting friend in a hut on the north coast of Spitzbergen, only about seven hundred miles from the North Pole. She was alone for much of the time while the men were out hunting, and in a hut completely buried under snow. She wrote:

For humans this stillness is horrible. It is days since I have been outside the hut. Gradually I have become fearful of seeing the deadness of the land. I sit in the hut and tire myself out with sewing. It makes no difference whether the work is finished today or tomorrow, but I know what I'm up to. I do not want to have my mind free for a moment to think, a moment in which to become aware of the nothingness outside. I have become conscious of the power of thought, a power which up here can bestow life or death. I have an inkling, or rather I know with certainty, that it was this, terror of nothingness, which over the past centuries has been responsible for the death of some hundreds of men here in Spitzbergen ...

There is no longer even a glimmer of day, not even at noon. Around the whole horizon only deep starry night. Day and night, throughout its circular course, the moon is in the sky ... No central European can have any idea of what this means on the smooth frozen surface of the earth. It is as though we were dissolving in moonlight, as though the moonlight were eating us up ... The light seems to follow us everywhere. One's entire consciousness is penetrated by the brightness; it is as though we were being drawn into the moon itself ...

We cannot escape the brightness. I take it particularly badly, and the hunters maintain that I am moonstruck. What I would like best of all is to stand all day on the shore, where in the water the rocking ice floes catch and break the light and throw it back at the moon. But the men are very strict with me. They do not let me out of their sight and often keep me under house arrest. And then I lie down in my little room, where the moonlight filters green through the small snowed-up window. Neither the walls of the hut nor the roof can dispel my fancy that I am myself moonlight, gliding along the glittering spines and ridges of the mountains, through the white valleys.[5]

What would have happened to her if her companions had not taken care of her? Quite likely she would have wandered out alone and succumbed to the enticing power of the moon.

Frank Mulville, a hardened singlehanded sailor, very nearly did just this, although in a very different climate. Somewhere in the region of the Caribbean he was taken with an overwhelming desire to see from the outside his yacht *Iskra*, on which he had lavished so much care in preparation for his voyage. Therefore, one calm day, he let himself down into the water and floated away from his boat. He wrote:

It made me quite dizzy to look at her. She seemed the most lovely thing dipping in and out of sight as she mounted the long Atlantic swell and then slipped into their hollows. This, it struck me, was the supreme moment of my life. I had never achieved anything to equal it before and I was never likely to again. This was the ultimate experience – alone in an ocean, surrounded by the calm beauty of the sea and the sky and with my boat, also a thing of beauty, on a string in front of my eyes. It was my dream and I had it. Why not let go the rope? To melt into the sea at this apex of experience would be the crowning touch – the only thing left. Nothing that could happen in the future could better this – all

future experience must fall short. Why not trump the ace and walk
out?

I stayed at the end of the rope for about a minute and then I
began to get frightened – not so much at what might happen to me
but at what I might do myself. Suppose the rope should break –
suppose there should be a shark – a sudden squall of wind.
Suppose I should take myself seriously. I glanced briefly down into
the womb of the sea – watched the bending shafts of sunlight as
they spent their energy uselessly in its density and wondered what
unknown things might lie in this close darkness. I slipped the
bowline off my shoulders – hung for an instant on the very end of
the rope – my fingers grasping the bare end of life itself – and then I
hauled myself back hand over hand. When I stood on the firm
familiar deck I swore I would never do this thing again. I was
running with sweat and shaking all over.[6]

Mulville literally held his life in his hands, and he realised just in time
that he belonged in life. Christiane Ritter was in a broadly similar
state of enchantment and sense of unity with all things, but she was
in a ferocious climate which would have killed her rapidly if she had
wandered, or had been allowed to wander, out of the snow-covered
hut.

What about those adventurers who do not return? Many disappear
without trace and carry their secrets with them, but did they 'let go' in
a state of bliss or did they die fighting against impossible conditions?
We can never know, but sadly, those moments of bliss, which may
come unexpectedly or after periods of supreme endeavour out in the
natural environment, must be treated with respect if one is alone, and
if possible resisted, because of the temptation to carry too far the
process of unity with all things, at which point – since all is one –
there is little distinction between living and dying.

The sense of mastery and control, and inner stillness

It is sometimes slightly uncomfortable to sail with an experienced
singlehanded yachtsman, especially, for example, shortly after he has
sailed the Atlantic on his own. He is in such a close relationship with
his boat and carries out all the manoeuvres with such economy of
effort that someone else on board feels hopelessly ineffective and
generally in the way. Rock climbers are also adventurers, and their
complicated technology can give them a feeling of mastery, since from
the technical point of view there is nothing that is unclimbable.

Mario Andretti, a racing driver, has put it thus: 'When a man is competing in a racing car, when he is pushing himself and his machine to the very limit, when the tyres are breaking free from the ground and he is controlling his destiny with his own two hands, then, man, he is living – in a way no other human can understand.'[4] The sense of mastery is often connected with an inner stillness, which, while accompanied with a high state of alertness, replaces the more usual anxiety which is necessary (through the production of adrenalin) to activate lesser people to their best efforts.

Jackie Stewart has described his feelings just before a race:

> By race time I should have no emotions inside me at all – no excitement or fear or nervousness, not even an awareness of the fatigue that's been brought on by pacing myself. I'm absolutely cold, ice-cold, totally within my shell. I'm drained of feeling, utterly calm even though I'm aware of the many things going on around me, the mechanics, people running about, the journalists and officials and everything else.[4]

Again, Billie Jean King, writing of the perfect shot in tennis:

> I can almost feel it coming. It usually happens on one of those days when everything is just right, when the crowd is large and enthusiastic and my concentration is so perfect it almost seems as though I'm able to transport myself beyond the turmoil on the court to some place of total peace and calm.[4]

Where personal danger is involved, mastery often means going as close to disaster as possible while still retaining full control, because it is in that narrow space, which holds the greatest risks, that supreme success lies. In motor racing this means driving the car to the limits of its capacity and the driver's ability. For the yachtsman, success in competition comes from carrying the maximum sail area for the particular conditions, although carrying too much sail in heavy conditions may cause the mast to break or the boat to founder.

The element of invulnerability has been discussed in Chapter 7 with regard to special troops such as the American Green Berets or the British Special Air Service. Their feeling of technical mastery may lead them to take unnecessary risks because they may almost come to believe that they are less vulnerable to bullets than the next man. However, I feel the real danger lies in adventurers who get a positive stimulation from danger itself, as they may seek it needlessly and so put at risk not only themselves and their companions but also all those who may be called upon to rescue them.

Depression and frustration

Considering how appalling conditions frequently are out in the natural environment, it may be surprising to the ordinary person that periods of depression are not more common.

Six of the sailors in the central part of my study of the 1972 Singlehanded Transatlantic Race complained of feeling depressed at times. Some felt it most acutely at the start, which had an element of anticlimax about it. On one hand it was the culminating moment after perhaps three and a half years of preparation, during which the sailor's life was totally dominated by the race, but on the other hand the start meant leaving people behind and facing three thousand miles of Atlantic Ocean on one's own. Depressive and negative feelings are virtually the norm before any adventure, because what is being left behind is still more evident than what lies ahead. One man was acutely conscious of this on the morning of the start. 'I became extremely depressed,' he said, 'on seeing the spectator boats heading back to Plymouth. In fact Saturday was a day of highs and lows, mostly the latter, which only left during the night. For instance I couldn't enter the saloon [main cabin], it reminded me too much that the boat was home.' Another competitor, a naval officer who did very well in the race, saw the schooner *Wild Rocket*, which was more than twice his own boat's length, blow her sails out shortly after the start, and he wrote in his log for the first day, 'I'd have taken any excuse to give up. *Wild Rocket* – lucky chap to have his sails blow out close to port.'

It is hard to be depressed when there is a great deal to do, as there usually is on board a small boat except when it is calm. Calms, however, were frequent in the 1972 race, and they imposed a tremendous psychological strain on those generally competitive people, so that the predominant negative emotion here was a mixture of depression and frustration. As one Polish competitor put it, 'These calms, they get me crazy, so I prefer storms.'

Here are some consecutive log entries on the subject of calms. The skipper of a 25-foot (7.6-m) sloop wrote: day 19 – 'It's calm and hot and driving me nuts.' Day 21 – 'The calm weather is becoming unbearable, been unable to use self-steering for almost three days.' Day 25 – 'It's now calm again and I'm getting to screaming pitch. A couple of reasonable days and now calm again.'

Another, in a 38-foot (11.6-m) cutter, wrote: day 24 – 'Considering that this is the fifth day of calms, I'm really very relaxed, and I have five kittens and mum all sleeping at my feet.' Day 28 – 'I want some wind, nine days without it is too much.' But then on day 46, after making eight miles of progress in the preceding three days: 'I'm pissed off. I feel like a prisoner in a well stocked cell but with no one around to tell me the date of termination of my sentence.'

A third, who had started late on account of illness, kept a diary, and as the calms continued the word 'becalmed' was written larger and larger on the page, until it covered the whole two-page spread and the pencil was driven through the paper. 'BECALMED. Another utterly miserable, miserable windless day in this forsaken area! CALMS. TORRENTIAL RAINS.' Another man who found the calms 'very frustrating' actually smashed a cupboard door during one period of desperation.

By contrast, two of the becalmed men adapted pretty well to the state. They were not highly competitive individuals and they had no reputation to maintain. One was a farmer who took a generally philosophical line, and his strongest log entry when he was becalmed – and he was becalmed quite often – was on day 31: 'Frustrated when *no wind*.' But it was he who smelt coffee on that same day though he had none on board. The other took an actually positive attitude, and on day 28 he could write: 'Becalmed in warm waters, shaking Sargasso weed into a bucket helps to pass the time. And you have as an end result one hell of an aquarium.' He had a child's fishing net and collected 'little monsters' from the weed. He also swam around the boat to check things. In Newport he explained: 'Becalmed days were shaping up days ... I never got frustrated [by calms] because I enjoyed them so much ... Oh, how I enjoy those calms.' This man had grown up on an island off the east coast of the United States where his father was a fisherman.

The worst experience of depression, frustration and general misery was endured by a man who would have lost the essence of its awfulness had it not been for a tape he made when at rock bottom. He was David Blagden, who made a magnificent crossing in fifty-two days in a 19-foot (5.8-m) sloop. For most of the time at sea he was soaking wet and afflicted with salt-water sores, because the tiny space inside the boat (I would hardly call it a cabin) and his own large size compelled him to sit hunched up on a sodden mattress. Nevertheless, he arrived in Newport in excellent shape. Back in London after the race, when we were talking about his experiences, there was little mention of bad times. Then, while he went out to the kitchen to make a cup of tea, he handed me a tape to play. Immediately David's anguish filled the room as I listened to the recording he made on day 39, after days of battering by adverse winds which had driven him badly off course so that the Gulf Stream might have carried him some way north past Newport Rhode Island.

It was agonising listening (which in no way can be captured on the printed page), and when David came back into the room with the tea, he could not bear it and rushed out again. It was just all too painful at that time, but later he was able to make use of it in his book.[7]

David Blagden's experience, in which the worst memories are virtually forgotten, is fortunately common – the most notable example being how the horrific events of combat usually fade while the good times are remembered. All the same, bad times will occur on adventures, just as they will in ordinary life, and people can benefit from the knowledge that there will be bad times in any adventure. At David Blagden's very worst, when he was sobbing into his tape recorder for a ship to come into sight, one might have expected that he was going to ask to be removed from his misery. But no, what he really wanted, even at that low point, was an accurate position so that he could plan sensibly what to do next. He could honourably have given up at that point, but he was a very experienced sailor who knew what he could do and what his boat could do, and he was not going to let his depression and frustration interfere with his plans.

Depressions are part of ordinary experience in a way in which illusions and hallucinations are not. Depression is characterised by lethargy and a sense of meaninglessness. Therefore routines are let slip, jobs are left undone, food is left uneaten and simple protective precautions are no longer taken. In ordinary life social contacts are avoided and personal welfare is liable to be disregarded; the depressed person can usually lie low until the worst of the feelings are past. Out in the natural environment nothing can be allowed to let slip. I do not know whether depressions are commoner out in the natural environment than in a domestic setting, but I suspect they are different in quality. More is happening on adventures, more crises and hence more frustrations. The adventurer may find himself plunged suddenly into the depths of despair, while the urban dweller may find events closing in on him slowly. The suddenness, or acuteness, of the episode in the course of an adventure can be consoling, because if one dips down that fast it means that one can come up again equally fast. However, there is much less latitude for the adventurer to function below his optimum.

Richard Byrd, alone in a hut in the middle of the Antarctic winter in June 1934, expressed a subtle and deadly lethargy in his diary just after having talked to his base camp on the radio link – and he was also suffering from the effects of toxic fumes from the stove. 'Why bother? ...' he wrote. 'Why not let things drift? That would be the simple way. Your philosophy tells you to immerse yourself in the universal processes. Well, the processes here are in the direction of uninterrupted disintegration. That is the direction of everlasting peace. So why resist?"[8] He did resist for another two months, and despite his depressed state he continued with his meteorological observations and other tasks, even though the temperature fell to an incredible −83°F (−64°C), until he was resued by a party from the base.

13

Disorganised Behaviour and Psychological Breakdown

So far in this discussion of reactions to external events, the main emphasis has been upon misperceptions, inaccurate interpretations of one's surroundings for various reasons, and fluctuations of mood. The external events involved have been pretty extreme but not overwhelmingly so; it is anxiety or fatigue that have as often as not reduced individuals' ability to function effectively.

This chapter will be concerned with what people *do* rather than how accurately they perceive their surroundings, and although all behaviour must follow on from perceptions of some kind, it is the behaviour which ultimately matters most.

The body has its way of responding to any crisis or threat by biological mechanisms well established throughout the animal kingdom. These are either for meeting the threat directly (fighting the adversary, taking decisive action in a crisis) or by skilful avoidance (running away). Unfortunately, most of the critical situations described in this book call not for basic biological responses but for restrained, deliberate and accurate acts often in the face of extreme pressure.

The ways in which people respond to circumstances they cannot deal with effectively are fairly uniform – provided the event is not too overwhelming in the first place – and they can best be described by referring to some experiments.

The Cambridge cockpit experiments, already referred to in Chapter 9, were important studies on pilot error carried out during the Second World War. In order to investigate how performance becomes impaired, the investigators first had to disrupt the equilibrium of the experienced pilots who were their subjects. They did this by giving them a course to 'fly' in the trainer cockpit in which it was virtually impossible to reach the standard of competence which they would normally expect of themselves. Thus, the pilots' efforts to reach a satisfying standard were frustrated, and they suffered the experience of failure; and these feelings were aggravated by having to perform a skilled task for a long time.[1,2]

Although the details would vary with individual temperaments, the subjects' responses to the built-in frustration were remarkably uniform and predictable. To begin with there was a period of overactivity, and I shall quote from Derek Russell Davis' original description:

> The subjects felt tense, under strain or irritable and, sometimes, frankly anxious. Corrections were made with impatience and were hurried, and subjects felt that correction was urgent. They were often preoccupied with one or other aspect of the task which had acquired a temporary urgency. Their attention was 'sticky' and was held by one aspect, instead of being distributed over the whole field of events. They were distractable in the sense that recent instructions or interventions gained the greater part of their attention. They tended to sit more erect and to grasp the controls more firmly. The tasks seemed more difficult, and this was sometimes felt to be unreasonable and was blamed on the working of the machine, while it was actually due to change in the nature of the movements which the subject made.[1]

This is all very similar to how many people respond to a car that will not start, or to some other piece of machinery that will not perform as expected. Extra energy is put into the task so that the various controls are manipulated with excessive vigour. Later on the car is blamed, and then all cars, and then mechanical devices in general. After that, the car itself may be attacked physically (although such attacks were unusual in the experiments), and then the subject will probably move on to the second phase of responses.

The second phase is characterised by apathy and withdrawal. To quote again: the subjects

> ... tended to relax, concentration failed and interest declined. The feeling of strain gave way to one of mild boredom, tedium or tiredness; sometimes, however, they felt satisfied with a standard of accuracy which was lower than when they were fresh. The task might appear easier because part of it was being neglected or, in other cases, because certain errors were accepted as inevitable faults of the machine and not as the responsibility of the subject ... Thoughts began to wander and careless mistakes were made. Manoeuvres were omitted or carried out in the wrong order ... In some cases there was ... a tendency to make larger and less

appropriate control movements [which were] reinforced by inattentiveness and, thence, by the larger size of errors before they were corrected.[1]

The motorist who has reached this stage sits slumped in the driver's seat, operating the controls in a desultory way, no longer really concerned whether the car starts or not.

The relevance of these experiments is to show how efficiency is liable to become impaired once things begin to go wrong. The physiological emergency mechanisms which lead to energetic activity are most emphatically not required when performing skilled tasks in a crisis, and equally inappropriate is the lethargic under-activity of the second phase.

The cockpit experiments created a small crisis through the relative impossibility of the subject being able to steer a satisfactory course in the trainer cockpit. The reactions of the subjects provide a good basis for considering the ways people react to crises of various kinds, especially when they are performing tasks which are important to them. One important factor, however, is inevitably missing from the experiments, and that is personal danger or risk to other persons. It is reasonable to assume that danger heightens the tension accompanying any act, probably leading to extra-careful performance in the ordinary way, but at times of great crisis it may well generate a level of anxiety that could further hinder efficient functioning.

When events are truly shattering and the threat to life is too great – such as in an earthquake, inside a building engulfed in flames, on board a small boat when one's sole companion is swept overboard in a storm – then extreme reactions may follow and behaviour may become totally disorganised, for a while at any rate.

Here are some of these reactions: shock or apathy, acute distress, useless activity, denial and misinterpretation of the crisis, compounding errors or persisting in inappropriate acts, panic, searching for explanation. They are not discrete entities, and aspects of some of them can be related to examples in previous chapters, but they give an idea of the range of responses.

Shock, apathy, or the inability to act

Shock is most intense after a major disaster, when not only is life threatened but the whole environment is disrupted. An observer of an earthquake at Messina in Sicily has caught the mood well:

> The immediate and almost universal effect that the earthquake had on those who escaped death at Messina was of stupefaction, almost of mental paralysis. They were stunned ... Lamentation was infrequently heard except when caused by physical suffering.

Tears were rarely seen. Men recounted how they had lost wife, mother, brothers, sisters, children and all their possessions, with no apparent concern. They told their tales of woe as if they themselves had been disinterested spectators of another's loss.[3]

The scene is re-enacted just about weekly in one part of the world or another, after floods, hurricanes, fires, explosions, air raids, terrorist attacks, transport accidents and the like. The impact may be sudden and unexpected and last only a few seconds, as in the case of an earth tremor, or it may go on for days if there is heavy flooding, but the nature of the initial reaction is remarkably constant. The severity of the state of shock and its duration will depend on the significance of the loss and disruption for the individual. Insofar as it is possible to imagine a hierarchy of suffering and loss, the worst experience as far as engendering a state of shock is concerned would be a severe earthquake such as the ones which struck southern Italy in 1980. There whole villages were destroyed and there was heavy loss of life. Just about everything that was familiar was in many cases lost or obliterated, and it was to be expected in such circumstances that people would remain shocked and unable to fend for themselves for days on end, unable even to protect themselves against common dangers such as the cold (as far as that was possible anyway) or to bother to eat. After a 'lesser' event such as a near miss from a terrorist bomb where there was no injury or personal or material loss, the shock would not last more than minutes or a few hours at the most.

This state of shock is a protective mechanism. The individual has endured just too much – either actual loss or the awful realisation of what so nearly might have been. No more horrors can be assimilated, so the person 'switches off' and ceases to react or even apparently to respond appropriately to what has already happened. But the response is appropriate from the psychological point of view, provided the physical needs can be taken care of by others. Such psychological responses tend to be adaptive, and although people may appear to be in danger of wandering into oblivion or stepping on live electricity cables and the like, I do not actually know of any examples of people dying because they have blankly walked into a fatal hazard. I mention this because I suspect there is yet another self-protective mechanism that will prevent the individual succumbing totally unless he is somehow rendered vulnerable by previous loss, depression or other bad experience.

Responding to the shock   Isolated groups can suffer catastrophe in the course of their ordinary activities. A party of climbers may lose someone from a rope breaking or through a fall down into a crevasse.

The crew of a small yacht may lose someone overboard in a storm. These are shattering events by any standards, even when they involve people who have lived for years with the knowledge of sudden disaster. A close friend with whom you have climbed, or sailed or worked, with whom you have a deep level of mutual trust, who at times has held your life in his hands just as you have held his in yours, is needlessly killed, possibly before your eyes, and there is nothing you can do to avert the tragedy. So easily it might have been you. You are shocked and stunned, but you must keep going and keep control of the situation, or you will go the same way.

Of course people do keep going – otherwise they would not be able to tell their story – but it may be that some of the disasters in which a whole party have perished began with the death of one person, with the others subsequently unable to act effectively in the short term, even to protect themselves. This is especially relevant in a small boat in a storm. One person is washed overboard. If a rescue is to be attempted, highly skilled manoeuvres are required *immediately* if the victim is not to drift hopelessly far behind (and probably upwind); and even if rescue is judged out of the question because of darkness or the severity of the conditions, effective handling of the boat must be maintained if it is not to slew round broadside to the wind and capsize. Similarly, wartime aircrews had to go on flying their planes even though a mate was seriously wounded and in need of attention. Climbers after a tragedy have a few minutes at any rate in which they can hold tight and take stock.

During the direct assault in 1965 of the 6,000-foot (1,800 m) precipice which is the north face of the Eiger, John Harlin fell to his death when some two thousand feet from the summit. After their initial shock the remaining climbers were able to continue, and this Anglo-American group joined forces with a party of Germans who were on the rock face at the same time.

In the course of the 1971 International Everest Expedition, Harsh Bahuguna fell into a crevasse and hung there on a rope with one glove off and part of his abdomen exposed. There was a storm blowing at the time and darkness would soon fall, and it seemed certain that not only would Bahuguna not survive the rescue attempt but that the rescuers would probably perish also. Thus the decision had to be made to leave their companion, even though he was not quite dead. The storm continued for another ten days, during which time the members of the expedition were confined to their tents. The expedition had been an uncomfortable one from the start. International cooperation is a nice idea, but national rivalries were never far below the surface, and furthermore there were disagreements about the best route to take which split the expedition down the middle.[4] Harsh Bahuguna had been a much respected companion and possibly something of a peacemaker, and I suspect that his death placed too much strain on the fragile integrity of the expedition, because after the storm had abated there was no more serious climbing and people began to drift home.

There were important differences between the Eiger group and the 1971 International Everest Expedition. To begin with, the Eiger group was small and composed of men who knew and respected one another; the Everest expedition was made up largely of strangers. The Eiger members were quite clear about the precise route they were taking; on the Everest expedition there were serious disagreements about routes, who should lead, and so on. Nobody actually saw Harlin fall, and by the time the disaster was appreciated he was two thousand feet down the precipice. By contrast, the Everest climbers had the horror of seeing their companion hanging there, still living but beyond rescue. Lastly, there is an intensity about climbing the six-thousand-foot wall of the Eiger which totally engaged the climbers' attention, and so it was probably easier for them to go on than it was for the others on the the lower part of Everest where that expedition was not nearly at the final 'assault' stage.

During the first Whitbread Round-the-World Sailing Race for fully crewed yachts in 1973/4, two men were lost overboard. One was from a boat skippered by Chay Blyth with a well-disciplined crew of paratroops. Blyth apparently got together a group of durable men and welded them into a team; then he taught them to sail. This may be a slight oversimplification, but it indicates that the team aspect came first, and sailing ability, second. By contrast, the other boat that lost a member overboard was crewed by highly expert yachtsmen, capable of being skippers in their own right. When Blyth's crewman was knocked into the Southern Ocean by a blow on the head from the boom, the remainder of the crew kept going, and their boat eventually won the race. The other boat retired, the crew demoralised.

Acute distress

This means 'going to pieces', and is liable to happen when inexperienced people of a nervous disposition become involved in a crisis to do with someone falling overboard or a climbing accident. The very experienced and hardy can also go to pieces, but their breaking point is naturally much higher. This is seen clearly with élite troops in combat. They can generally tolerate more bloodshed and exposure to danger than ordinary troops, but when their limit is reached their breakdown is complete.

More common is the person who hangs around wailing and weeping, contributing nothing and upsetting those trying to retrieve the situation.

Useless activity

After a period of inactivity in a state of shock, or perhaps as an initial reaction, some people throw themselves into feverish activity almost as a distraction against the awfulness of the events. So when someone falls overboard, our useless crewman starts lowering the mainsail or dropping the anchor, without any real understanding of the needs of the moment: it is just that some kind of activity makes him feel less distressed. This is commonly seen after motor accidents: feeling a great need to 'do' something, spectators pull the wretched victim out of the smashed car, thus aggravating his injuries.

At the scene of disasters it is common to see people clawing uselessly at the rubble to try and free relatives they imagine to be trapped alive somewhere below. This was poignantly evident at Aberfan in 1967, when a coal tip collapsed engulfing a school and killing 116 children and twenty-three adults. Even people directly involved in the rescue effort were so overwhelmed by the horror of the disaster that they were unable to act in a coordinated manner and had to go searching hopelessly for their lost children. Doctors may become so bewildered by the sheer scale of the casualties confronting them, especially when their facilities have been destroyed too, that they cease to function effectively even within their limited resources. After a tornado in Worcester, Massachusetts, a doctor was found to be suturing infected wounds[5] – something that should never be done under any circumstances. And at Hiroshima:

> ... bewildered by the numbers, staggered by so much raw flesh, Dr. Sasaki lost all sense of profession and stopped working as a skilful surgeon and a sympathetic man; he became an automaton, mechanically wiping, daubing, winding, wiping, daubing, winding ... Near the entrance to the park, an Army doctor was working, but the only medicine he had was iodine, which he painted over cuts, bruises, slimy burns, everything – and by now everything that he had painted had pus on it.[6]

Unfortunately, people in a distressed state – such as when recently bereaved or after a disaster – become highly suggestible, just as people can be rendered suggestible by first making them fatigued and anxious. So someone with a forceful personality who develops a conviction about what needs to be done in a crisis may become a positive menace. In 1963 after the cruise liner *Lakonia* caught fire and was sinking in the Atlantic, someone describing herself as a nurse went amongst the passengers telling them to remove as much clothing as possible before jumping into the sea, and once in to move as vigorously as possible to generate warmth in the body. This ridiculous advice doubtless contributed to the 113 deaths from exposure, since people going into the sea should put on as much clothing as they can and then once in move as *little* as possible.

Useless activity relates to the processes of preoccupation and distraction described in Chapter 9. The difference is merely one of degree. In each case the individual cannot cope with the current realities when comprehended as a whole, and therefore becomes totally preoccupied with some detail. In the case of preoccupation and distraction the concern is with some detail related to the main task; in useless activity it is likely to be with some quite extraneous matter.

Denial or misinterpretation of the crisis

This is a variation of 'seeing what you want to see' (Chapter 9) transposed to the setting of possible disaster. For example, two liners, the Italian *Andrea Doria* and the Swedish *Stockholm*, were in collision off the east coast of the United States. The *Andrea Doria* soon began to sink and passengers and crew rapidly abandoned ship. The *Ile de France* happened to be passing at the time and came in close to help with the rescue. Passengers on board the *Île de France* observed the searchlights playing on the people in the water and thought that a water carnival was in progress, despite the fact that they were two hundred miles out to sea. Presumably carnivals better matched their mood and expectations than marine disaster.[7]

The inherent improbability of most disasters is an important factor in people misinterpreting the warning signs, and nowhere is this more conspicuous than with warnings of the ultimate disaster of nuclear attack. In February 1971 someone put on the wrong tape when the weekly test of missile defences was due. What went out across the United States was a genuine warning of impending nuclear attack.[8] Radio and television stations, on receiving the signal, were to go off the air immediately and await further orders from the White House. To all intents this warning was ignored. A few stations did close down, but when they found that others were still transmitting they resumed their own transmissions. Perhaps they thought their advertisers might be annoyed. So what went wrong? Probably it just seemed too improbable. There was no major East-West tension at the time, and anyway there had been previous false

Mike McMullen at the helm of the 46-foot (14 m) trimaran *Three Cheers*. Three days before the start of the 1976 Singlehanded Transatlantic Race, his wife, Lizzie, was killed while working on the boat. Nevertheless, he started in the race, which he had a good chance of winning, but was never seen again. *(See p. 239.) (Jonathan Eastland)*

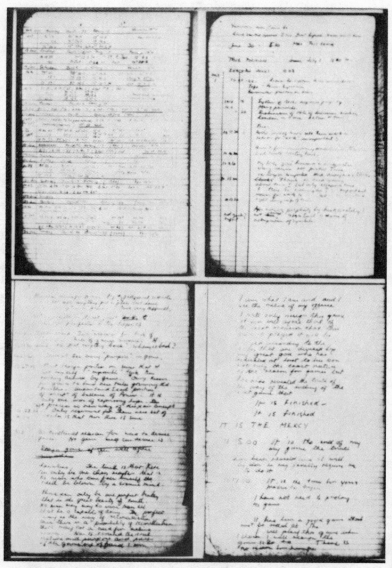

Donald Crowhurst's last navigational entries and last writings between 12 June and 1 July 1969. The progressive disorganisation of the written page exactly matched his psychological disintegration which led him to lower himself over the side of his yacht to merge with the Atlantic Ocean. (*See pp. 63 and 190.*)

Brian Cooke and his 52-foot (16 m) trimaran *Triple Arrow*, in which in 1976 he hoped to set a record of 4,000 miles (6,400 km) in twenty days, but on his way to the start he must have fallen overboard as his upturned abandoned trimaran was later found floating in Mid-Atlantic (*see p. 239*). He had previously sailed successfully in Singlehanded Transatlantic Races (*see p. 113*). (*Jonathan Eastland*)

David Blagden in his 19-foot (5.8 m) sloop *Willing Griffin*, before the start of the 1972 Singlehanded Transatlantic Race, puzzling how to stow sufficient stores in such a tiny boat for what turned out to be a fifty-two-day passage to Newport, Rhode Island (*see p. 170*). Six years later he was drowned when a yacht he was sailing foundered in a storm in the Irish Sea (*see p. 240*). (*Glin Bennet*)

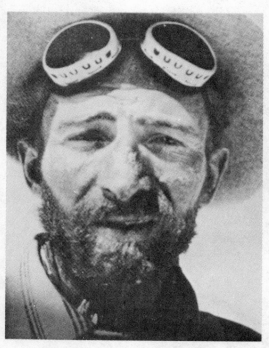

Hermann Buhl (*left*) and Dr David Lewis (*below*) shortly after their ordeals. Buhl had just staggered down from the first ascent of Nanga Parbat (26,670 ft; 8,125 m) which he climbed without oxygen and alone as his companion dropped out. He made his descent without ice axe and one crampon, experiencing hallucinations of another person present with him, and arrived back badly frostbitten and in the last stages of exhaustion (*see p. 153*). David Lewis was photographed on arrival at Palmer Base in the Antarctic after twelve weeks at sea in which he was capsized twice and suffered a broken mast, as well as complete disruption of the interior of *Ice Bird* (*see p. 147*).

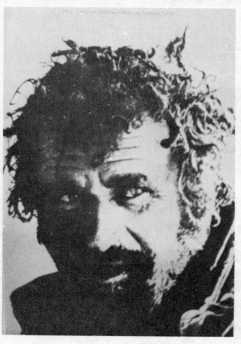

alarms. Since then there have been further false alarms which make it even more likely that people will believe what they want to believe and so become less likely to act effectively in a real crisis.[9]

Compounding errors or persistence in inappropriate acts

A small error or minor crisis – in this case, the activities of a bird – can trigger off a sequence of events which can end in disaster.

Preparing for a long downhill run into Hatfield station, north of London, the driver and fireman of a diesel train were startled by a bird flying into the front window. Instinctively they raised their hands in front of them, which made them laugh. Dropping his hand, the driver began to apply the brakes at the usual time and place, about a mile and a quarter from the station. At the same time he cancelled the automatic warning system. Gradually he realised that the train was hardly slowing at all from the 70 miles per hour (110 kph) he had been travelling at, and that it was going to overrun the station. Since he had a full load of passengers on board and there were regular shunting movements in the busy station ahead, he began to whistle furiously in order to warn the signal box to give him a clear run. But the two signals ahead of him remained at red, and it was only when he had passed them both that he looked at his vacuum gauge, which showed a considerable pressure. He realised at once from this high pressure that he had not been applying the vacuum brake at all. Instead, he had been persistently working the air brake handle which lies next to the vacuum brake handle: the air brake has no effect at all on the speed of the train. He had persisted in two inappropriate actions – applying the air brake and whistling – even though they were being ineffective, and an appreciable time had elapsed before he began to question the wisdom of these manoeuvres and to consider other possible actions.[10]

Another driver, bringing his train into Royton Station, near Manchester, in February 1961, began to brake slightly later than he should have done, and so when he did apply the brakes he did so more sharply than usual – too sharply for them to take maximum effect. Then, becoming anxious about his excessive speed, he was seized with the idea that the wheels throughout the train were locked solid and that the train was skidding. In fact this was not the case, and only the bogie wheels under the cab were sliding, but to check this imaginary skid he released the brakes. Convinced that the wheels were still locked he began to apply engine power to free them, so that by the time he reached the station the train was not only unbraked but was actually running under power at 40 miles per hour

(64 kph). Fortunately the driver was able to jump clear and no one was hurt, as the train smashed into the buffer stops at the end of the platform.

Three years later a somewhat similar incident occurred at Bradford (Exchange) Station in Yorkshire. This time the driver was not so lucky and lost his life, when his diesel ran into the station without slowing down and collided with a stationary parcels train which was waiting there. Eye-witnesses in the front passenger compartment (who have a clear view of the driver in local trains of this design) said they saw the driver apply the brake repeatedly as he approached the station, but none of the applications was made for long enough to be fully effective. Soon realising that the train was out of control, the passengers escaped to the rear carriages, but the driver remained at his seat, motionless and impassive. A post-mortem on him showed that some time previously he had had a heart attack (myocardial infarction), and the report suggested that he could have been in such pain at the time of the collision that he was temporarily incapacitated. It was further postulated in the report that pain itself may have been precipitated by the fearful realisation that the braking was ineffective and that the train was going to run out of control on the downhill gradient ahead of him.

Part of this incident was observed by the driver and guard of a steam engine standing stationary nearby. They said they had seen the driver of the ill-fated train attempt to leave his seat just before the collision. One of them said the driver had actually left his cab by the centre rear door; the other said he had seen the driver try to move sideways. When this situation was reconstructed it was found impossible for either of these men to have seen into the driver's cab, and they both had to withdraw their statements, presumably given in good faith. Here is an example of people misperceiving an event, relating to their own job, in a manner which would conform to their expectations of how one ought to act. The guard at the rear of the runaway train also demonstrated an inappropriate reaction in an emergency after the accident had actually happened. Although he was trained in first aid, he wandered right away from the scene of the collision and the injured passengers. He made his way along the track to the nearest signal box where he merely asked what the time was.[11]

In these three examples the drivers had persisted in inappropriate actions even though they were quite evidently ineffective. At Hatfield the driver eventually realised his mistake: at Royton and Bradford Exchange the drivers' inappropriate reactions persisted until a crash was inevitable.

Take a more familiar situation. A motorist driving downhill in icy conditions applies the foot brake to slow himself down. When the car loses control he simply presses harder, and then pulls on the hand brake until he crashes or someone in the car tells him to take off the brakes and change down to a lower gear. Pressing the foot brake is the normal way to slow down; when this does not work there is momentary anxiety which somehow prevents a rational appraisal of the conditions, and so the vicious circle starts.

Panic

Panic develops from the fear of what *might* happen rather than as a consequence of what *has actually* happened. Most dramatically it occurs in a crisis if the escape routes are closing down and avoidance of the disaster seems unlikely, and the most terrible examples are fires in public buildings where large numbers of strangers gather together, sometimes drunk, and amongst whom there is no sense of cohesion. A notorious example was when the Iroquois Theater in Chicago caught fire in 1903. The theatre itself was so little damaged that a performance could have been put on two days later, but when a few panicked there was a stampede in which 602 people died.[12] The same kind of thing happened in the Cocoanut Grove night-club fire in Boston in 1942. Two hundred of the 491 dead were piled behind one revolving door, and another hundred bodies were found behind a door that would only open inwards.[13]

Football matches provide even clearer examples of panic as a major cause of loss of life. After a disallowed goal at a football match in Peru in 1964, a dispute developed amongst the spectators; later the police intervened and lobbed tear gas into the crowd. There were fifty-three thousand spectators in the stadium at the time, and in the rush to escape between 287 and 328 people died (the exact number was never ascertained).[12]

Panic is also likely after there has been a disaster and when there is a threat of further danger and destruction. Port Jervis, in New York State, was badly flooded by the rains connected with hurricane Diane in 1955. The emergency had been handled fairly well by the inhabitants, but anxiety developed later about the security of a dam some forty-four miles up-river. Rumours spread quickly. Then during the night the police chief announced that water was going to be let off the dam to relieve pressure. In their highly sensitive state the populace misinterpreted the information in a predictably un-favourable way, and assumed that the dam had burst. To make matters worse, the fire department assumed the same thing, and firemen then went about the streets with sirens wailing, shouting at people to evacuate. The panic to get out of the town might easily have been more disastrous than any flooding.[14]

Quick thinking

This is the antithesis of panic and it supplies some examples of positive activity in a chapter concerned mainly with disorganised behaviour. Albert von St Gallen Heim, whose studies of falling climbers were described in Chapter 3, was able to record his own responses when he fell between the front and rear wheels of a horse-drawn wagon in the Italian Alps in 1881:

> For a fleeting moment I was still able to hold onto the edge of the wagon. The following series of thoughts went through my mind: 'I cannot manage to hold on until the horse comes to a stop; I must let go. If I simply let go, I will fall on my back and the wheel will travel forward over my legs. Then at the least a fracture of the knee-pan or shinbone will be unavoidable; I must fall upon my stomach and the wheel will pass over the backs of my legs. If I will then tense the muscles, they will be a protective cushion for the bones. The pressure of the street will be somewhat less likely to break a bone than the pressure of the wheel. If I am able to turn myself to the left then perhaps I can sufficiently draw back my left leg; on the other hand, turning to the right would, by the dimensions of the wagon, result in both legs being broken under it.' I know quite clearly that I let myself fall only after these lightning-fast, wholly precise reflections, which seemed to imprint themselves upon my brain. Thereupon through a jerk of my arm, I turned myself to the left, swung my left leg powerfully outward, and simultaneously tensed my leg muscles to the limit of their strength. The wheel passed over my right ham, and I came out of it with a slight bruise.[15]

Neil Williams was part-way through an aerobatic sequence in a Zlin Akrobat in 1970 when his left wing buckled upwards under him. He could not control the aircraft effectively and began to lose height; in addition, he was carrying no parachute, which he would certainly have used if he had been. He reasoned to himself, partly on the basis of the experience of another pilot who had once been in a similar predicament, that if he inverted the aircraft the wing might 'snap back' into position. So he gave the engine full throttle and rolled over to the left. The wing did snap back and he was flying under control again, but upside down. He then had to work out how he was going to get down to land. After considering various possibilities, he decided to make for a grass strip parallel to the runway, still upside down, and then flip the aircraft over at the very last moment. This is how he described the end of a crisis which lasted sightly less than ten minutes:

> As the speed fell to 87 mph (140 km/h) a full aileron roll-out was made to the right, and just a trace of negative g [thrust away from gravity] was maintained in order to hold the left wing in place. The aircraft responded well to the controls at this stage, but as it approached level flight the left wing started to fold up again. The nose was already down as a result of the slight negative g, and subsequent examination of the impact marks showed that the left wing tip touched the ground during the roll, although this could not be felt inside the aircraft. As the wing folded the aircraft hit the ground hard in a slight nose-down, left-bank attitude, I released the controls and concentrated on trying to roll into a ball, knees and feet pulled up and in, and head down protected by my arms. I had a blurred impression of the world going past the windscreen sideways and then with a final jolt, everything stopped.[16]

The search for explanation
There is a basic human need to make sense of one's condition, and the worse the conditions are the greater is this need. When the town of Skopje in Yugoslavia was devasted by an earthquake in 1963, people there, especially the elderly, went around saying things like, 'people in Skopje have lived too well', they had grown 'much too conceited', there was 'too much building going on', and people were prone to forget 'how small and insignificant they were'.[17] Similarly in 1970, after large-scale earthquakes in Peru, some mountain people who had lost everything said to a relief worker, 'The God of the mountains did it because he was angry with the people in Lima.' Townspeople also saw the event in terms of divine retribution. When a black community in Mississippi was struck by tornadoes, with over thirty children killed and scarcely a family left untouched, they saw the disaster as the work of God and blamed themselves for being sinful and deserving of punishment; some compared their lot to that of Job.[18]

More 'westernised' communities, meaning perhaps those with less of a religious tradition and possibly also less social cohesion may give their explanation in more temporal terms. After the explosion of a munitions ship in 1917 which destroyed part of the port of Halifax, Nova Scotia, all the German residents were immediately placed under arrest – a tacit way of assigning blame, at least in the short term, when emotions carried more force than facts.[19] During the bombing of London in the Second World War, air raid victims would quite indiscriminately blame the prime minister, Hitler, the Royal Air Force, the Luftwaffe and even the local air raid warden.[20] And after the Cocoanut Grove fire the survivors blamed 'the owners' and the Boston City officials for it, even though in fact there was only one owner and it was known early on that the fire had been started by a 'bus boy'. Even stranger, the bus boy, far from being blamed, received fan letters and gifts of money.[21]

Relatively close communities can handle major calamities better: Aberfan, for example, which suffered the terrible pit tip collapse in 1967; and the group of north Somerset villages, the homes of the 104 people, mostly mothers of young children, who were killed in April 1973 when the aircraft taking them for a day's shopping and sightseeing in Switzerland crashed into a hillside after having failed to land at Basle airport in a snowstorm.[22] My impression of these communities is that they were more interested in coping with the daily realities than in assigning blame for what had happened – and could not now be undone – even though subsequent inquiries showed that they had good grounds for complaint against the authorities. However, these disasters aroused so much publicity, particularly in the case of Aberfan, that the villagers could hardly avoid controversy. They were inundated by the media, who feed on controversy, and in a democratic society there will always be politicians, local and national, ready to make personal capital out of any event.

As with all the other reactions to catastrophic events, the behaviour of large groups is merely an extension of what happens to a stricken individual. A bereaved person has a need to comprehend the death of a loved one. There may be no problem if the death was expected and occurred in the fullness of years, but if the father of young children is killed in an accident or dies after a minor operation in hospital, then there is an intense need for an explanation which will make some sense of the event and integrate it into some larger framework of meaning. In a non-religious society this can be very difficult, and so authorities and organisations (such as hospitals) may catch the blame. Those at the receiving end of such blame, assuming they have done no wrong, must be forbearing and understanding and not try to justify themselves even though it is painful to be wrongly accused.

Adventurers develop a fairly philosophical attitude towards death in the natural environment, and I am being forced to acquire it myself. Three of the twenty who comprised the main part of my study of singlehanded sailors have so far died at sea, as have a number of other ocean-sailing friends. A climber in his late forties recently said to me quite calmly, 'Most of my close friends have been killed climbing.'

Disorganisation and breakdown

Another way of reacting to disaster, besides going into a state of shock, panicking, or misinterpreting the crisis altogether, is to withdraw from the unmanageable reality into a calmer psychological environment: in common parlance, to go mad.

In the late 1940s Ann and Frank Davison bought the virtual wreck of a 70-foot (21.3-m) ketch, *Reliance*, with something of a post-war dream of sailing away from Britain to a pleasanter land and a less complicated way of life. Unfortunately their expenses mounted, creditors became impatient, and they were threatened with a writ. Such a writ would literally be nailed to the mast and would prevent them from leaving harbour, and in all probability the boat would then be seized and auctioned off to pay their debts. They therefore secretly provisioned the boat and slipped out of Fleetwood harbour days before the ultimatums from the creditors were due to expire. Their plan was to sail across the Atlantic, probably to Cuba, but from reading Ann Davison's account[23] it is not at all clear how they hoped to achieve this. Their experience was limited, and the boat was almost certainly not suitable for an ocean passage and was inevitably inadequately equipped and provisioned on account of shortage of time and money.

The trip seems to have been a disaster from the start. They had heavy weather and never seemed to know where they were. Eventually, much weakened by the storms and consequent lack of sleep and proper food, they passed Land's End, hoping to strike out into the Atlantic. South-westerly gales, however, forced them up the English Channel instead, as their engine was unreliable and the boat clearly would not sail well to windward. Ann was beginning to suffer blackouts and was weakening from the endless buffeting of the sea, but the real trouble was going to be with Frank.

Frank sat in the wheelhouse hour by hour trying to steer the boat through the crashing waves, refusing to let Ann help him in any way. He began to sense that something was wrong with him, that he had perhaps driven himself too hard. Then his mood changed. 'The lost look had gone from his eyes but his expression was very strange,' Ann wrote. Frank turned on her, 'Had a bit of a party, haven't you?'; then he shouted menacingly, 'Ship's a bloody shambles.' Ann pointed out that it was bound to be a shambles in a gale, but he snarled, 'Don't think you can get away with that. You can't fool me.' She realised she could not handle the boat and her husband in that state and that she must get help, yet when she made for the flares to give warning of her predicament he snatched them from her, and then, to continue in Ann Davison's own words:

> I grabbed him by the coat and we fought, horribly. He got the door open, threw the flares out, over the side, whisked away by the screaming wind. With a supreme effort I thrust him aside and slammed the door. He threw himself upon the wheel, opened the throttle wide, and in a paroxysm of frenzy pulled the wheel first one way and then the other.
>
> Something had to be done. And quickly. With the vain hope that a counter-shock might restore his senses, I screamed at the top of my voice, simulating hysterics. And thought at first it had succeeded, for he quietened and slowly throttled down: said, 'Ann, Ann, this isn't like you.'
>
> At this point the engine stopped.
>
> 'My God, you've stopped it!' The words were out, in a whisper, my hysterical act forgotten. He had turned the throttle wheel too far.
>
> He said in a perfectly normal voice, 'I'll tell you something' – I turned to him hopefully – 'we are not at sea at all. We're in harbour. Tied up along a quay.'
>
> Anguished, I could only stare helplessly ...
>
> Suddenly he caught me off my guard as I was racking my brain for some solution to the dreadful problem, and was out of the wheelhouse door, shouting he was going ashore and I could not stop him. I was after him, terror-stricken, and had him by a bulldog grip on the arm. But he would not come back, and it was no place to fight out there. I thought if he saw what it was like, felt the force of it, perhaps the truth might penetrate to his tired, blind brain. We made our way, step by step, up the heaving, pitching deck, with spray stinging our faces, wind tearing our hair, clutching our clothes, water swirling about our feet. Nothing of which he seemed to realise. Right to the stemhead we went. The storm had moderated, of course, or we should never have got there. And we stood, I fast hold of his arm, he shouting to imaginary boatmen to take him ashore.

Then quite suddenly Frank acquiesced and allowed himself to be led down to the cabin. Fortunately also, the wind gradually abated and the crisis was temporarily over. In psychiatric language, Frank had had an acute paranoid reaction as a way of dealing with a totally unmanageable situation, namely that he was trying to get away from

England, where there would be a writ awaiting him, in a boat that was incapable of making headway against the south-westerly gales. He could not win; therefore he reconstructed reality, so to speak, to match his needs.

Once below, Frank collapsed asleep. Next morning he was so much restored in mood that Ann felt she could let go at last, and then, with the boat in Frank's now capable hands, she fell into a deep sleep. Frank was later able to relate his perception of the night before. He felt that something was wrong, and that Ann was

... keeping something dreadful from him. Then when he went below he passed out again in the saloon, and came round with the conviction that he had been attacked and laid low by a blow from behind. The chaos in the saloon being evidence of a fight having taken place there. He knew, as one knows in a dream without question or reason, there was a plot afoot in which [Ann] was involved together with other unknown invisible persons (presumably responsible for the attack) to deprive him of the ship. Make away with him, in fact, and take *Reliance* off on some unspecified, nefarious purpose.

When they then went up on deck together, he was convinced that they were in harbour, tied alongside the quay wall.

Thereafter there was no further psychological disturbance, but the weather deteriorated again and they were driven further and further back up the English Channel; I suspect that neither of them was functioning very effectively by then (which is hardly surprising) as, unless the boat was totally uncontrollable, it should have been possible at least to stand out to sea. They were driven into the tide race off Portland Bill and eventually ran aground there. They got off the boat onto an open raft where they were tossed about for hours in the fierce seas of the race. Frank succumbed, but Ann was washed ashore and lived to go to sea again in another boat and become the first woman to sail the Atlantic singlehanded.

I have related this story at some length because it illustrates how a combination of factors, both remote and immediate, can lead to total psychological breakdown. The remote factors were the long-standing financial anxiety about the boat and all the distressing dealings with creditors, plus a certain dissatisfaction with life leading to a desire for a fresh start together, with dreams of how life might ultimately be for them. The immediate factors were their unsuitable boat which would not handle safely in heavy weather, their lack of sailing experience and knowledge of the sea, the over-hasty fitting out and lack of sea trials so that nothing seemed to work properly once they were out of the harbour, and their misfortune with the weather.

Around twenty years later, another modestly experienced sailor with a fantasy of success was to set off from England on an even more adventurous voyage in a probably even less satisfactory boat. He was Donald Crowhurst, whom I have referred to several times so far in this book. Inspired by Sir Francis Chichester's circumnavigation of the world and triumphant homecoming to Plymouth in May 1967, he resolved to do the same himself. A number of others had been similarly inspired, and this prompted the *Sunday Times* to devise a contest which would bring together all the prospective round-the-world sailors (whether they actually entered or not), and offer prizes for the first home and for the fastest time.

Unfortunately their rules only allowed Crowhurst about eight months in which to acquire or have built a suitable boat. He chose to have one specially built, a trimaran of novel design, and of course there were snags. All the same, amid desperate scenes at Teignmouth, his port of departure in Devon, he did leave on the last permissible day.

Two weeks out he realised, I think, that his boat was incapable of sailing round the world non-stop. He had staked his whole future (and that of his wife and four children too) on this enterprise, and he hoped it might revive the fortunes of his ailing electronics company. He had to consider his financial backers, and media interests as well. What on earth was he to do? To drop out at this stage would have precipitated an intolerable personal and financial crisis for him, but to take on the Southern Ocean in his flimsy trimaran would have been suicidal. Thus, as with Frank Davison, there was no rational solution, but, as we have seen, Crowhurst came up with something entirely novel: he would fake a voyage round the world. He would circulate around in the South Atlantic where there are few shipping lanes, and then at the 'appropriate' moment announce that he had 'rounded' Cape Horn. After that he could sail home conventionally. He would come in third or fourth, everybody would congratulate him and he would gain the much needed publicity for his firm and the nautical navigating device he manufactured.

This plan worked quite well at first. At the end of April 1969 he broke his long radio silence, and was going to sail openly back to England. Robin Knox-Johnston had already arrived home, but having made a very slow passage. Nigel Tetley, in a trimaran very similar to Crowhurst's, was somewhere ahead. The publicity machine got into action again now that there was a real race between two people, and needless to say, Tetley soon became aware that Crowhurst was on his tail. Tetley therefore drove his boat even harder until it began to disintegrate and eventually sank on 21 May in a storm off the Azores. Now, with the irony of a Greek tragedy, Crowhurst found himself in a position where he could not fail to win the race. He had sent out such convincing messages of his progress that he misled Tetley into believing he would soon be overtaken – which was the last thing he actually wanted to happen. And he could not now sail so slowly as to allow Knox-Johnston to beat him on time, as the media were beginning to watch his progress closely. As winner, of course, his log-books would be scrutinised carefully and his deception would be sure to be discovered.

He became progressively more aware of his predicament, and all this time he was unable to manage a radio-telephone link with his wife, to whom he might have been able to confide his plight – insofar as anything is private on radio transmission. So he gradually ceased effective sailing, and from 23 June spent most of his time writing furiously in his log-books.

Over the next seven days he wrote some twenty-five thousand words which were intended to be his message to the world. It is a remarkable pencilled testament, written sometimes neatly, sometimes illegibly, but always with an urgency that stands out from the page. The content of these writings I have discussed at length elsewhere,[24] and so have Nick Tomalin and Ron Hall in their book.[25] What matters here is the significance of the act of writing this testament and Crowhurst's state of mind during these final days. Clearly he had become embroiled in a trap. His simple deception had escalated into something far more complicated than he could ever have imagined: a private fraud was at risk of becoming an event which would rouse interest throughout the world. As far as Crowhurst could see, there was no possible way out, except one: to retreat from reality into a private world where he was in command – in other words to go mad, which is precisely what he did.

Isolated on the ocean in his private world, his thoughts took off, and he developed progressively more exalted ideas about his own powers. To begin with he took issue with Einstein, then he surpassed him in his insights. Eventually he tackled God, then became God with the power to create gods at will. By this time he had transcended all the trifling realities of publicity and exposure to public obloquy that had been confronting him, he had become able to readjust the whole system of realities in the world; and he had in his mind reached a level of total mastery over everything such that there was scarcely any point in remaining in the world that most people regard as real. On 1

July, therefore, after having written what was in effect a countdown
to his own end, he slipped over the side of his boat, to merge with the
ocean and the universe.

Nine days later his intact boat was found floating peacefully in
mid-Atlantic. It was untidy from eight months at sea, but undamaged,
and on board were found log-books, tape-recordings, film, details of
cables sent and received, and of course his own voluminous writings.
From this, and from a good deal of external evidence, it has been
possible to piece together what happened.

In presenting the stories of Frank Davison and Donald Crowhurst
together, I am not implying that they were men of similar
temperament, although they may have been. Nor am I suggesting that
they were basically unstable, meaning that their ability to withstand
psychological strain was limited, as I have no evidence to support
that view. Of course, they may have been rather romantic, idealistic
characters, but so are many adventurers, and when they succeed
these are the very qualities that are admired. All I can say about these
men is that when faced with a reality which they could not handle,
they did what many many people do in ordinary life – they retreated
into a psychological 'space' where the issues were once again
manageable. In principle the mechanism is satisfactory; in practice
out on the high seas or on expedition it is liable to be disastrous.

PART IV

Coping and Preventing

14

Surviving Against the Odds

Why does one group succeed while another fails? Why does one man survive a catastrophe and another succumb? These are simple questions to ask, but difficult to answer directly.

Some of the people struggling for their very survival have got into difficulties as a direct consequence of their own adventurousness: a great many, probably the majority, have suddenly found themselves up against it when both physically and psychologically unprepared, such as when taken hostage, shipwrecked or isolated after an air crash.

This chapter will examine the factors which can lead certain people to come through certain kinds of ordeal – the attitudes of mind, the types of behaviour, and the different responses called for by different circumstances. I will give a series of vignettes rather than a systematic account, general observations rather than instructions for survival.

Surviving in a concentration camp
It is one thing surviving out in the open in a hostile climate where the forces are impersonal, but quite another to come through an ordeal which has deliberately been contrived. Through no fault of your own and after having committed no wrong, you find yourself incarcerated with thousands of others in an environment created expressly for the purpose of your destruction, where death is the only realistic outcome. It may seem insensitive to attempt to discuss the effects of the forces of nature alongside the horrors that occurred in concentration camps, but I believe lessons were learned there which have an application in the wider world of adversity.

The most important factor affecting survival in a concentration camp was the whim of the guards. There was so little the prisoners could do in their debilitated and demoralised state. Escape was virtually impossible – only a tiny number out of millions – and survival strategies therefore refer to a fairly narrow band of coping behaviours. Since the inmates could exercise no initiative, survival depended on a person's ability to adapt to the physical surroundings, to the guards and to the regular casual brutalities that had to be witnessed and endured.

I have drawn here on experiences in camps in Germany run by the Gestapo, because a great deal is now known about Nazi concentration camps in the form of personal accounts and statistical studies.

Bruno Bettelheim,[1] a psychologist, was incarcerated in Buchenwald and then Dachau for one year before the outbreak of the Second World War, simply because he was Jewish. As a trained observer, he was in a good position to comment on the processes involved. He has compared the attitudes of the 'old' prisoners – that is, those who had been there more than one year – with what he calls the 'new' ones. It follows that the old prisoners had adapted to a fair degree simply because they had survived that long. The great struggle was to keep going for the first few days, and then for the first few weeks. A very large number died within the first few weeks 'either because they did not care to survive by means of adapting themselves to the life in camp or because they were unable to do so'.[2] Later, if they had got through the first three months it was held that they would last the next three years.

There were a number of features which differentiated the old from the new prisoners. The main concern of the old prisoners was how to live as well as possible in the camp. Only camp news, which directly affected their lives, was of any real interest. Concern about international matters, the progress of the war, and even about the welfare of family and friends, receded. If they did speak about people outside it was in a somewhat detached way, and there was a tendency to forget names and places which were no longer immediate. Money and any spare energy was used to secure better living conditions or a lighter job. During the first year or so there was a tendency to split off, to imagine that the horrors around one were not really happening, at least not involving oneself. After two years this defence mechanism subsided, and the daily events in the camp were accepted as totally real. I have heard, in an interview, a Polish cavalry officer describing sitting in the sun joking with fellow prisoners while five hundred yards away hundreds were at that moment being gassed, and they knew it might be their turn tomorrow.

The Polish officer cut out his past, thought little about the future, and lived completely in the present. He accepted in full consciousness the actuality of what was going on before him, although he suppressed any awareness of the implications of these events. There was an intellectual acceptance of the realities, but not an emotional one, because that would have been intolerable.

Bettelheim observed a child-like regression on the part of the prisoners, so that they might come to speak appreciatively of their guards, to emulate their aggressive behaviour towards newer prisoners, and even to try to make their clothing resemble a Gestapo uniform. This often backfired, as did being 'cooperative' with the guards in managing the crematoria, for example, as such prisoners usually ended up in them themselves or might be done to death by their fellow prisoners. It is hard to say what was the best line to take towards the guards, since their attitude and behaviour were totally capricious. Nevertheless, the Nazis valued *esprit de corps*, and if the individual guards were not too vicious they would allow some grudging admiration for those who tried to help, rather than destroy, their fellows. This is a subtle line. A considerable measure of passivity and acceptance is required to adapt to circumstances where you have no rights at all and where the objective is to break your spirit, but at the same time you must not be so limp as to arouse the guards' contempt.

Paul Matussek,[3] a psychiatrist, has compiled, together with eight associates, a statistical study of a sample of 245 out of 210,000 concentration camp survivors. They were mainly concerned about the after-effects of incarceration, but they did pay attention to factors favouring survival.

They distinguished those who made a successful adaptation from those who did not. Those who adapted well actively sought social contacts, took an active part in a politically organised group, had frequent contact with people with similar religious beliefs, struck up associations with various groups, had frequent contacts as a result of holding a supervisory position, comforted fellow prisoners, showed new inmates how to protect themselves, occasionally shared food with others when they were in dire need, carried on trading activities in the camp, succeeded in getting work in the camp kitchen, had a useful skill such as hair-cutting that made possible connections which could be exploited, forced respect from the guards because of a brisk manner, and displayed an 'opportunistic submission'.

By contrast, the kind of person who adapted badly was regarded variously as an 'odd character', one who mistrusted everyone, was only interested in forming special advantageous relationships with the guards, was uncomradely towards fellow prisoners and only looked after his own interests, clung on to the other prisoners, was a mere hanger-on in politically organised groups, was completely apathetic and wanted to die, attributed survival to chance or fortune, tried to seek safety in illness, was frequently punished and always given the worst work, was hostile and stubborn towards the guards and was frequently tortured because of disobedience.

Matussek and his associates further claimed that those coped better with imprisonment who had formerly 'taken an active part in the general life of society' and who 'reacted with active counter-measures to the onset of persecution'. Going further back still, they claimed those people who previously had had a good and supportive relationship with their mothers were subsequently better able to cope with the traumas of camp life.

Surviving as a hostage[4]

Vulnerable people in certain countries can be alert to signs that they are being watched or followed, such as by seeing the same person in different parts of the town. They can also put their affairs in order so that they will at least not have certain practical worries if they are later seized.

There will be a period of shock and paralysis from fear for minutes or hours after seizure, but after that composure will return. The victim needs to remember that he is expendable, and that his captors are afraid and want to get him away as quickly as possible with a minimum of fuss. The captors may belong to nationalist or ethnic groups, or else have a primary ideological motivation (usually Marxist), or perhaps all these together; and the potential victim should be informed about the different viewpoints and practices of the particular groups.

Urban terrorists are liable to isolate their victims in a cellar or other confined space cut off from daylight, at least for an initial few weeks. The conditions will be disorientating, and may be exceedingly cramped. One American was held for almost three months in a cell too low for him to stand upright, but people do survive these suffocating conditions. In fact, in a survey of three hundred kidnap victims of international terrorism, only twelve were 'executed'.

Passivity and acceptance

One of the greatest aids to survival is the ability to recognise and differentiate the times which demand vigorous action from those which require passivity and acceptance.

The state of passivity and acceptance is a subtle one. It involves 'flowing with the current' and not trying to fight overwhelming forces, human or natural, but at the same time not losing one's sense of identity and self-respect or the feeling of being in command of one's own destiny. Bruno Bettelheim[1] was able to observe this distinction in the hopeless environment of a Nazi concentration camp where many people just gave up and earned the label 'moslem' (based on an erroneous view of moslem fatalism). They gave up when they came to believe that they no longer had any power to influence their condition.

But even the 'moslems', being organisms, could not help reacting somehow to their environment, and this they did by depriving it of the power to influence them as subjects in any way whatsoever. To achieve this, they had to give up responding to it at all, and become objects, but with this they gave up being persons. These walking shadows all died very soon ... They had given up all action as being utterly pointless; then feeling, because all feeling was merely painful or dangerous or both ... The deterioration began when they stopped acting on their own ...

Nobody and nothing could now influence these persons or their characters, because nothing from inside or outside was reaching them any more. Other prisoners often tried to be nice to them when they could, to give them food and so forth, but they could no longer respond to the emotional attitude that was behind someone's giving them food.

Bettelheim came through the ordeal. He recognised that

... to survive as a man not a walking corpse, as a debased and degraded but still human being, one had first and foremost to remain informed and aware of what made up one's personal point of no return, the point beyond which one would never, under any circumstances, give in to the oppressor, even if it meant risking and losing one's life. It meant being aware that if one survived at the price of overreaching this point one would be holding on to a life that had lost all its meaning. It would mean surviving – not with a lowered self respect, but without any.

This point of no return was different from person to person and changed for each person as time passed. At the beginning of their imprisonment, most inmates would have felt it beyond their point of no return to serve the SS as foreman or block chief, or to like wearing a uniform that made them look like the SS. Later, after years in the camp, such relatively external matters gave way to much more essential convictions which then became the core of their resistance. But those convictions one had to hold on to with utter tenacity. About them, one had to keep oneself informed at all times, because only then could they serve as the mainstay of a radically reduced but still present humanity. Much of the tenacity and relentlessness of political prisoners in their factional warfare is thus explainable; for them, political loyalty to party was their point of no return.

Those prisoners who blocked out neither heart nor reason, neither feelings nor perception, but kept informed of their inner attitudes even when they could hardly ever afford to act on them, those prisoners survived and came to understand the conditions they lived under. They also came to realize what they had not perceived before: that they still retained the last, if not the greatest, of the human freedoms: to choose their own attitude in any given circumstances.[1]

Walter Gibson was on board a small steamer with five hundred others escaping from the Japanese invasion of Malaya in 1942. They were torpedoed, and 135 people crowded into the only lifeboat which could be launched in time, and which had been designed to carry no more than twenty-eight persons. Over the next twenty-six days this boat drifted over one thousand miles. Only five survived, the remainder having died through dehydration, starvation, suicide and murder, as Gibson has recounted in his book *The Boat*.[5] Walter Gibson was often asked what led to him surviving. He felt it was partly due to the fact that he had broken his collar bone and so had been excused spending up to four hours a day in the water to ease overcrowding in the boat in the early days. But also, he said:

I feel that I started with advantages over most of the other soldiers in the boat. I had been a regular, on foreign service, for 13 years. I was toughened to the climatic conditions of the East ... Perhaps because long service had taught me a philosophy, I early on adopted a mood of passivity. It seemed to me useless to butt in when so many were making plans and giving orders, and I imagine that my quiescence had in it something parallel to the stoicism of Doris Lim [a Chinese girl on the boat, and one of the five survivors], and it served me in equal stead. Then – and possibly this is the most important reason of all – I was determined not to die. It never crossed my mind that survival would come about because our boat drifted to land – but somehow I never had any doubt that we would be picked up. Only very rarely did utter hopelessness descend on me.

And I do believe that it was the little matters of procedure and the adherence to my self-made rules about gargling, cleaning my teeth, etc., which served to maintain my morale. Once and once only did I surrender to the contagion of the suicidal urge.

This urge came over him shortly after an episode in which some of the soldiers were evidently murdering their comrades and tipping them over the side. These men were eventually thrust over the side themselves in a brief skirmish in which Gibson showed that, despite his passive philosophy, he was able when the occasion demanded to give a decisive and courageous lead. A few days later he joined with a young soldier in drinking sea water copiously, and actually jumped into the sea. Fortunately, he came to his senses in time and clambered back on board.

The other four survivors were three Javanese (who the day before being washed ashore in Sumatra had murdered the only other European on board), and the Chinese girl, Doris Lim, who 'from the first day to the last day in the boat, had been completely passive'. Once ashore, however, Doris Lim was able to take some initiative while Gibson was prostrate. The two were cared for by local tribespeople, but were in due course picked up by the Japanese. Doris Lim disappeared after that, and probably was shot.

Maurice and Maralyn Bailey[6] survived their 118 days in a life-raft and rubber dinghy in the Pacific, largely, I think, through their ability to accept calmly what was inevitable and could not be affected by energetic activity. They are two quiet and gentle people, but whether they were always like that or became so after their ordeal I cannot say. Nonetheless they had proved their ability to be resolute when the need arose by the fact that they both gave up their secure jobs in England, acquired and fitted out a yacht and sailed it to the Pacific. And, incidentally, since their rescue they have had a new boat built and are sailing again.

In the Arctic Circle, August Courtauld volunteered to spend the winter of 1930/31 alone on the Greenland ice-cap. Until he was completely snowed in, he went out six times a day to make weather observations. During the month before his rescue he was in total darkness because his lamp fuel had run out, but when found in May 1931 he was in reasonably good shape physically. He had never had any doubts about his rescue. He wrote:

> The complete silence all round seemed to urge one to keep in tune with it by being silent oneself. After a time I got over this, and used to get great satisfaction out of a sort of singing. All the time I was not sleeping, and while the light lasted, I used to read, or draw plans of boats, dinners, meteorological instruments and other

things. ... Many doubts presented themselves to me at the start, and for a while they grew in number and in weight. But as each month passed without relief, I felt more and more certain of its [rescue's] arrival. By the time I was snowed in, I had no doubts on the matter, which was a great comfort to my mind.[7]

Photographs taken of him at the moment of rescue[8] show him looking limp and effeminate, in strong contrast to pictures taken at another time of the firm-jawed naval officer. C. G. Jung[9] likened his appearance to that of a man without a 'persona', that is without the front, or mask, that most people need to show to the world. Jung said: 'The expression on his face is like a woman who has been intoxicated, and then put into cold water till she was nearly drowned, and then pulled out again. Completely demoralised ... He looks like an egg without a shell, like a sort of sentimental Jesus by Guido Reni.' Jung's point was that without ordinary human contacts the persona no longer has any function, and so it disappears. That leaves the unconscious feminine side unsuppressed and free to emerge into consciousness. Possibly this was related to Courtauld's ability to be passive and accepting of his situation, which I feel contributed to his ability to cope and ultimately to survive.

How would the energetic and competitive men who became so frustrated during the calms in the 1972 Singlehanded Transatlantic Race have fared if a prolonged period of passivity and acceptance had been called for? True they were in a race, but is this ability to be passive when the occasion demands an inherent attribute, or can it be acquired?

These active, energetic people have been called 'Type A' personalities, and this description fits most of the ambitious, competitive and successful people in Western society – who are always striving after what they have not got, who set deadlines for themselves and who are always trying to do better than before. These personalities also have a high rate of coronary heart disease.[10] By contrast, the Type B personality is generally more contented with his lot, values personal relationships more than material success, and sees little point in striving. His rate for coronary artery disease is conspicuously low. The usefulness of the classification is that it enables Type A to recognise their normal mode of functioning and then to do something about it – at least to do something about it should they find themselves in circumstances where only passivity and acceptance will see them through. The records of Walter Gibson, the Baileys and August Courtauld have shown them to be people capable of resolute action, in the best Type A manner, but they also had this life-saving ability to adapt when conditions demanded it. I would like to think also that the frustrated singlehanders, if conditions became really critical, would recognise current realities and needs and manage to adapt to them.

Climbers have to alternate between intense and perilous activity on the rock face and periods of total inactivity when stormbound. Some appear almost to go into a state of hibernation or to sit in a tent for days on end, methodically organising their hardware, with a perfect acceptance of the superior forces of nature.

In April 1977 Jacobo Timerman, the Argentine newspaper editor, was able to give himself up to the torture sessions:

> I realized that, instinctively, I'd developed an attitude of absolute passivity. Some fought against being carried to the torture tables; others begged not to be tortured; others insulted their torturers. I represented sheer passivity. Because my eyes were blindfolded, I was led by the hand. And I went. The silence was part of the terror. Yet I did not utter a word. I was told to undress. And I did so, passively. I was told, when I sat on a bed, to lie down. And, passively, I did so. This passivity, I believe, preserved a great deal of energy and left me with all my strength to withstand the torture. I felt I was becoming a vegetable, casting aside all logical emotions and sensations – fear, hatred, vengeance – for any emotion or sensation meant wasting [useful] energy....
>
> I had a similar experience during those long days of solitary confinement. More than once I was brusquely awakened by someone shouting: 'Think. Don't sleep, think.' But I refused to think. I behaved as if my mind were occupied with infinite diverse tasks. Concrete, specific tasks, chores. To think meant becoming conscious of what was happening to me, imagining what might be happening to my wife and children; to think meant trying to work out how to relieve this situation, how to wedge an opening in my relationship with the jailers. In that solitary universe of the tortured, any attempt to relate to reality was an immense, painful effort leading to nothing.[11]

Geoffrey Jackson was British ambassador in Uruguay when he was kidnapped by the Tupamaros guerrillas in 1971 and imprisoned by them for the best part of that year. For most of the time he was in solitary confinement, but was not otherwise badly treated. He devised his own 'four-point plan' to keep his 'inmost core intact'.

> (1) I am in a totally passive situation – a prisoner, guarded and immobilized. It is up to me to turn this into an active situation, by

seeking survival through the preservation of my health and, when it comes to the point, my life.

(2) I am in a totally negative position – no freedom, no family, no friends, no news, no time, no light, no faces, no green growth, no world. It is my obligation to turn all these negatives into a positive by identifying in them a purpose, pursuing it, and attaining it.

(3) There is no reason to hate these people (my 'hosts'). Nor however may I be sentimental about them. I must therefore make no concession to them, and give them no satisfaction.

(4) These people, however objective I force myself to be, have done my family, my government and my country an immense injury. I have no right to add to it by anything I may do, and conversely the absolute obligation to seek by any means I can, to transform that injury into a good, for my family, my government and my country.[12]

Jackson has emphasised how he tried to isolate himself from his past, although retaining the warmest feelings for his wife and family. He tried to see himself as a person without any existence, concerns or commitments beyond his cell. These seemed to give him strength and helped prevent him from pining for what he could not have. It also made him a difficult person for his captors to deal with, as he was a non-person, a being suspended totally in the present, without a past and without any evident awareness of a future, so that threats and promises lost their impact – since they tended to relate to matters like freedom or death which could have no relevance for a 'non-person'.

Jackson's technique worked for him, as it may for many under certain circumstances, but it is only fair to say that for the majority it is the thought of loved ones at home that keeps them going. A recent example of this comes from a study made by two Australian psychiatrists who interviewed seven survivors of a shipwreck.[13]

The small cargo vessel, *Blythe Star*, capsised and sank off Tasmania in 1973. All ten crew escaped in the life-raft, but one died on the fifth day at sea and two more on reaching an uninhabited beach on the ninth day. Seven survived and were interviewed within five days of their rescue. All seven spoke of their preoccupation with wives, mothers, children and girlfriends, and regarded such thoughts as of prime importance in their survival. These men also possessed a powerful drive to survive – 'You don't want to die – desperately you don't want to' – whereas the man who died on the fifth day seemed to have given up quite early on. Other factors reported, which helped these men, were good leadership, prayer, hope, humour, deliberate suppression of distressing thoughts, denial of the harsh realities, altruism towards others, redirected activity (distracting the men) to reduce anxiety, and fantasies about rescue, food and warmth.

The Chinese concept of *wu-wei* seems to catch the essence of the kind of passivity and acceptance that can enable a person to survive. Wu means 'not' or 'non-', and *wei* means 'action', 'making', 'doing', 'striving', 'straining', 'busyness':[14] the injunction is to refrain from activity which is contrary to nature and the cosmic process, because only if one is in harmony with nature will one's actions be successful. In no way is this a prescription for lethargy. One should be fully alert to what is going on, and have a realistic enough grasp of events and circumstances to judge when energetic action is called for and when it is not, as the examples have shown.

Leaders

So many groups owe their survival to a leader – one who was in command at the outset or else who emerged to meet the crisis – that the phenomenon of leadership needs to be considered here, even if it cannot be explained.

The ten men just referred to who were cast adrift off the south-west coast of Tasmania were fortunate in the chief officer they had.

All the men spontaneously reported his being a major factor in their survival. He became the acknowledged leader within a few hours of the sinking. He displayed admirable leadership in the following ways: he was the principal decision-maker, and demonstrated his technical ability to be so, in relation to winds, currents and the use of survival apparatus; he was largely responsible for schedules of rowing and for rations; he could behave firmly with men who were reluctant to pull their weight or who threatened the group's mood with displays of anger and hopelessness; and he could show gentleness and compassion, particularly to the youngest man. Above all, he provided a model of competence, rationality and hope.[13]

Tragically, this admirable man became delirious on the beach and died four days before rescue. It is not recorded what previous experiences he may have had which would have fitted him for this life-saving role, but clearly he had a latent ability to inspire confidence and to think calmly at a time of crisis.

In the aftermath of Scott's heroic failure at the South Pole, Sir Ernest Shackleton planned for 1915 a crossing of the entire Antarctic continent from the Weddell Sea to the Ross Sea. Unfortunately, his ship *Endurance* was beset by pack ice for ten months; the ice then crushed the ship until it sank, leaving Shackleton with twenty-seven men and forty-nine dogs marooned on the ice, 1,400 statute miles (2,240 km) from their base on the island of South Georgia – without radio and without the remotest possibility of anyone coming to look for them. When the ship failed to return to base, it was assumed to have been lost in the ice with all hands, or in the storms of the Southern Ocean. In fact, they all survived. One man lost five of his toes through frostbite, but there was no other lasting injury to the twenty-seven men whom Shackleton brought through seventeen months of continuously appalling conditions, spanning the best part of two Antarctic winters. It is, as far as I am aware, the supreme epic of leadership in totally impossible circumstances, and the men, as they fully realised, all owed their lives to this extraordinary man.[15,16,17]

For five months after they had to abandon the ship, the party camped on ice floes which drifted slowly northwards and gradually broke up, even splitting right under their tents. When the ice finally became too untrustworthy, and after a total of fifteen months of living on 'the accursed heaving, restless ice', they took to the three small boats they had dragged with them against this eventuality and made for Elephant Island. It was now that the desperate hardship really began. Although the men were fairly well accustomed to the cold, they were not equipped to deal with the wet as well, and the seas which broke regularly over the bows and sterns froze in great masses there and on to the men as well. Added to this was the misery of seasickness, but after four days in which Shackleton feared they had all nearly reached their limits, they sighted Elephant Island. It was a desolate, inhospitable and then unexplored place, which, where it was not covered with snow and ice, offered merely rock and broken stones with no vegetation at all; but it was solid land.[18]

Almost straight away they started preparing the 'largest' of their boats to go off and seek help. This was the *James Caird* – 22 feet (6.7 m) overall with a 6-foot (1.83-m) beam. A crude decking was constructed out of boxes, and the bottom filled with stones as ballast. Two masts were fitted, and the total effect, from contemporary photographs, is rather quaint. It was the kind of makeshift boat in which one might potter around in an estuary, but never out into the open sea, let alone with six men on board on an 800-mile (1,280-km) journey through the wildest ocean in the world. Yet on 24 April 1916 Shackleton set off with five others for South Georgia, which was the nearest inhabited place sufficiently well downwind, as there was no possibility of sailing broadside across the ferocious gales of the Southern Ocean.

The sixteen-day voyage, cramped in this tiny boat, permanently saturated with icy water from the continuous storms whipped up by the polar winds, is beyond my imagining. The story should be read by all adventurers, especially those on the sea, before they ever again speak of hardship; and the *James Caird* has been preserved and can be seen in the National Maritime Museum at Greenwich. The story has been told vividly by Shackleton himself,[15] and also by Frank Worsley,[16] who managed somehow to navigate in utterly absurd conditions, making his calculations from books of navigational tables that had virtually been reduced to pulp by the wet. Nevertheless he hit his target, which was a mere twenty-five miles across. If they had missed it, the next land would have been three thousand miles away and there would have been no conceivable hope of surviving.

Shackleton was a complicated character. He was Irish, a merchant navy officer, and while at home an ambitious and flamboyant entrepreneur. In the Antarctic he inspired a special kind of devotion, but at times he could be ruthlessly authoritarian. There is a story that in 1901, when Scott was unable to deal with a seaman who refused to be repatriated, Shackleton simply knocked the man down, then knocked him down a second time, whereupon he agreed to go.[16] And as we have seen in Chapter 5, when conditions were beginning to get really bad during his own expedition in 1915, the carpenter, like the seaman on the previous expedition of 1901, began to rebel because he felt his rights were being infringed. Shackleton called the company together on the ice floe and simply read out to them the agreement they had all signed before leaving England.[17]

Most of the time, however, it was his caring that came through. David Thomson, a commentator on Captain Scott's expeditions, has described Shackleton's style, mainly with regard to his earlier Antarctic journeys, contrasting it with the more austere ways of Scott:

> The atmosphere of Shackleton's expedition was consistently united and cheerful. He was known as the Boss, yet it was his practice to discuss problems openly before coming to decisions. Those who worked for him were unusually fervent in praising his sympathy for all sorts of men; they trusted his judgement and responded to his humorous treatment of danger and difficulty. There grew up about Shackleton the notion that he was most shrewd and quick in a crisis. For an 'adventurer', his journeys are notably free from disaster; time after time he brought men unscathed through spectacular perils. Some credit for this should

go to the way he solicited and listened to others' opinions. But Shackleton also charmed his men, and made them feel so privileged that, in the words of Jameson Adams, they all recognised in their leader an 'almost supernatural intuition for selecting men who believed in him implicitly and who were proud to have the honour of participating in his great adventure' ...

Because Shackleton went for the sake of adventure, he tolerated very few of the myths and barriers that Scott observed: rank, duty, science, patriotism and orders. Shackleton says in effect to his men 'we are here because we want to be, and we will not get through unless we live and work together'. This stance smacks of equality, yet it depends on the glowing conviction of its casual boss. Shackleton led by encouragement and jokes, by being the most boyish of the boys. Scott was far more detached, a middle-aged man in charge of boys. But the difference in style does not mean that Shackleton was any less autocratic. Only a dazzling tyrant could have made men perform as he did: men strove to carry out Scott's orders, but they wanted to please Shackleton.[19]

Writing about the proposed voyage from Elephant Island to South Georgia, Frank Worsley has described what lay behind Shackleton's decision to risk 'the lives of a few for the preservation of the party':

It was certain that a man of such heroic mind and self-sacrificing nature as Shackleton would undertake this most dangerous and difficult task himself. He was, in fact, unable by nature to do otherwise. Being born a leader, he had to lead in the position of most danger, difficulty and responsibility. I have seen him turn pale, yet force himself into the post of greatest peril. That was his type of courage; he would do the job that he was most afraid of ...

Looking back on his great boat journey, it seems certain that some of our men would have succumbed to the terrible protracted strain but for Shackleton. So great was his care of his people, that, to rough men, it seemed at times to have a touch of woman about it, even to the verge of fussiness.

If a man shivered more than usual, he would plunge his hand into the heart of the spare clothes bag for the least sodden pair of socks for him.

He seemed to keep a mental finger on each man's pulse. If he noted one with signs of the strain telling on him he would order hot milk and soon all would be swallowing the scalding life-giving drink to the especial benefit of the man, all unaware, for whom it had been ordered.

At all times he inspired men with a feeling, often illogical, that, even if things got worse, he would devise some means of easing their hardships.[16]

Emergent leaders   The effective leader in a disaster or other crisis is the person with the skills and temperament to match the situation. If the leader for normal times proves unable to meet the demands of the emergency he will be replaced by the crisis leader, who will be recognised and accepted at once and will equally readily be discarded when the crisis is over or the needs of the people change. On a national scale this could be said of Winston Churchill or General de Gaulle, who perfectly matched the needs of their people at a certain period but who were discarded when they had played their part.

In bad flooding in Winnipeg in the 1950s, five or six leaders emerged in different parts of the city. They played crucial roles

... but have subsequently disappeared almost completely and have had no particular civic responsibility since. One of them literally took over behind the scenes, directing the activity in the central part of the city and in fact had administratively displaced the mayor. In all municipalities that made up this city there was only one mayor acting in that capacity, that is, as the leader of his community following the bursting of the dykes. In the suburbs of St. Boniface, despite feverish activity, they were making little progress building defences until about 11 o'clock at night when a hypomanic contractor appeared on the scene. This man took over and started ordering heavy earth-moving equipment from all over Manitoba. He took responsibility that no one else was ready to take. He just didn't bother about who was going to pay for this, who was going to return the equipment and so on. And by about 4 o'clock the next morning St. Boniface was surrounded by a dyke. It is still there. The man disappeared and has not been seen since.

Another emergent leader, [a former] Army officer who had been quite restless in civilian life, appeared in another part of Winnipeg and organized convoys taking workers to the dykes in a sort of regular fashion with out-riders and orders snapping in all directions ... the population was ready to put up with it just so long as they felt this kind of organization was desirable. As soon as things started to settle down again, he returned to his job in the grain exchange, as a clerk.

Another example is the boy in the severe department store fire in Halifax, Nova Scotia, which killed about thirteen people.

The fire occurred at about 5 o'clock in the afternoon and started on the ground floor. This lad was on the third floor and he saved about two dozen people who were milling around by taking them out through a skylight in the roof. He was extremely cool, quite calm and collected, and was very effective for this group of people whom he collected and took away. He was their emergent leader.

The interesting thing about him was that he had not been particularly outstanding in the store before. He was a messenger in the store. He had been in the habit of climbing to the roof and, at the time of the fire, he simply went in the direction to which he was accustomed and took a large number of people along with him. But the fact is that he functioned as a leader and this seems to be not just a matter of familiarity with the setting but also something beyond this, because a good many people capable of getting themselves safely out of the building had not concerned themselves with others.[20]

At the Springhill coal-mine in Nova Scotia in 1958, seventy-five miners were killed by an underground shift of the coal seam known as a 'bump'. Two groups, one of twelve men and the other of six, were separately trapped by the rock falls for six and a half and eight and a half days respectively. To begin with, both groups explored all possible escape routes and made energetic efforts to free themselves. After two or three days they realised they were getting nowhere, their lamp batteries had almost failed, and water (which they had used carelessly while they were digging) became short. They therefore changed their style so that they were no longer trying to escape so much as just to survive.

During the 'escape' phase leaders appeared in each group. When escape was finally accepted as impossible, the energetic style of the escape leaders was no longer relevant, and fresh leaders emerged who were to guide the men through the 'survival' phase. The survivors of this ordeal, as well as the relatives going through their own agonies up on the surface of this mile-deep (1,600-m) mine, were studied by a team of researchers, and a useful contribution to the literature of reaction to disaster has resulted, especially where leadership is concerned.[21]

They identified various characteristics that distinguished the two types of leader.

During the *escape period*:

1. They made direct driving attacks on problems.
2. They perceived problems as involving physical barriers rather than interpersonal issues.

3. They associated with one or two friends: the whole group was not their frame of reference.

4. They were rather individualistic in their opinions and actions, outspoken and aggressive.

5. They were not particularly concerned with having the good opinion of most others.

6. They lacked empathy and emotional control.

7. Their performance abilities were better than their verbal abilities.

During the *survival period*:

1. They were sensitive to the moods, feelings and needs of others, rationalising and sympathising with them when appropriate.

2. They sought to avoid conflict and discussion.

3. They were intellectualisers, using communication rather than action to satisfy group needs (their verbal abilities being better than their performance).

4. Their role in the survival period was to a considerable degree a function of their need to have the general good opinion and recognition of the whole group, rather than the specific good opinion of a special friend or partner.

5. They perceived themselves as making an important contribution to the group.

The transition between the two sets of leaders was managed with remarkable smoothness, which must have been helped by the fact that they were a fairly homogeneous group from a traditional mining community, over which the threat of disaster always looms. The choice of leaders depended on the amount of action each had initiated. At first this related to seeking out new escape routes; in the survival period it comprised organising concerted banging on pipes to attract the hoped-for rescuers' attention, or initiating the drinking of urine or eating coal.

Lack of leaders   The worse the predicament, the greater the need for a leader, but leaders will not always appear spontaneously, as these two examples may show.

In 1846 a group of families migrating from Illinois to California were snowed up in the Sierra Nevada mountains. Of the eighty-one men, women and children in the Donner party, as it has come to be known, only forty-five survived. They were ordinary people, though adventurous enough to be making such a trip in the middle of the nineteenth century, but without any preparedness for extreme conditions. It seems that the interests of individuals and families prevented any concerted group action. They had cattle with them, but a number were lost unnecessarily. They ate those they could, but, unable to find suitable food in the mountains, they resorted to various unpalatable and inedible substances, and eventually consumed some human bodies – for which this ill-fated group has become famous. Throughout all this and the departure of several break-out parties, no leader emerged. True, the party was large, composed mainly of family groups and physically spread out, but although a firm leader would seem to have been in everybody's interests, none was found.[22]

Perhaps the most terrible of all the well documented accounts concerns the 150 castaways from the *Medusa*. This was a French sailing ship, carrying 160 crew and 240 passengers to Senegal in 1816. Through a mixture of arrogance and incompetence the ship was needlessly grounded some fifty miles off the west coast of Africa, north of Cape Verde. The captain, a number of the officers, and a future colonial governor made their escape comfortably in various of the seaworthy boats carried by the ship. The remaining 150 men and women had to make do with a raft 60 by 20 feet (20 by 7 m) constructed of solid timbers. With that number on it, together with six casks of wine and two of water, it was floating submerged, and those at the edge had great difficulty preventing themselves being washed off it.

Worse still was that this unruly collection of sailors and soldiers of different races and nationalities, army officers and civilians, was under the command of a twenty-three-year-old midshipman who was recovering from a wound received in the Napoleonic wars. The officers took the safer positions at the centre of the raft, but on the second night there was a mutiny, when they were rushed by a ferocious, drunken and undisciplined rabble, well armed with knives. 'Get rid of the officers,' they cried. By the following morning there were only sixty people left on the raft. Most had been killed in the fighting, though a good many had been swept overboard or had jumped off the raft to commit suicide (a quite commonly reported act among castaways). Despite the lightening of the load, the raft was still partially submerged, and it was impossible for anyone to lie down. By the third day adrift, some of the survivors started eating the bodies of their dead comrades. Sub-groups formed: soldiers stayed together, as did groups of Spaniards and Italians, and 'Negroes' – who remained less badly affected by the intense heat. Then more fighting occurred, and in the end only thirty remained alive, with only twenty of them capable of standing. After that there was little activity. They firmly believed that a search would be made for them once the seaworthy boats had reached the coast, which they all succeeded in doing. A ship was dispatched from the African mainland – not, however, to look for survivors on the raft but to pick up those who had landed from the boats further up the coast and to try and rescue some of the gold from the stranded *Medusa*.

Those on the raft had been given up for dead, and it would have caused serious embarrassment if they had been found, on account of the cowardice of the captain and the officers, for when it proved impossible for the boats to tow the raft effectively, they cast it adrift. The rescue ship did not find the survivors of the boats, but the drifting raft with fifteen people still alive on it, although five of these later died in hospital.

The *Medusa* was located fifty-two days after its grounding. Its hull was still in sound condition, indeed it was visible above the water nine months later. Seventeen men had remained on board, of whom three were still alive, which was especially damning for the captain, who should have been the last to leave his ship. Even allowing for the avoidable grounding, the whole complement of the ship could have been ferried ashore, and there was never any need for 150 people to be cast adrift on a makeshift raft.

The ship was abandoned with quite unnecessary haste, as a result of incompetent leadership. It is hard to see how the crowd on the raft could have been controlled by anybody, but there was not even any attempt to establish a chain of command, since those in a position to do so were mainly interested in getting away themselves. The wounded midshipman was clearly unequal to the task, and only after the numbers had been reduced to thirty was there any semblance of leadership. This came jointly from the surgeon and from an engineer on the raft, who all along were stabilising figures but who later asserted themselves more. Even so, one can only describe those on board the raft as a disorderly rabble, until they were so weakened by hunger and thirst that they could no longer take decisive action of any kind. Probably the surgeon and the engineer were able to keep themselves in better shape than most because they were observing and thinking about what was going on. The terrible tale of the *Medusa* has been carefully reconstructed and told by Alexander McKee.[23]

Women
Naomi James sailed round the world in 272 days after only two years of sailing experience. She made two stops for repairs, but hers is still the fastest passage to date. Two women have made solo flights

around the world in light aircraft, and at least nine women have climbed Everest. Women participate in virtually all sports, even downhill ski racing in which the unprotected body hurtles down icy slopes at up to 80 miles per hour (139 kph), and so quite exceptional courage, speed of reflexes and physical stamina are called for.

There is nowadays virtually no activity that women do not pursue if they have the inclination, but how do women cope when conditions are extreme? I do not know of many instances of women in extreme conditions in the natural environment, but that may be because they are less strongly motivated to go in the first place, being less vulnerable to the spell that lures men to high and lonely places.

When women are in extreme conditions not of their own choosing they cope every bit as well as men, if not better. At the risk of over-generalising and of inviting attack from sexist groups, I think that the attribute of acceptance is more highly developed in women than in men, because of what happens to female bodies (menstruation, childbearing) and because of the social role forced on women in many cultures for centuries past. At best this engenders adaptability and a readiness to make the best of things, which are good starting points for surviving hardship.

Women prisoners of the Japanese in the Second World War stood up to their ordeals conspicuously well, especially when one bears in mind that as well as being prisoners, they were regarded by their captors as objects of particular contempt on account of their sex. Lavinia Warner and John Sandilands have contrasted the responses of men and women to the horrors of imprisonment by the Japanese on Sumatra:

> ... the misery of defeat and subjection did not leave the males. The glumness which the women had observed before their separation from the men persisted, unleavened by the sort of absurdly optimistic gestures which the women contrived. The displays of cemetery flowers, the tea-parties, the exchange of little, impractical gifts would anyway have been a little out of place. It would scarcely have been in the mould of ex-Empire builders, oil-men, planters and District Commissioners to display the kind of hilarious skittishness that led cockney Maudie James to visit her friends in the Irenelaan [prison camp] bungalows one day, dressed as a bride. Her veil was an old mosquito net and her outfit was complete down to a bouquet made from the ghastly water-spinach and marred only by the ragged bandages round the tropical ulcers on her ankles and the ungainly lump of wood, known as 'trompers', which those without shoes wore on their feet.

There were many acts of kindness and selflessness among the men but broadly the imprisonment, as it continued, drew the men away from each other into a dogged, solitary battle with their circumstances whereas it drew the women more closely together ... The women were never to be as devastated as the men by the outward signs of their subjugation, perhaps from having been cast in a more acquiescent role long before this dramatic oppression occurred.

Although in the camps certain women might be looked to for guidance, it is likely that women in general do not have the same need as men to organise themselves hierarchically and so are better placed to cope with circumstances where no effective power structure is possible.

'Grin and bear it. Growl and go'

This was an expression of Frank Worsley's that related to the men on Shackleton's *Endurance* expedition,[16] and it exemplifies the attitude, conspicuous in that group, that when conditions are really bad you just have to keep going and put up with it.

Few people outside Australia have ever heard of Douglas Mawson, yet he made major Antarctic explorations, and the story of his survival is both awe-inspiring and horrific.[25,26] He reached the Antarctic in January 1912 just as Captain Scott, from a base some 1,500 miles (2,400 km) to the west of him, was struggling towards the South Pole. Mawson had in fact turned down a very pressing invitation from Scott to accompany him on his fateful journey to the South Pole, because he wanted to pursue his own explorations of the Antarctic coast adjacent to Australia.

After wintering over on the Adelie coast through 1912, members of Mawson's expedition set off in small groups to explore different parts of the coast. Mawson set off with two redoubtable companions: Dr Xavier Mertz, a Swiss ski champion, and Lieutenant Belgrave Ninnis, an English army officer. They planned to travel some 400 miles (650 km) eastwards, using sledges drawn by huskies.

From the start conditions were dreadful. There were ferocious winds which for days on end could blow at an *average* speed of 60 miles per hour (96 kph), poor visibility, a steeply rutted snow surface with hard snow ridges, and also, since they were travelling over snow-covered ice, hidden crevasses. Despite these hardships they made good progress and maintained their programme of topographical and climatic observations.

Then a snow bridge collapsed, and Ninnis, his sledge and the six strongest huskies fell to their deaths in an immensely deep crevasse. That left Mawson and Mertz 320 miles (500 km) from base with their much loved companion gone, and with him their tent and main food supply. It was 14 December and already they had been out for five weeks.

Their immediate need was for shelter, and they fashioned a crude tent from a canvas tent cover and struts of wood. Next day they shot and ate their first husky. Although exhausted and hungry, the two men made forced marches, keeping their westerly heading from the north-south alignment of the snow ridges, as they were too close to the South Magnetic Pole to use their compasses. Mawson continued to log his observations meticulously.

Christmas dinner was dog stew with an ounce of butter, and by then they had only two dogs left to eat. They were fairly cheerful but noticed that their skin had begun to peel off (desquamate) and that their hair was falling out. Thereafter Mertz began to decline, and by January 1912 he was incapable of any effective action. The two men remained in the makeshift tent for six days, but Mawson realised they would have to move on if they were not both going to die. Mertz struggled on for a couple of painful miles but then could move no further. Next day he became disorientated and raving, and to make matters worse, developed a severe dysentery. Mawson tried to clean him up and make him comfortable. Mertz later put one of his fingers into his mouth and bit it off. He became violent, thrashing his arms about until he lapsed into a coma, and died soon after.

Now Mawson's ordeal really began. He was alone in the un-explored Antarctic. He had lost his two companions and seventeen dogs, he was ill and debilitated and near-frozen, and about one hundred miles (160 km) from his base. Already he had been living in the snow for nine weeks, four of them near starvation on a daily diet of 8 ounces (230 grams) of dried food plus dog flesh. He staggered forward with his sledge, taking the shorter but more treacherous route over the glacier. Mawson's own account, partly from his diary, captures best what happened next:

> Going up a long, fairly steep slope, deeply covered with soft snow, broke through lid of crevasse but caught myself at thighs, got out, turned fifty yards to the north, then attempted to cross trend of crevasse, there being no indication of it; a few moments later found myself dangling fourteen feet below on end of rope in crevasse – sledge creeping to mouth – had time to say to myself, 'so this is the end', expecting the sledge every moment to crash on my

head and all to go to the unseen bottom – then thought of the food uneaten on the sledge; but as the sledge pulled up without letting me down, thought of Providence giving me another chance. The chance was very small considering my weak condition. The width of the crevasse was about six feet, so I hung freely in space, turning slowly around.

A great effort brought a knot in the rope within my grasp, and, after a moment's rest, I was able to draw myself up and reach another, and, at length; hauled myself on to the overhanging snow-lid into which the rope had cut. Then, when I was carefully climbing out on to the surface, a further section of the lid gave way, precipitating me once more the full length of the rope.

Exhausted, weak and chilled (for my hands were bare and pounds of snow had got inside my clothing), I hung with the firm conviction that all was over except the passing. Below was a black chasm; it would be but the work of a moment to slip from the harness, then all the pain and toil would be over. It was a rare situation, a rare temptation – a chance to quit small things for great – to pass from the petty exploration of a planet to the contemplation of vaster worlds beyond. But there was all eternity for the last and, at its longest, the present would be but short. I felt better for the thought.

My strength was fast ebbing; in a few minutes it would be too late. It was the occasion for a supreme attempt. New power seemed to come as I addressed myself to one last tremendous effort. The struggle occupied some time, but by a miracle I rose slowly to the surface. This time I emerged feet first, still holding on to the rope, and pushed myself out, extended at full length, on the snow – on solid ground. Then came the reaction, and I could do nothing for quite an hour.

The tent was erected in slow stages and I then had a little food. Later on I lay in the sleeping-bag, thinking things over. It was a time when the mood of the Persian philosopher appealed to me:

> Unborn To-morrow and dead Yesterday,
> Why fret about them if To-day be sweet?

I was confronted with this problem: whether it was better to enjoy life for a few days, sleeping and eating my fill until the provisions gave out, or to 'plug on' again in hunger with the prospect of plunging at any moment into eternity without the great luxury and pleasure of the food. And then an idea presented itself to me which greatly improved my prospects. It was to construct a ladder from alpine rope; one end of which was to be secured to the bow of the sledge and the other carried over my left shoulder and loosely attached to the sledge harness. Thus, if I fell into a crevasse again, it would be easy for me, even though weakened by starvation, to scramble out again by the ladder, provided the sledge was not also engulfed.

Notwithstanding the possibilities of the rope ladder, I could not sleep properly at all; my nerves had been so over-taxed. All night considerable wind and drift continued.

On the 19th [January] it was overcast and light snow was falling. I resolved 'to go ahead and leave the rest to Providence'.

As they wallowed through the deep snow my feet and legs kept breaking through into space. Then I went right under, but the sledge was held back and the ladder 'proved trumps'. A few minutes later I was down again, but I emerged again without much exertion, half-smothered with snow. Faintness overcame me and I stopped to camp, though only a short distance had been covered.[25]

Two days later Mawson was clear of the glaciers and, although he was weakening, the going was easier. He continued his painful progress and as ever kept his diary entries up to date. Food was pitifully short, and by 28 January – twelve weeks out and three weeks since Mertz' death – he had only about two pounds (1 kg) of dog meat left. It was imperative that he find the ice cave they had made months before where there should be proper shelter and some food. He was now becoming ill with joint pains and nose-bleeds, and he found it increasingly hard to haul his sledge, even by crawling on all fours.

Then he came across a black shape in the mist which he knew was not a natural object. It was a freshly made cairn. Someone had been there to look for him, and, as he discovered later, they had been there only six hours before. They had left him some food: he knew he would survive.

He reached the ice cave, and found shelter and food but not the crampons he needed to descend the icy cliffs to the base camp. So he hammered nails into boards and strapped them to his feet. They worked, though they cut his now raw feet terribly. The final blow came when he looked out to sea and saw the rescue ship steaming away over the horizon: he thought he would be marooned alone in the base camp for another whole year.

As Mawson approached the camp he saw men – so he had not, after all, been left there quite alone. One of them ran up to him – someone he knew really well – but the man did not recognise him: 'My God,' the man said, 'which one are you?' Normally Mawson weighed 15 stone (210 lb, 96 kg) but on his return he weighed less than 8 stone (112 lb,

51 kg). It took him some months to recover, so it was a blessing in disguise that he had to remain quiet in the hut until the next summer ship arrived.

Later, Douglas Mawson could write of the Antarctic: 'We came to probe its mystery, to reduce this land in terms of science, but there is always the indefinable which holds aloof yet which rivets our souls.' After his return to Australia he made a further trip to the Antarctic and led a productive life as a geologist until he died in 1958 at the age of seventy-six.

A combination of exceptional physical strength and a total commitment to his scientific objectives seems to have kept Mawson going, as well perhaps as a sense of obligation to his dead companions. He had come to do a job, had done it, and now had to get his findings back safely to the outside world. Mawson's incomparable ability simply to keep going is caught so well in the words of Robert Service, which Mawson repeated over and over to himself:

> Buck up! Do your damdest and fight;
> It's the plugging away that will win you the day.

The physical ailments of Mertz and Mawson, and Mertz' psychological breakdown, were probably the result of an overdose of vitamin A from eating the livers of the huskies, especially in the presence of vitamin C deficiency from which they were suffering, and which caused their scurvy. Polar bear livers and some seal livers are also rich in vitamin A, and eskimos have long known to avoid them.

15

Investigating and Understanding

Investigating accidents

From the bulky and meticulous reports produced after a major accident it might be supposed that accident investigation was a sober and logical matter. It is not sober and logical: it is highly emotive.

After an air crash there is the most detailed study of every aspect of the aircraft's functioning; huge sums are spent reconstructing what happened, gathering pieces of wreckage, examining bodies, and interviewing witnesses, air traffic controllers and survivors, if any. And much of this may be done on an inaccessible mountainside thousands of miles from home.

No one can complain that the engineers and other technologists have not done their work thoroughly: their reports are exemplary. The trouble is that only 8.5 per cent of accidents are due to 'material or system failure',[1] and a further 4.5 per cent are due to 'weather'. That leaves a massive 87 per cent due to 'human failure'. This figure needs to be broken down into: crew, 62 per cent; operational (design, procedures, etc.), 15 per cent; non-operational (sabotage), 6.5 per cent; and maintenance, 8.5 per cent. But even that leaves some two thirds of accidents due to crew failure. These figures refer to the 124 total losses in the ten years 1962 to 1971.

In a study of 2,258 consecutive road accidents reported to the police in the state of Indiana, human factors were the 'probable or definite cause' in 91 per cent. Environmental factors (such as view obstructions, glare, slippery roads) were 'probable or definite causes' in 34 per cent, and vehicle faults in about 11 per cent (usually more than one cause). Out of this group a sample of 420 accidents was taken for 'in depth' analysis. Here, human factors were regarded as 'definite causes' in 70 per cent, environmental factors in 12 per cent, and vehicle faults in 4.5 per cent.[2]

These surveys do not reveal anything new, and will in no way surprise those who follow these matters. What is surprising is that the meticulous enquiries go on without proper attention ever being paid to what is overwhelmingly the commonest category of explanation for transport accidents, namely, the human factors. To emphasise this point, I shall review three major accidents which were the subject of an official inquiry as well as a good deal of public interest. These accidents are the Trident air crash in June 1972, the Moorgate underground train crash in February 1975 – both already referred to in Chapter 1 – and the Fastnet yacht disaster of August 1979.

The Trident air crash

On a June afternoon in 1972 a fully laden aircraft crashed in a field 150 seconds after take-off from London Airport, killing all 118 people on board. The normal public inquiry procedure was followed. A judge who had been a bomber pilot in the Second World War was appointed as commissioner, and there were two expert assessors. Their eighty-four-page report is a thorough and carefully considered document, compiled after interviewing sixty-nine witnesses – mostly experts – hearing from nineteen lawyers representing various parties, visiting the reconstituted wreckage of the aircraft, and flying in a similar Trident 1.

The intact flight data recorder – the 'black box' – made it possible to reconstruct accurately what had happened, since height, speed, attitude of aircraft and movement of the controls were all recorded. It became clear to the commission that the captain had failed to achieve and maintain adequate speed and had retracted the droops prematurely. The flight crew had failed to monitor these irregularities; they had failed to diagnose the reasons for the repeated visual and auditory warnings about the imminent danger of stall, and they had ultimately overridden the automatic stall recovery system.

The question, then, was *why* these extraordinary events occurred – and, especially, how not one but three pilots had overriden the safety devices, not once but three times. The commission felt that the underlying reason for this lay in the captain's abnormal heart condition, 'leading to lack of concentration and impaired judgement sufficient to account for his toleration of the speed error and (possibly) his retraction of or order to retract the droops on the leading edge of the wing in mistake for the flaps on the trailing edge'.

Other factors they considered relevant were distraction and lack of experience on the part of the other flight crew.

Although the captain's undoubted heart abnormality was eventually singled out as the explanation for his fatal errors, human factors were considered. There was a dispute running with the airline, with the possibility of strike action over a claim for higher pay; the captain had been involved in a fierce row in the crew-room, an hour and a half before take-off, about whether or not to take the proposed strike action (Captain Key was against it). One eye witness said it was 'the most violent argument he had ever heard'.

On a table-top on the flight deck of the Trident graffiti were found: 'KEY MUST GO.' 'STRIKE NOW.' 'WHEN STANLEY KEY DIES, WHO WILL BE GOD'S NEXT REPRESENTATIVE IN B.E.A.!.' 'BLOODY STIRRER.'[3]

There was also some evidence from a doctor about the captain's 'worry and concern about his failure for a time to achieve the position of route check captain [more senior supervisory position]'. This was judged to be 'irrelevant to the heart condition', as was all the evidence about the crew-room row and the graffiti. The captain had made errors 'in completing the last page of his log-book. Certain entries had been put in inappropriate columns.' But, they said, 'We do not regard this as being of any material significance.'

The commission, with commendable openness, realised they did not have all the facts and that 'there may well be some vital piece of information missing which would, if known, change the whole picture'.[4] They had in mind information that might have come from a cockpit voice-recorder, had there been one, which might well have been illuminating about the mental state, in particular, of the captain, and thus about the psychological processes involved. There is a great deal more background information that I, for one, would certainly want before I would feel in any way able to comprehend the behaviour in the cockpit. I would want to know details of the dispute and the captain's feelings about it, about his career and where he was going in life, and of course details about his personal life, the acquisition of which naturally poses delicate and painful problems.

The whole emphasis of the commission was technological and traditionally medical, which is entirely characteristic of such bodies. Information about behaviour and psychological processes was presented, but it was discounted for the simple reason, I presume, that none of the investigators knew what to do with information of this kind. Their conclusion was that the captain was 'mentally fit except insofar as his acute abnormal physical condition may have affected him mentally'. There was never any question of mental illness, rather the possibility of an abnormal psychological reaction under extreme circumstances, which is quite a different matter.

The heart abnormality may have caused pain, and this possibility, I feel, was seized upon by the investigators as an explanation for his irrational behaviour at the end. It is hard to say how a man will react when stricken with cardiac pain, with not only the pain itself but the fear of death that cardiac pain can engender, but I do feel he would have indicated his distress to one of the other three pilots in the cockpit, so that he could take over, rather than just carrying on with his totally inappropriate actions. What seems to me to be more significant is that psychological processes were never taken seriously as possible explanations for behaviour. It is not possible to do more here than offer an approach to this particular incident, but certainly two familiar processes would at least seem to demand some consideration. These are persistence in inappropriate behaviour (perseveration), and misperception of orientation.

There was clearly perseveration on the part of the captain in repeatedly overriding the stall recovery mechanisms, and perhaps at the same time insisting that the crew abide by his actions – a cockpit voice-recorder would have been helpful here. Perseveration has been described along with a number of abnormal behavioural responses mostly with regard to trains, but that is because train drivers more often live to give their own evidence.

Another mechanism which might have been considered is the misperception of attitude or orientation during climbing and acceleration (described on p. 141), so that the pilot supposes that his angle of climb is steeper than in fact it is. This might have made Captain Key and his crew extra sensitive to the action of the automatic stall recovery mechanism but presumably it did not. Or was there possibly an orientation error of some other kind? At least it would present a single factor which could have affected all four pilots in the same way at the same time.

These two processes are not of course offered as explanations for the tragedy, but simply as fresh ways of looking at the evidence.

The Moorgate train crash

The Moorgate train crash has proved altogether more puzzling. Here an experienced driver, aged fifty-six who had talked normally to his wife and colleagues earlier that day and who had already completed the same run three times before the accident at 8.46 a.m., drove a crowded underground train under power into a dead-end tunnel. Forty-three people were killed and seventy-four required hospital treatment. The front car, 52 feet (16 m) long, was collapsed into 20 feet

(6 m), and it was some five days before the dead driver could be reached. He was found in the correct driving position. Post-mortem evidence showed that his hands had been on the controls, and mechanical evidence showed that he could not have released the power less than two seconds before impact. He was found to have no abnormality of the brain or heart. There was a raised level of alcohol in the blood (to 80 mg/100 ml, which is the legal limit for motorists in Britain), but there was disagreement among the expert witnesses as to whether this was the result of alcohol intake or post-mortem putrefaction.[5]

The investigator sums up the perplexity of people trying to understand what really happened. The train left the previous station thirty-six seconds before the accident.

> During this period of 36 seconds the train continued in what was almost certainly an unlit single-bore tunnel for some 25 seconds before entering the illuminated crossover chamber [where lines cross]. The sudden change in environment, both in respect of the change in noise level and the opening up of a direct view through the crossover chamber into the station ahead, with the red light on the sand drag [heap of sand in the dead-end tunnel to absorb impact] clearly visible at a distance of some 200 yards, should have been enough to bring to his senses a man whose mind had merely wandered from his job and, even at this stage, Motorman Newson had only to release the deadman [handle] in order to avert the accident. As it was, he took no action of any kind as the train ran through the station and into the overrun tunnel, although he was seen by several witnesses to be sitting up and looking forward in an apparently alert position with his hands in the normal position on the controls, and the medical evidence indicated that his hands were still on the controls when the impact occurred.

Two speculative explanations were offered by one of London Tranport's medical officers.

> The first, 'akinesis with mutism', is caused by a tiny clot in the area of the mid-brain which could cause a person to freeze in such a way that his muscle tone would not be affected, thus leaving him sitting up and depressing the deadman's handle. Such a condition could only be diagnosed by a microscopic examination of the brain and this was not possible owing to its condition. The second possibility was 'transient global amnesia' caused by a spasm of

blood vessels in part of the brain which could cause a complete obliteration of all Newson's previous training and experience but would not otherwise affect his physical ability to drive a train. This latter condition would leave no trace whatever at post-mortem since it would not have prevented normal muscular movement.[5]

The doctor told the investigator that he 'would have expected Newson to have raised his hands in a last attempt to protect his face'. In his view the absence of such a gesture was one of the most inexplicable things of the whole incident.

After the inquest and the official inquiry there was an informal meeting of neurologists, psychiatrists and other interested people, to consider further this hitherto inexplicable act. It was noted that the driver had had £270 on him and was intending to buy a car for his daughter with it; he also was going on sixteen days' leave starting the following day, and he had some plans to go camping (it was late February). There was no other firm personal information available that might have indicated that the man was under some psychological pressure, which in turn might have led to disorganised behaviour or even to suicide, but certain explanations have been put forward.[6] On the basis of his wife's reported statement that the level of rum in the bottle at home was lower than when she had last noticed it, it is inferred that he could have drunk the equivalent of three measures of rum early that morning (around five hours before the crash) and that this uncharacteristic act was to give him 'Dutch courage' if he was intending to commit suicide or to reduce anxieties about other matters. It has also been suggested variously that he had shortly before consulted his doctor about impotence (the doctor is said to have prescribed placebo tablets), that he was bored with an uninteresting five-stop run, and that he was generally unsatisfied in his personal life.

I mention these conjectures, which came from responsible newspaper articles, to indicate some of the difficulties in trying to explain the driver's actions. Information concerning personal habits is very difficult to obtain where an accident has attracted widespread publicity and there are complex questions waiting to be asked about responsibility and blame: it is hard under such circumstances to interrogate relatives who are distressed enough anyway. But even if one did have answers to all the personal questions that could be asked, what would one do with the information and what quantity and quality of details would be required before a causal connection could be proposed?

The medical group did not appear to follow this approach of

exploring antecedent factors, which might have given some indication of the man's state of mind before going to work that day. Instead of considering the psychological processes which might have been involved, they preferred the traditional medical style where human behaviour is 'explained' in terms of disease entities: they seized on the diagnostic tags proposed by the London Transport medical officer of 'akinesis with mutism' and 'transient global amnesia', which even their proponent admitted were advanced in the absence of any evidence.

Once more, we have a situation where a familiar psychological process is disregarded. As with the Trident accident, there was an example of perseveration (persistence in an action inappropriate to the needs of the moment) – in this case, persisting in holding the master controller and keeping the train under power instead of braking. Compare the very similar accident that occurred eleven years before at Bradford (Exchange) Station, when a driver drove his train under power into the back of another train which was standing in the station. It is described in Chapter 13 along with two other examples of perseveration of behaviour on the part of train drivers.

It is not possible to say that this is the explanation for the Moorgate disaster, merely that it is a plausible mechanism for it, and that these kinds of processes should be considered if we are ever going to make sense of such tragedies. The process is one thing, the state of mind which triggered it off is another, and for that we are thrown back on to a fairly thorough exploration of antecedent events.

Commissions of inquiry like medical evidence, especially if it involves a diagnosis, but the investigator of the Moorgate accident, to his great credit, was not taken in by grand-sounding diagnostic labels and sought to find out on what evidence these were based. The medical profession, too, likes such labels, and doctors regularly delude themselves that once they have applied one they have actually revealed some new information or insight. Labels such as 'akinesis with mutism' and 'transient global amnesia' contribute no information: they are merely descriptions of behaviour meaning respectively 'motionless and silent' and 'briefly forgetting everything'. They are not, I must add, terms commonly used in medical practice, but they have been used on this occasion to reduce the anxiety of uncritical doctors and others by a false appearance of knowledge and understanding.

The Fastnet yacht disaster

The Fastnet yacht disaster of 1979 claimed the lives of fifteen sailors, and twenty-four yachts were abandoned. It was a tragedy occurring in the course of a leisure activity as opposed to a transport accident, but it has attracted more interest than any recent disaster I can think of. In addition to a formal report[7] there have been to date three books,[8,9,10] a full-length television documentary and numerous articles dealing with various technical aspects.

The Fastnet race covers a course from Cowes, in the Isle of Wight, round the Fastnet Rock off the south-west coast of Ireland, and back to Plymouth, a distance of 605 miles (1,115 km). It is one of the few occasions when the British high-performance yachts of the so-called 'ocean-racing' fraternity actually venture out from the relatively sheltered coastal waters where their main competitions occur. The yachts have lately become quite extreme in design to cope with rating rules, and new materials, amongst other developments, have made possible short keels and slimmer rudders, and higher masts capable of carrying an ever greater area of sail. 'Ocean racing' is also a highly competitive activity, with huge sums of money invested in the yachts for the kudos of success in this high-status pastime; the pressure to win, therefore, is tremendous, and it is worth blowing out sails and damaging gear if it will get you first past the winning post. In this respect it is a very different activity from the singlehanded transatlantic race or other races involving thousands of miles of open ocean, where the emphasis is on nurturing the boat and indeed developing a relationship with it.

For the previous sixteen years – spanning the memory of most of the competitors – the Fastnet race had been run in light conditions. In 1979 this fleet of high-performance yachts was hit by a terrible storm with winds of up to 55 knots, and the inevitable happened. There is a special sort of horror being in a tiny boat (all ordinary sailing boats are 'tiny' in a storm like this), being rolled over through 360°, which breaks off the mast, and being pounded by tons of water from immense waves with the feeling that at any moment the fragile shell known as the hull will disintegrate completely. This is how one man described his experience:

> On the first roll, we lost the mast, half-filled with water, and a man was badly injured. On the next roll, we lost a man overboard. Had we done a third roll, which was almost inevitable, we might have lost another man or been badly injured by the hard-pointed interior of the boat; we might have sunk without being able to launch the life raft; or we might have lost the life raft. Also, having been bailing the boat for a long time, we would probably have been too exhausted to cope with another knockdown.[9]

This man was defending his entirely understandable decision to 'get out' and launch the life-raft. He emphasised 'the terrific feeling of security once we were in the life raft, and I'm sure that the psychological boost gained from this enabled us to keep going for a few minutes longer – very valuable time in my case'.

He was one of the only two survivors of the yacht, *Ariadne*. One man was swept overboard, the skipper died of hypothermia floating in the water, and two were killed when their life-raft was swept under the stern of the rescue boat. *Ariadne* was later found drifting but with the mast gone, and was towed into Penzance harbour where she lay for a while before she was eventually sold.

The inquiry comprised a computer analysis of replies to a questionnaire from 235 of the competitors, plus interviews with relevant people.[7] Characteristically, all aspects of design, equipment and mechanical functioning were considered in great detail: the human aspects were passed over relatively lightly, partly of course because it is difficult for computers to deal with the subtleties of human behaviour in a realistic way, since they deal with the quantity of things rather than their quality, and also because the yachting establishment does not feel comfortable with such issues. Hardly anywhere in the numerous commentaries on the race were fear, or distress or fatigue mentioned, nor were questions relating to the quality of decision-making explored.

Many of the crews were operating under tremendous pressure. In this culminating race of the season, which counts heavily towards the final placing in the Admiral's Cup and brings its own special distinction as well, every effort would be made to keep the boat at maximum speed. Then the weather turns bad. Do you plough on regardless, straining the boat to its limits, or do you run off downwind before the seas become too fierce? And if you take the safe course, what do you say to the owner or to your fellows afterwards in the clubhouse? This is not the fellowship of men who sail the oceans and are adapted to the ways of the elements: it is a ferociously competitive world in which sailing boats happen to be the chosen intruments.

My reason for bringing the Fastnet tragedy into this discussion is to try to find out what part human factors played – or was this an instance where no human actions of any kind could have adapted to such a storm? Yet I wonder how David Lewis and a number of other experienced ocean sailors would have coped with this storm of 13 August 1979. They would certainly never have chosen to take out into the ocean a yacht primarily designed for manoeuvring adroitly around markers, since such a boat by definition lacks directional stability. They would have had a much stronger (and thus heavier and slower) boat, which could be thrown about by the waves, and they would have made more realistic survival arrangements. Information about such protective measures is readily available.[11] There is a large though limited literature about safety at sea, and a conservatism prevails regarding physiological and medical issues – as I know from having had a paper on the shortcomings of ordinary life-rafts and other measures for combating hypothermia rejected by a well-known British yachting magazine in 1974.

A glance at examples of the two kinds of boat lying side by side at a berth – that is, the lightweight highly competitive racing machine and the ocean-going sailing boat – shows that they represent almost two different cultures, neither of which seems to want to learn from the other. There were cruising boats about in the area of the Fastnet storm, and they did not all succumb.

I would like to see a much more detailed analysis of the factors that led one boat to founder and another to survive. These are difficult things to measure, but there was an ideal opportunity with so many boats in trouble at the same time. Forget the technology, I would say, in this instance, and consider the people, how well they organised themselves, how decisions were made, how important it was to keep on racing, how well navigators coped when conditions became really bad, and so on.

In fairness to the compilers of the formal report, they did make some attempt to approach these issues, if only very tentatively. They were able to say: 'In general the yachts with more experienced skippers fared slightly better, their crews certainly seemed to be better fed, and lack of sleep or exhaustion were less widespread.' I only wish they could have taken these matters further.

Interpretation

If I was an engineer I would find little fault with the formal reports which follow accidents, yet, where aircraft are concerned, mechanical matters only account for some 8.5 per cent of accidents. Figures for other forms of transport are not to my knowledge available, but there is no reason why they should be very different, except that trains and boats are much simpler than aeroplanes.

In medical practice, some 30 to 40 per cent of all people consulting their doctor do so for reasons which are primarily psychological. They may present with a physical symptom, since that is the expected admission ticket for visiting the doctor, but it is the underlying or real issue which is so often found to be of psychological origin. Despite this, there is relatively little interest paid to these matters by the medical profession as a whole. There is an inveterate leaning towards the physical rather than the psychological, which is understandable if only because physical issues are so much more clear-cut and manageable. Unfortunately the desire to restrict one's range of explanations to the purely physical leads to such anomalies as the medical explanations for the Trident and the Moorgate accidents.

The undoubted heart pathology found in the unfortunate captain of the crashed Trident, and the symptoms it might have engendered, were seized upon by the investigators and their medical witnesses as a plausible explanation for the whole catastrophe. A diagnosis had been made and everybody was reassured that the problem had been solved. In the Moorgate accident, a quite bizarre pair of 'diagnoses' was presented, in this case based on no evidence at all. The investigator was unimpressed, but because a statement of certainty had been made, however improbable, anxiety had been reduced and everyone felt better.

Commissions of inquiry need to do what good scientists do: when one model of explanation does not explain the observed phenomena, then look for another model. This presupposes that people will be quite open about their adoption of explanatory models, but they are not, especially where psychological models are involved. Most explanatory models are based on principles enshrined in the physical sciences, but these are notoriously weak where human behaviour is concerned because simple chains of cause and effect cannot be employed here.

For example: a sailor hit some bad weather; therefore he did not rest; therefore he became fatigued; therefore his powers of observation and judgement became impaired; therefore he misread the lights; and therefore he piled his boat onto the sandbank. But the chain of cause and effect is seldom so clear: two people in the same situation would probably not react in the same way. So many factors are always involved that a model is required which does not insist on 'X' causing 'Y'. Instead, as when approaching a person who is in psychological difficulties of some kind, I would try to take account of the person's life as a whole, and in the case of the tired sailor, of as many as possible of the factors – immediate and remote – that might be affecting him. These factors tend to be interrelated, such as shortage of sleep, seasickness, hunger, having had to hurry through the traffic to get to the boat and so forgetting some important item of equipment or food, some worry from the office or some conflict in a personal relationship. Such matters cannot be quantified, arranged in order of importance or placed in any kind of sequence. It also, I believe, requires a certain kind of flexible temperament to handle such elusive variables, but it is vital to be flexible if people and their behaviour are going to be understood. When investigators try to be 'scientific' in the old-fashioned physical sense they lose altogether or make nonsense of the whole human dimension. People can be studied with great intellectual rigour, but different concepts have to be used from those that serve well when studying inanimate matter.[12,13]

Finding out what really happened

In their report on the Trident disaster, the investigators rather ruefully confess that 'there is a danger in assuming that we have all the facts before us and that the only problem is to assemble them in the right order'. How right they are, but since only mechanical, technological and organic medical questions are generally ever asked, answers can be framed only in these terms.

Another difficulty in finding out what really happened lies in the composition of boards of inquiry. As one observer of marine accidents has put it: 'Official inquiries held after a collision have a close family resemblance to the "post-mortems" after a game of bridge, with this difference that the unlucky, or the less skilful guessers, face legal penalties, and sometimes professional ruin.'[14] In air accidents the issues are more intense and, as the Trident investigation exemplifies, there is a tendency to keep matters within the establishment, with government servants engaged to scrutinise the crash of a government-owned aircraft.[15] True outsiders – by temperament or employment – might rock the boat a little, but they would help get the procedures on to a more realistic level.

Also, when traditional investigators stray beyond the purely technical, they are not impressive. British Rail investigators are almost always retired army officers, and they impart a military style to their inquiries. After a derailment at Leeds station in 1961 (leading to the death of one passenger), because the driver, for reasons which were never explained, passed a signal set at danger, there was the usual formal inquiry. In the course of almost forty pages of evidence the investigator did try to consider human factors, but unfortunately not in a manner likely to be illuminating:

Colonel: Had any illnesses?
Driver: No Sir.
C: Any troubles at home?
D: No Sir.
C: Any family?
D: Wife and son.
C: Quite well?

D: Yes Sir.

C: You were going off duty at 4 o'clock that afternoon. Was there anything special you were going to do that evening?

D: No, only the usual gardening.

C: You were not going to take the Mrs out anywhere?

D: No Sir.

When there has been loss of life, the atmosphere of an official inquiry is clearly not the right place for personal revelations, however pertinent they may be, but there is every reason to suppose that the drivers, who are on the whole very conscientious about their work, would welcome an opportunity to discuss their own part in the accident, their patterns of reaction and various antecedent factors which had occurred to them to be of possible relevance. Derek Russell Davis' studies of train drivers, with reference to signals passed at 'danger',[16] showed that in the setting of a private interview a wide variety of psychological factors would emerge which would facilitate more realistic explanations for the accidents than is usually the case. These might concern psychological processes such as preoccupation, distraction or false expectations, or anxieties about remote matters, such as a driver's worries about his daughter's illness.

Another problem with official inquiries lies in a requirement of the law to assign blame. Compensation is nearly always an issue, and it cannot be awarded unless an accident can be shown to have been someone's fault. This in turn can lead to a complex network of factors being absurdly oversimplified and distorted to satisfy the needs of the law, and for a man having unjustly to be blamed because in no other way can the victims receive any recompense.

No matter how sophisticated the modern investigator may be, and no matter how well versed in the problems of trying to understand human behaviour, he has to contend with a matter of great subtlety – and the greater the calamity, the greater the complexity. Thus the airline pilot will be more difficult to scrutinise than the train driver, who will be more elusive than the mountaineer or lone yachtsman and so on.

When I am consulted, say, by a flight engineer who has bouts of depression, who is unhappily married and who has some organic illness (not obviously affecting judgement) as well, I am placed in a difficult position. I want to help him, but I want to be reassured that he is functioning optimally. The only people who can answer that question are his employers, but if they knew about his condition they might take him off flying duty, and then he could no longer afford the mortgage repayments on his house or the school fees for his children.

He comes to me, working as I do fairly far away from an international airport, in the hope that I will not communicate with the airline. If I undertake not to communicate with any other body then I compromise myself; if I refuse to make any such commitment then I may cause him to avoid seeking help from anyone, with the result that his difficulty may only become manifest when something goes wrong.

The disturbingly high consumption of alcohol and tranquillising drugs by flight crews[17] must be due in part to their reluctance to seek professional help for fear that these advisors will 'tell on them'.

In the case of the two jumbo jets which collided at Tenerife airport in 1977 killing 528 people, the final bill in terms of insurance payments, when it is all eventually settled, will run into many millions of pounds. Therefore the inquiries set up by the Spanish government and the two airlines concerned take on an intensity that is absent in the case of a train driver passing a signal set at danger. It is simply not good enough for the pilot to say that he was worried about his daughter's health or that he was having an 'off day', but the fact of having hundreds of lives and millions of pounds' worth of aircraft dependent on your good functioning does not automatically make you more efficient and less vulnerable to human weakness. So what is the worried pilot to do? Is he to stay away from work unless he is feeling at the peak of condition? Does he avoid work after every domestic tussle – and pilots have stormier lives than most – or before every major decision or other event which might preoccupy him? Does he telephone the relevant official in the morning and say: 'I might be under a little stress today, so I think I'd better not turn up for work.' Well, he might do that once or twice, but no employer is going to take kindly to such absences if they become too regular, and no organisation could operate efficiently if staff could absent themselves in an apparently haphazard way.

The issue is being presented here with regard to civil aircraft and trains, but the same factors would apply to a surgeon, a senior business executive or a political leader. They can make catastrophic decisions and blunders but, unlike the airline pilot, they usually survive their mistakes. This is important for two reasons. First, the intensity of a crisis is lessened if one's own safety is not involved, and the chances of rational action are that much greater (although the fact that *all* your actions affect your chances of survival may have the effect of concentrating the mind).

The second, and more important, reason is that if the pilot is killed in the accident, how is the relevant information going to be obtained? Cockpit voice-recorders and more sophisticated flight data recorders can provide information about the pilot's functioning in the last minutes and so make it possible to piece together something of the psychological processes which led to the destruction of the aircraft, but they can reveal nothing of the antecedent factors. For this, some kind of personal inquiry is inevitable, and here there are tremendous problems.

After someone dies, especially if the death has been sudden or the circumstances unusually tragic, the bereaved relatives will have need to talk over all kinds of matters relating to the dead person. These can involve questions of personal relationship, unresolved conflicts, financial commitments, unfulfilled aspirations and so on, and an opportunity to talk through these matters can be profoundly helpful to a bereaved person who so often in Western society feels shunned by family and friends. However, when someone has died in the circumstances prevailing when a pilot is involved in a major transport accident, the matters are no longer private. All kinds of issues which may be a source of intense distress to the bereaved person may be of distinct relevance in making sense of what has happened and now become fodder for public appetite, but who on earth can go to the bereaved woman and ask questions about her intimate relationship with her late husband, however illuminating such information might be?

Even if the bereaved woman would tolerate such questioning, other pilots would object and so would their union, and the same would apply to any other groups one could think of. It is the kind of action that would offend the public's sense of propriety, but whether we can go on seeing fellow citizens killed, or being killed ourselves, when more searching though painful personal inquiries could perhaps lessen the death toll, is an issue that only society can decide. Unfortunately, even if such inquiries became the rule, there would still be questions left unanswered – human nature and the vagaries of human behaviour being notoriously elusive. But the fact remains that 80 per cent of aircraft accidents are due to human factors, and so the search for more understanding of them goes on.

Covering up

The majority of accidents go unreported because they involve small private groups or isolated individuals, and others never become a subject for careful study because the people involved close ranks. The Whitbread Round-the-World Sailing Races and other large-scale adventures of recent years have produced a fund of stories of distress, conflict, psychological breakdown, disputes over leadership and the like, which may be related over a drink in the bar or in a watered-down form in the subsequent books but which would be actionable if printed in full. After hearing an account of someone's death on a mountain or in a storm at sea, I have grown accustomed to hearing: '... and of course he had recently split up with ...'. The domestic lives of adventurers are liable to be more erratic than most people's, not only because the mountain or the sea or the open space is ultimately more alluring than the wife or girlfriend but also because they are simply never at home for much longer than is needed to organise the next excursion into the unknown. And when the tragedy occurs it is understandably the good and affectionate qualities that are remembered.

A good many expeditions from Britain are sponsored by the armed services or government agencies, who require their members to sign the Official Secrets Act. This means that all articles, books and interviews have to be cleared with the appropriate authorities, so as to avoid any potential embarrassing revelations. When Roger Banks[18] submitted his book about his two years in an Antarctic weather station for clearance, he was compelled to excise his account of the suicide of one of the party there – an event clearly of significance, but which conflicted with what he called 'the Captain Scott crap' and so could not be allowed.

It is rather more serious when, for example, the Royal Navy keeps information secret. Towards the end of the Second World War, a committee was set up to investigate causes of death at sea.[19] They found that two-thirds of all naval casualties were from drowning or exposure, and that the great majority of these apparently died from immersion hypothermia – loss of body heat while in the water. For reasons that we shall never know, this report was placed on the secret list, and it was another decade before the importance of hypothermia became generally known. If this information had been available in the late 1940s, then Ann Davison and her husband might not have placed their trust in an open float and he would probably not have died as he did, in the sea off Portland Bill. More recently, in an effort to maintain its image and to avoid the risk of litigation, the Royal Navy suppressed a report dealing with hypothermia which could have been of value to rescuers and hospital staff dealing with the victims of prolonged immersion in the sea.

Learning more
How can we learn more about all these errors of perception, judgement and behaviour in order to reduce their incidence? It is good to be able to monitor our own functioning but it is not sufficient in itself, and there is a need for systematic research.

In a new field of inquiry isolated anecdotes or case reports may be collected which give a clue to the existence of a problem. After that questions are formulated and systematic studies set up to test the validity of the suggestions contained in the original case reports. Thereafter, more specific questions are asked and more refined methods of analysis used.

With lone sailors, I collected a large number of individual accounts, and then in the 1972 Singlehanded Transatlantic Race I was able to make some systematic observations. Further studies in this area would involve making more precise measurements (using the compact recording devices now available) and correlating performance more accurately with environmental conditions. And these techniques could be extended to monitor performance and physiological function in any of the activities referred to in this book. Studying the interactions between people, as opposed to individual behaviour, is more complicated, but if discreet video cameras can be tolerated, an enormous amount can be learned about group dynamics under difficult conditions.

All this presupposes that people are prepared to be studied, but most people, for understandable reasons, cannot be expected to lay themselves open for detailed scrutiny. The threats of losing one's job, having insurance claims rejected, being criticised at a board of inquiry, being sued for damages or even being sent to jail are pretty powerful deterrents; but the information needs to be obtained, and here some kind of system of confidential reporting can be invaluable as a starting point.

For nearly twenty years now, doctors in Britain and the United States have been regularly reporting any adverse reactions to drugs which they come across in their patients.[20] There is no implied negligence in such reporting, so the system works quite smoothly. There is also a regular inquiry into the causes of death of women before, during and after childbearing, although, since maternal death is quite often due to clinical error, this is a much more sensitive matter. Nevertheless, these confidential inquiries have been going on for years now, and are published periodically so that everyone can learn from them.[21] Doctors also report to their legal defence agencies any events which might lead to litigation, and these bodies publish annual reports to alert doctors to likely pitfalls in clinical practice.

Flight crews in the United States can, in complete confidence, report any incident to the National Aeronautics and Space Administration (NASA); and the American magazine *Flying* has a regular feature entitled 'Aftermath', in which air accidents are analysed critically for the lessons which can be learned from them. The accumulation of detailed examples or case reports is an essential preliminary to any systematic research into human behaviour, and the study of human behaviour in extreme conditions is still, with a few exceptions, at this fairly rudimentary stage. Specific questions can then be formulated to discover under what conditions and in relation to what circumstances in a person's life errors and accidents are likely to occur. Equally important are inquiries about the psychological processes involved and the sequence of events leading up to the final catastrophic act.

The scene is right for research into human behaviour under extreme conditions. Psychologists of various kinds have on the one hand all the expertise and measuring equipment they need, and on the other a problem to study of great human and economic importance. A slight difficulty is that these psychologists are very rigorous people as far as their experimental methods are concerned, and were horrified, for example, when I described how I proposed to study lone sailors and people caught in a disaster. They felt I could not control the variables well enough to make the work scientifically respectable; this kind of anxiety can inhibit researchers from exploring new fields, however interesting and important these might be. I would like to think that potential researchers reading this book will take note of the many pressing and fascinating questions that await serious study, that they will accept that the research design will be dictated by the subject matter and the conditions under which the observations are going to be made, and that the carefully controlled laboratory experiment is by no means the ideal to which everyone should aspire.

16

Drawing It All Together

This book has been dedicated to the memory of three men who died at sea, and I want to say something about them and about the circumstances of their ends. I knew Brian Cooke and David Blagden well, and Mike McMullen only moderately well. They all helped me greatly in my researches (even though Mike McMullen did throw my record cards overboard, as he said he would, in the 1972 Singlehanded Transatlantic Race), and I liked them very much as people. They also appreciated what I was trying to do in my studies and gave me leave to say whatever I wanted to about them.

Brian Cooke died on his way to attempt a record of 4,000 miles (7,400 km) of singlehanded ocean sailing in twenty days, that is, two hundred miles a day for twenty days. He was a sailor of proven ability, toughness and conscientiousness. He had a boat, the trimaran *Triple Arrow*, which was fast enough and strong enough, but it had capsized in a freak squall during the 1974 Round Britain Race. Trimarans do capsize, but they are by far the fastest type of sailing boat at the present time and so are a natural choice for racers and record-breakers, who simply hope and pray that they will not meet the kind of huge wave that will overturn any small vessel. The four-thousand-mile run was to start fifty miles up the estuary of the Gambia river in West Africa, and end at Belize in Central America. It was on his way from England to Gambia that his boat was lost.

So what happened, and why did it happen? Without the boat and log-books this must be a matter for speculation. The question why is more difficult to write about, but I am sure Brian would not mind me trying. I had misgivings about this trip and was not surprised at its fatal outcome.

Brian Cooke was an ocean sailor held in the highest esteem by his fellow sailors. In his seagoing life he excelled, and it was a delight to sail with him. He was meticulous and supremely confident on board, yet patient of the shortcomings of his crew: back on land he was much less comfortable or sure of himself. His personal life had not been happy. Shortly before the 1974 Round Britain Race his wife died, and after that he did not settle. He threw himself more energetically into long-range ocean sailing and developed a hopeless affection for a young woman, which brought him pain, as it was bound to do.

Late in 1974 Brian Cooke made his first attempt to break the four thousand miles in twenty days barrier, but he had to abandon the venture after he broke his back in a fall from his mast. When he had recovered from this injury he set about preparing for a second attempt. By late 1975 he was well prepared and had happily made a new and much more promising friendship – at least that was his view in the last conversation I had with him in December 1975. I hoped he was right, but I feared he was unduly vulnerable to the forces that drew men repeatedly back to sea. There was a radio message from him shortly before Christmas, but after that nothing. The next news came some weeks later – a sighting of *Triple Arrow* abandoned and floating upside-down in mid-Atlantic. Most likely he was capsized in a squall, or possibly he fell overboard and the unattended boat later capsized on its own. No effort was made to recover *Triple Arrow*: it was left to break up at sea or somewhere along the American coast.

Mike McMullen's story is pure tragedy. He started in the 1976 Singlehanded Transatlantic Race with every chance of winning in his beautiful yellow trimaran *Three Cheers*. He set off bravely and was never seen or heard of again.

Three days before the race, his wife, Lizzie, was working with him polishing the hull to reduce water resistance to the minimum. She was standing in the water using an electric polisher. She dropped it into the water, bent down to pick it up and was electrocuted. She died almost immediately. Her funeral took place the day before the start of the race.

At first sight, Mike McMullen was everybody's party-going extravert – he enlivened any group he joined with his warm voice, his laughter, his guitar-playing and songs. He was rather overweight at thirty-three, but even by his Marine commando standards he had an incredible toughness and ability to withstand cold and lack of sleep. Having grown up with sailing, he could do anything in a sailing boat – from coping with a storm on the ocean to coming in under sail into a crowded marina, with precision and perfect control – and for such a good sailor he was unusually well engaged with life on land. He had had hard times after leaving the Marines, and great hopes were invested in success in the 1976 race, indeed it was economically vital for him to do well, as he had committed himself to the sailing industry and to writing.[1] Therefore Lizzie and he had devoted themselves totally to preparing the boat, and I do not think any boat came to the starting line of a great race better tried or in better condition. But Mike set off to race over three thousand miles of ocean just three days after his wife's sudden death. At the start it was the extravert Mike, waving and blowing his foghorn as he sped past the spectator boats in Plymouth Sound, but before long he was to be entirely on his own.

Mike received all kinds of advice about whether or not he should sail, and since his loss there have been all kinds of explanations about what happened. Almost certainly he took a northerly route where severe storms occurred which could easily have capsized any small boat. Whether he was inattentive because he was still stunned from his loss, we can never know, but he died on a voyage that he had to make. If he had remained behind he would have been mourning his wife and he would have seen the collapse of his business plans: hence a sense of double failure and probably a feeling that he was letting Lizzie down on what they had worked at so hard together for the preceding three years. It was a heavy predicament. Mike chose the way of action and he lost, but it was the way that was true to his nature. One of his close sailing friends said simply: 'What a way to go.'

David Blagden was a professional seaman in the Merchant Navy as well as an experienced small-boat sailor. He had a singular ambition to sail a small boat across the Atlantic, and his voyage in the 1972 Transatlantic Race was quite an epic.[2] He demonstrated great ability in translating his dream into reality: finding the sponsors, planning the modifications to the boat, equipping it and finally sailing for fifty-two days across 3,500 miles (6,450 km) of ocean. *Willing Griffin* was a mere 19 feet (5.8 m) overall. When he had achieved his ambition, he left sailing and returned to his other career, acting; but after a while he branched out again to become administrator in an organisation concerned with personal psychological growth. In this he was highly successful and much respected.

His geniality concealed a prolonged pain at the breakup of his marriage, and then he had to endure the collapse of the organisation he had been administering. By early 1979, at the age of thirty-five, he was over the worst of it, and his personal and working life were again bringing a feeling of fulfilment. Then in September of that year, when he was sailing with a friend from the Isle of Man to Fleetwood in Lancashire, they were hit by a sudden storm. Their fairly ordinary yacht was not equal to the battering, and foundered, drowning David and his friend.

Of these three men we can ask ourselves, why did they die? Why did they die in the manner they did, and *when* they did? We can ask ourselves these questions endlessly, and never get an answer. All through this book I have related examples of *how* things went wrong, the circumstances in which mistakes are made and the processes by which they occur. *Why* is a very different question.

I never thought when I began my studies of sailors that I would make so many friends among them, and least of all that I would ever be in a position to write about the deaths of some of them. I do have a sense of intruding even though I know it would not be seen as such by Brian, Mike and David; but also I feel a certain obligation to the original aims of my study, which was to learn about how people react in extreme conditions.

There is no 'objective' or 'scientific' way of comprehending why these men died as and when they did. In Thornton Wilder's novel called *The Bridge of San Luis Rey*, about five people were crossing a bridge when it collapsed, killing them all. Wilder went back over their lives and came to the conclusion that there was an inevitability about their deaths and that they were destined to be crossing the bridge on that fateful day. It can be tempting, even consoling, to take such a view, whether as a manifestation of predestination or as the result of a conjunction of events which makes death inevitable.

If death is predestined by superior forces, then there is nothing further to be said. If it occurs as the apparent outcome of the confluence of a number of factors, then it is open to some respectful consideration. A person may die following a series of events that deprive that person's life of meaning, and there may have been experiences earlier in his or her life which would increase the vulnerability to later misfortune. Alternatively, death may occur at what seems to be a crowning point in someone's life, after which there can only be decline. In either instance there can seem to be an inevitability about the death which somehow makes sense of it, although it is impossible after death realistically to imagine events taking any other course.

One thing that strikes me about Brian Cooke, Mike McMullen and David Blagden is that each of their lives seemed to be near a point where things were going to change for the better. Brian was at last freeing himself from the bondage of a hopeless affection, Mike was on the brink of success in the 1976 race which could have opened his life up in every way, and David was emerging from a long spell of personal pain. I can say no more than that.

The 'why?' and the 'how?' of accidents

The ultimate question *'why?'* can never be answered directly, and anyway the issue is metaphysical rather than psychological. All we can really do is to look more deeply into the processes – into the *'how?'*, then further back at the antecedent events and at as many as possible of the current issues in the person's life.

At the beginning of the book I said that many of the lessons learned about human behaviour out in the extremes of the natural environment could be applied to ordinary life. The converse also applies, that lessons which can be learned in the narrow domestic environment have an application in the exciting outside world. The small boat on the ocean is one kind of laboratory for studying behaviour over a period of time under conditions of physical and psychological hardship. Another is the home where a mother is looking after small children, where the strains may not be life-threatening but can last for a much longer time, and on the whole with less respite.

Housewives are easier to study than sailors and other adventurers: there are more of them, and they tend to stay longer in the same place. George Brown and Tirril Harris have studied a group of working-class mothers in Camberwell, in south London.[3] They were interested in the social factors which led to the women becoming depressed, just as I have been interested in the factors which lead to someone breaking down at sea. Brown and Harris identified what they call *vulnerability factors* and *provoking factors*. The vulnerability factors (three or more children at home under fourteen, lack of a confiding relationship, loss of own mother before the age of eleven) are long-term difficulties that render the woman extra-susceptible to the effects of the more obvious and acute crises which are the provoking factors (sudden illness, loss of job, death of a relative).

This model is quite applicable to the adventurer, train driver, airline pilot, motorist, or to any of the others mentioned in this book, even though their environments may fluctuate violently and there is equipment or a vehicle of some kind to contend with. For example, the sailor may be vulnerable by being short of sleep, careless with his navigation so that he does not know exactly where he is, neglectful about maintenance of the boat, and rather short on general sailing experience. In addition he may have worries concerning personal matters remote from the present scene. All these factors can act together to make the sailor more susceptible and thus potentially less well able to cope with the provoking factors which are the unavoidable crises connected with any kind of travelling – in this case, say, having a sail blow out or running aground.

The vulnerability factors set the scene; the provoking factors upset the equilibrium and trigger off the kinds of reaction described in Part III. In ordinary life the commonest of these reactions is depression; and associated with it may be anxiety and sleeplessness. The more severe reactions involve disturbance of thinking (mistaken ideas that people are spreading malicious stories about one) or perception (hearing voices, seeing things). These are all essentially psychological reactions to psychological threats, although physical factors may be quite overwhelming in their own right. Most of the time, however, the physical factors merely increase vulnerability, because what matters, in the ordinary way, is not so much the actual event as the person's psychological response to it and the special significance the event holds for him. There may also be physical responses to psychological threats, as we have seen with the air traffic controllers and their high rates for peptic ulcer, hypertension and diabetes.[4]

It is fairly easy to see how various factors can bring someone to the point of displaying one or more of the adverse reactions already described or of lapsing into some variety of mental disorder or complete psychological breakdown. It is much more difficult, if not impossible, to know the precise means by which these psychological threats are translated into abnormal behaviour. All behaviour is mediated by physical or physico-chemical processes of some kind. In most cases these processes are poorly understood; the real gap in our knowledge is in understanding just how a psychological threat that is perceived via the senses, such as vision and hearing, is dealt with *in the brain*, so that the brain transmits the appropriate signals to initiate depression, simple errors and misperceptions, or a peptic ulcer. In fact, it is such an opaque area that one can only speculate about it.

Depression can be understood as a reaction to difficult conditions; to a great extent it is adaptive, since it draws attention to the person's plight and permits a measure of withdrawal from the conflicts.[5] Many of the reactions, such as simple errors and misperceptions, although not adaptive in the sense of meeting a person's current needs, are at least useful as warning signs that the system is being pushed beyond its effective limits. Many of the reactions are also positively dangerous, and none more so than the perseveration in inappropriate actions – for instance, holding the train on full power until it crashes into a wall. In these cases, the processes can be identified even if the precise mechanisms involved remain obscure.

It is useful to know that we may embark on any enterprise (or simply that we make our way through life) with a number of limitations and vulnerabilities, as it gives us a realistic way of taking stock of ourselves. Deficiencies can be made good; weaknesses can be recognised and allowed for. The successful adventurer has a gift for anticipating every eventuality and a plan of action for every possible crisis. He knows the limits of his endurance and can sense when he is approaching them. He does not experiment out in the unknown: he is like Amundsen, who takes well tried dogs with him to the South Pole, as opposed to Captain Scott who chooses this occasion to innovate with ponies and motor sledges.

As I write this I think of Brian Cooke, Mike McMullen and David Blagden, who were all exemplary planners. In *British Steel* and *Triple Arrow*, Brian Cooke seemed to have thought of everything and allowed for every possible catastrophe. By contrast, Mike McMullen had *Three Cheers* starkly simple in order to keep the boat light, yet he lacked nothing that was essential for sailing. David Blagden's tiny *Willing Griffin*, packed with about two months' supplies of food and water, was a masterpiece of careful planning. In the event, even on such a long voyage, he ran short of nothing. Nonetheless, despite the flawless preparation of *Triple Arrow* and *Three Cheers*, both were lost, drowning their skippers; and David died sailing an ordinary cruising yacht in a gale.

Trying to predict the behaviour of other people is unsatisfactory. 'Head-hunters' are employed in industry to sign up promising executives who will reverse the company's fortunes, and football clubs spend huge sums for the stars they hope are going to carry them to the top of the league. On what criteria are these decisions made, and how successful do their choices turn out to be in practice? Even American presidents, with virtually the whole country to choose from, seem to be singularly unlucky in their selection of aides and advisors.

Self-monitoring and inward preparation

It is much more important to learn how to deal with ourselves, in particular to ensure that we remain optimally efficient while we are working. This book has dealt with the issue mainly by indicating some of the ways in which people fail or lose efficiency. Knowing what happens in others can make us more alert and better prepared. It can also encourage us to develop the habit of monitoring our own function so that we can be sensitive to any small errors we may make

– to a momentary lapse of attention when driving a car, a flash of irritability or frustration, unusual lethargy or feelings of depression. All this applies to domestic and urban life as much as to adventure out in the wider world. In the natural environment, the more spectacular pressures produce more spectacular reactions, but fundamentally the processes are the same. Hearing voices, seeing things or having odd ideas about the motives of others is not evidence that the sufferer is different in kind from the so-called 'normal' population, but merely that the person concerned has been subjected to extreme psychological pressures – even if we cannot identify why the particular pressures evoked such a drastic response.

Reinhold Messner systematically trained himself to climb Mount Everest solo and without oxygen. A few years ago this would have been regarded as physically impossible. Today the ability of some Buddhist monks to withstand cold by the practice of *gtum-mo* seems physically impossible mainly because there is no way of comprehending it within the framework of Western physiology. Yet the limits of human endurance are always being pushed further on,[6] and this is mainly because of a greater awareness of the importance of the mental attitude: a recognition that more is involved than better training techniques.

The great athletes, adventurers and other high achievers have supreme technical mastery, but technical mastery is merely the launching point for real attainment. These people work on themselves. They recognise that in order to enhance what they can *do*, they have to discover more about what they *are*. This essentially inward exploration does not come easily to everyone, but the inward state determines the quality of the outward behaviour.

Throughout the book I have dwelt on the heights and the depths of human experience – in success and in suffering. The difference between high adventure and domestic life is one of intensity only. People who are handicapped, poor, bereaved, lonely, exploited economically, divorced, locked in the conflicts of the nuclear family or trapped by social circumstances, are every day for years on end grappling with physical and psychological hardships that outsiders will scarcely notice or care much about anyway. When such people succeed there is no summit of Everest, when they fail there is nothing heroic about it. All too often failure in the face of overwhelming pressures in everyday life is seen in terms of personal defect or mental illness, and that is regrettable.

The adventurers and the achievers, and ordinary people, choose their external circumstances or have these thrust upon them. In any given crisis some come through while others do not, some are strengthened by their ordeals while others are crushed. For the survivor the extreme external conditions are matched by an inward strength and detachment, so that amid all the struggle and activity there remains a calm centre.

There will be times when no amount of composure will prevent annihilation, but many, many more times when the inward attitude will enable the individual to transcend seemingly impossible conditions and challenges. The stories related in this book will, I hope, be instructive and inspiring as examples of what can be accomplished; and there are lessons to be learned from those who faltered or failed. I have tried to avoid too much explanation, because people cannot be explained. Their experiences are the most eloquent testimony, and my function has been to present them with humility and admiration.

Summary

Introduction
Personal interests and experience indicate my approach to the study
of behaviour in adverse conditions. These interests are: my work as a
psychiatrist, studies of people in disasters and of singlehanded ocean
sailors. The contributions from experimental psychology, such as
problems of cause-and-effect and single versus multiple causes, are
discussed, and the fact that people in arduous environmental
conditions may exhibit emotions and behaviour that are conventionally regarded as 'mad' (which should make people reconsider their
attitudes to those labelled as mentally ill).

1   How Things Go Wrong
Large-scale transport disasters are described where there has either
been heavy loss of life or extensive environmental damage: among
these are the Moorgate train disaster, the Trident (Staines) and the
Boeing 747 (Tenerife) crashes, and the stranding and breakup of the
Torrey Canyon and Amoco Cadiz. Human judgement, decision-
making and communication were factors in most of these disasters
whether or not each could clearly be ascribed to human error.

2   Working Environments
Small boats on the ocean, large ships, aircraft, trains, motor cars,
mountains at high altitude and polar regions can all be seen as
special environments which impose particular strains on the
individuals involved. Leaders and decision-makers are included here
because in many ways their positions of authority impose the
greatest strains of all.

3   Extreme Predicaments

Major disasters – natural and man-made; sudden captivity by being taken hostage or by arrest; concentration camps; interrogation and thought reform; risking death (bomb disposal), expecting death (in accidents), and accepting death are described as circumstances where almost everything familiar and valued is in danger of being lost.

4   Isolation

Experimental isolation by total sensory deprivation or the creation of a monotonous environment can produce quite severe temporary mental disturbance. Such conditions can be experienced in polar regions, in caves, in solitary confinement in prison, alone on the ocean, in intensive care units in hospitals. Various psychological processes are involved.

5   Isolated Groups

The Andes air crash of 1972 is a powerful example of an accidental isolated group. Most expeditions are planned isolated groups – the best studied of these have been in the Antarctic. Physical hardships are borne well; it is the psychological problems that are the main threat to the integrity of the group; some of the desirable and undesirable qualities of group members are outlined.

6   Physical Conditions

Physical factors such as oxygen lack at high altitude, cold, heat, hunger and thirst, noise and vibration can have an effect on overall efficiency. So also can sleep loss, the disruption of body rhythms caused by crossing time zones, and drugs and alcohol. These factors seldom occur singly, so that people are often trying to function effectively while grappling with a multiplicity of adverse influences.

7   The People

Individual styles and attitudes are described. There is no one personality type predominant amongst adventurers, but there are certain common features amongst those who have accidents. Accurate perception requires a clear signal, intact eye and brain, and some knowledge and theories about what is being observed, yet there are individual differences in perceptual style. Anxiety and personal threat impair efficiency in proportion to their severity; so also does fear except in the most highly motivated, but efficient training can mitigate its effects on behaviour. Danger, which is closely related to fear, is consciously sought by some for reasons that are usually undesirable.

8 Simple Errors, Poor Concentration and Forgetfulness

Examples of simple errors are given, concerning doctors, sailors, a bomb disposal officer and airline pilots. Sometimes the problem is mainly within the individual (tiredness), sometimes outside (poor visibility), and sometimes extraneous anxieties may interfere with efficient functioning.

9 Faulty Judgements and Perceptions

Making sense of the environment involves making guesses (or hypotheses) about what is there, and modifying them as the input becomes clearer. Indiscriminate guessing, or rigid adherence to one early interpretation which remains unchanged in the light of new information, can lead to serious errors: to seeing what one wants to see and not what is there, to faulty judgements and irrational plans. Related sources of error are preoccupation and distraction, excessive concentration on details at the expense of the whole, and the relaxation that is so tempting after a period of anxiety and demanding activity.

10 Illusions and Misinterpretations

Even under good conditions errors can be made in the perception of size, distance, shape and movement of objects; the errors will increase as conditions deteriorate. Pilots are at extra risk because of the high speed they travel at and the powerful gravitational and inertial forces which can act upon them. When a person is fatigued, misinterpretations of the surroundings (of varying degrees of severity) can occur; usually these are visual, but they may also involve the sense of smell and the perception of space.

11 Hallucinations and 'The Other Person'

Hallucinations have physical, chemical and psychological causes. In the natural environment they are usually experienced by fatigued people, and are generally visual or auditory. Sometimes an actual person (the 'other person') is seen, who may or may not be identifiable, but who is recognised as a benign and helpful presence. People may find they are looking at themselves from a distance (out-of-body experiences), or they may feel that parts of their bodies or inanimate objects take on personalities as though they were people. One feature common to all these experiences is that they happen only when people are close to the limits of their resources.

'Other person' experiences can also occur as a result of certain brain disorders.

12   Ecstasy to Black Despair
Ecstatic feelings of unity with all things, a sense of mastery, control and inner stillness, can alternate with profound depression and frustration. Both the ecstasy and the depression are potentially lethal for lone adventurers.

13   Disorganised Behaviour and Psychological Breakdown
Experimental frustration shows how easily purposeful behaviour can become disorganised. When a major crisis strikes, there may be a period of shock and apathy, followed by acute distress manifesting itself in useless activity and, under certain circumstances, panic; sometimes there is a total denial of the crisis. After a mistake has been made there is a tendency to compound the error by persisting with the initial erroneous behaviour – an important factor in transport accidents. In times of crisis some people can display remarkably quick thinking which saves them. There is a basic human need to explain catastrophe, which can sometimes lead to apparently irrational acts. The breakdowns of two men at sea are considered in some detail.

14   Surviving Against the Odds
Specific factors that improve the chances of survival in a concentration camp or when an individual is taken hostage are described; and also the life-saving ability to become quite passive in conditions where energetic activity will be useless. Shackleton exemplifies most of the qualities required of a leader in desperate circumstances; other crises are mentioned in which leaders have emerged spontaneously to save the day, and also disasters which have occurred through lack of any effective leader. Lastly, there is just grinning and bearing it when conditions are really bad; and just keeping going when it seems quite hopeless, as epitomised by Douglas Mawson.

15   Investigating and Understanding
Most transport accidents are caused by human factors, which are largely disregarded by investigators, who concentrate on mechanical and environmental factors. The Trident air crash, the Moorgate train crash and the Fastnet yacht disaster are reviewed to see what human factors might be relevant. Some of the problems in identifying the human factors are discussed, including the tendency to conceal potentially life-saving information because it might place individuals

or organisations in a bad light. The possibilities for serious research into human behaviour in extreme conditions are examined.

16 Drawing It All Together

The deaths of Brian Cooke, Mike McMullen and David Blagden are recounted. The question of why things happen is elusive, but more can be learned about the 'how' through studying vulnerability and provoking factors. Ultimately people must work on themselves, to make themselves as capable as possible to deal with crisis, whether in high adventure or in ordinary living.

Further Reading

A selection of useful and authoritative accounts

General
Environment and Human Efficiency, E. C. Poulton (1970), Springfield,
    Ill.: C. C. Thomas
Behaviour and Perception in Strange Environments, Helen E. Ross
    (1974), London: Allen and Unwin
The Psychology of Anomalous Experience, Graham Reed (1977),
    London: Hutchinson

Special topics
Air
    Aviation Medicine, vol. 1: *Physiology and
    Human Factors*; vol. 2; *Health and Clinical
    Aspects*, G. Dhenin (ed.) (1978), London:
    Tri-Med Books
    The Human Factor in Aircraft Accidents,
    David Beaty (1969), London: Secker and
    Warburg

Concentration camps
    *Internment in Concentration Camps and its
    Consequences*, Paul Matussek (1975),
    Berlin: Springer Verlag
    *The Informed Heart: The Human Condition
    in Mass Society*, Bruno Bettelheim (1960),
    Illinois: Free Press; London: Thames and
    Hudson

Disasters	*Disaster: a Psychological Essay*, Martha Wolfenstein (1967), London: Routledge and Kegan Paul
	Management of Human Behaviour in Disaster, H. D. Beach (1967), Ottawa: Department of National Health and Welfare
Heat and cold	*Man – Hot and Cold*, O. G. Edholm (1978), London: E. Arnold
Leaders	*Fit to Lead?*, Hugh L'Etang (1980), London: Heinemann Medical Books
Mountains	*Man at High Altitude: the Pathophysiology of Acclimatisation and Adaptation*, D. Heath and D. R. Williams (1981), London: Churchill Livingstone. 2nd edn.
	Mountain Medicine: A Clinical Study of Cold at High Altitude, Michael Ward (1975), London: Crosby Lockwood and Staples
Poles	*Polar Human Biology*, O. G. Edholm and E. K. E. Gunderson (eds) (1973), London: Heinemann
Railways	*Red for Danger: a History of Railway Accidents and Railway Safety Precautions*, T. T. C. Rolt (1955), London: Bodley Head (Pan, 1960)
Roads	*Psychology of the Road: the Human Factor in Traffic Safety*, David Shinar (1978), New York: Wiley
Sea (large ships)	*Black Tide Rising: The Wreck of the Amoco Cadiz*, David Fairhall and Philip Jordan (1980), London: André Deutsch; New York: Stein and Day
Space	*Human Factors in Long-Duration Spaceflight*, Space Science Board (1972), Washington, D.C.: National Academy of Sciences
Sport	*The Psychic Side of Sports*, Michael Murphy and Rhea A. White (1978), Reading, Mass.: Addison-Wesley
World problems	*The Seventh Enemy: the Human Factor in the Global Crisis*, Ronald Higgins (1982), London: Hodder and Stoughton; New York: McGraw-Hill

Single events

Alive: the Story of the Andes Survivors, Piers Paul Read (1974), London: The Alison Press/Secker and Warburg (Pan, 1975)

Endurance: Shackleton's Incredible Voyage, Alfred Lansing (1959), London: Hodder and Stoughton (Granada, 1980); New York: McGraw-Hill

The Boat, Walter Gibson (1953), Boston: Houghton Mifflin; London: W. H. Allen (Star Books, 1979)

The Strange Voyage of Donald Crowhurst, Nicholas Tomalin and Ron Hall (1970), London: Hodder and Stoughton (Penguin, 1971)

This Accursed Land, Lennard Bickel (1977) (the story of Douglas Mawson's survival), London: Macmillan

Scott and Amundsen, Roland Huntford (1979), London: Hodder and Stoughton

References

* indicates a review article or general account of the subject.

Statements or accounts in the text not accompanied by references have been given personally by their authors.

Introduction

1 Bennet, G. (1970), 'Bristol floods 1968: controlled survey of effects on health of local community disaster', *British Medical Journal*, **3**, 454–8
2 Bennet, G. (1974), 'Psychological breakdown at sea: hazards of singlehanded ocean sailing', *British Journal of Medical Psychology*, **47**, 189–210
3 Tomalin, N., and Hall, R. (1970), *The Strange Voyage of Donald Crowhurst*, London: Hodder and Stoughton (Harmondsworth: Penguin 1971)
4 Bennet, G. (1973), 'Medical and psychological problems in the 1972 Single-handed Transatlantic Yacht Race', *Lancet*, **2**, 747–54
5 Bennet, G. (1973), 'The tired sailor and the hazards of fatigue', *Yachting Monthly* (London), **133**, 1393–9; *Sail* (Boston, Mass.), **4**, No. 11, 69–76
6 Davis, D. Russell (1946), 'The disorganisation of behaviour in fatigue', *Journal of Neurology and Psychiatry*, **9**, 23–9
*7 Davis, D. Russell (1958), 'Human errors and transport accidents', *Ergonomics*, **2**, 24–33
*8 Davis, D. Russell (1966), 'Railway signals passed at danger: the drivers, circumstances and psychological processes', *Ergonomics*, **9**, 211–22
*9 Fells, J. C. (1977), 'A motor vehicle accident causal system: the human element', *Human Factors*, **18**, 85–94

Chapter 1   How Things Go Wrong

1 Marks, L. (1976), 'Was it suicide?' *Sunday Times*, 29 February 1976
2 McNaughton, I. K. A. (1976), *Railway Accident: Report on the Accident that occurred on 28th February 1975 at Moorgate Station, on the Northern Line London Transport Railways*, London: Her Majesty's Stationery Office
3 *Sunday Times*, 7 March 1976
4 Lane, G. (1973), *Trident I G–ARPI, Report of the Public Inquiry into the causes and circumstances of the accident near Staines on 18 June 1972*, Civil Aircraft Accident Report 4/73, London: Her Majesty's Stationery Office
*5 Bignell, V., Peters, G., and Pym, C. (1977), *Catastrophic Failures*, Milton Keynes: Open University Press

*6   Godson, J. (1974), *Papa India: The Trident Tragedy*, Salisbury, Wilts.: Compton Press

7   *Observer*, 22 August 1976

8   Spanish Ministry of Transport and Communication (1978), *Report on Accident at Los Rodeos Airport, Canary Islands, on 27 March 1977* (in translation), *Aviation Week and Space Technology*, 20 and 27 November 1978

9   Keesing's Contemporary Archives (1967), 'The *Torrey Canyon* Oil Disaster', p. 22002

*10   Fairhall, D., and Jordan, P. (1980), *Black Tide Rising: The Wreck of the Amoco Cadiz*, New York: Stein and Day; London: André Deutsch

Chapter 2   Working Environments

1   Lewis, D. (1975), *Ice Bird*, London: Collins, p. 60

2   Davison, A. (1951), *Last Voyage*, London: Heinemann, p. 217

3   Knox-Johnston, R. (1969), *A World of My Own*, London: Cassell and Corgi

*4   Radloff, R., and Helmreich, R. (1968), *Groups Under Stress: Psychological Research in Sealab II*, New York: Appleton-Century-Crofts

*5   Ross, H. E. (1974), *Behaviour and Perception in Strange Environments*, London: Allen and Unwin

*6   Miles, S. and Mackay, D. E. (1976), *Underwater Medicine*, 4th edn., London: Adlard Coles

7   Kinsey, J. L. (1959), 'Psychologic aspects of the "Nautilis" transpolar cruise', *US Armed Forces Medical Journal*, 10, 451–62

8   Serxner, J. L. (1968), 'An experience in submarine psychiatry', *American Journal of Psychiatry*, **125**, 25–30

9   Carruthers, M. (1976), in *The Times*, 12 April 1976

*10   Danaher, J. W. (1980), 'Human error in ATC operations', *Human Factors*, **22**, 535–45

11   Cobb, S., and Rose, R. M. (1973), 'Hypertension, peptic ulcer, and diabetes in air traffic controllers', *Journal of the American Medical Association*, **224**, 489–92

12   Finkelman, J. M., and Kirschner, C. (1980), 'An information-processing interpretation of air traffic control stress', *Human Factors*, **22**, 561–7

*13   Space Science Board (1972), *Human Factors in Long-Duration Spaceflight*, Washington, D.C.: National Academy of Sciences

*14   Shinar, D. (1978), *Psychology on the Road: The Human Factor in Traffic Safety*, New York: Wiley

*15   Black, S. (1966), *Man and Motor Cars*, London: Secker and Warburg

*16   Nicholl, A. M. (1970), 'The motorcycle syndrome', *American Journal of Psychiatry*, **126**, 1588–95

17   Gillman, P., and Haston, D. (1966), *Eiger Direct*, London: Collins, p. 164

18   Cherry-Garrard, A. (1922), *The Worst Journey in the World*, London: Constable, Introduction

19   Byrd, R. E. (1938), *Alone*, New York and London: Putnam, p. 83

20   Banks, R. (1962), *The Unrelenting Ice*, London: Constable, p. 116

*21   L'Etang, H. (1969), *The Pathology of Leadership*, London: Heinemann Medical Books, p. 71

*22   L'Etang, H. (1980), *Fit to Lead?*, London: Heinemann Medical Books

23   Blair, J. and C. (1976), *The Search for JFK*, New York: Berkley, Putnam

24   See also Dixon, N. (1976), *On the Psychology of Military Incompetence*, London: Cape; and Robinson, R. S. (ed.) (1977), *Psychopathology and Political Leadership*, New Orleans: Tulane University

Chapter 3   Extreme Predicaments

1   Nugent, T. (1973), *Death at Buffalo Creek: The 1972 West Virginian Flood Disaster*, New York: W. W. Norton

2   Erikson, K. T. (1979), *In the Wake of the Flood*, London: Allen and Unwin (previously published in USA: *Everything in its Path*, 1976, New York: Simon and Schuster)

3   Grieve, H. (1959), *The Great Tide: The Story of the 1953 Flood Disaster in Essex*, Chelmsford, Essex: Essex County Council

4   Higgins, R. (1982), *The Seventh Enemy: The Human Factor in the Global Crisis*, New York: McGraw-Hill; London: Hodder and Stoughton

5   Scott, G. (1975), *Building Disasters and Failures – a Practical Report*, Lancaster, UK: Construction Press

6   *Observer*, 5 May 1974

7   Bignell, V., Peters, G., and Pym, C. (1977), *Catastrophic Failures*, Milton Keynes: Open University Press

8   *Sunday Times*, 29 February and 12 September 1976

9   Westgate, K. (1975), *Flixborough: The Human Response*, Occasional Paper No. 7, University of Bradford Disaster Research Unit

*10   *Lancet* (1981), 'Seveso after five years', **2**, 731–2

11   *Observer*, 13 February 1977

*12   Humphrey, N. (1981), 'Four Minutes to midnight', *Listener*, 29 October

*13   Phillips, D. (1973), *Skyjack: The Story of Air Piracy*, London: Harrap, ch. 3

14   Jacobson, S. R. (1973), 'Individual and group responses to confinement in a skyjacked plane', *American Journal of Orthopsychiatry*, **43**, 459–69

*15   Miron, M. S., and Goldstein, A. P. (1979), *Hostage*, New York and Oxford: Pergamon

16   Bloom, A. (1970), *School for Prayer*, London: Darton, Longman and Todd

17   Solzhenitsyn, A. (1968), *The First Circle*, New York: Harper and Row; London: Collins and Harvill (Fontana, 1970, p. 632)

*18   Solzhenitsyn, A. (1974), *The Gulag Archipelago*, vols 1, 2 and 3, New York: Harper and Row (1975); London: Collins/Fontana (1978)

19   Bondy, C. (1943), 'Problems of internment camps', *Journal of Abnormal and Social Psychology*, **38**, 453–75

*20   Lifton, R. J. (1961), *Thought Reform and the Psychology of Totalism: A Study of 'Brainwashing' in China*, New York: W. W. Norton; London: Gollancz; Harmondsworth: Penguin (1967)

*21   Goffman, E. (1961), *Asylums, Essays on the social situation of mental patients and other inmates*, New York: Doubleday; Harmondsworth: Penguin (1968)

22   Erikson, E. H. (1958), *Young Man Luther: A Study in Psychoanalysis and History*, New York: W. W. Norton; London: Faber

23   Timerman, J. (1981), *Prisoner Without a Name, Cell without a Number*, London: Weidenfeld and Nicolson

24   Koestler, A. (1937), 'Dialogue with Death', in *Spanish Testament*, London: Gollancz (Hutchinson, 1966)

*25   Patrick, D. (1981), *Fetch Felix: The Fight Against the Ulster Bombers*, London: Hamish Hamilton

26   Heim, A. St G. (1892), 'Remarks on fatal falls', in 'The experience of dying from falls', by R. Noyes and R. Kletti (1972); *Omega*, **3**, 45–52. Also in *The Games Climbers Play*, ed. K. Wilson, London: Diadem (1978)

27   Bluestone, H., and McGahee, C. L. (1962), 'Reaction to extreme stress: impending death by execution', *American Journal of Psychiatry*, **119**, 393–6

*28   Bennet, G. (1979), *Patients and their Doctors: the Journey through Medical Care*, London: Bailliere Tindall

29   Greer, S., Morris, T., and Pettingale, K. W. (1979), 'Psychological response to breast cancer: effect on outcome', *Lancet*, **2**, 785–7

30   Hackett, T. P., Cassem, N. H., and Wishnie, H. H. (1968), 'The coronary care unit: an appraisal of its psychological hazards'. *New England Journal of Medicine*, **279**, 1365–70

*31   Cherry-Garrard, A. (1922), *The Worst Journey in the World*, London: Constable, Introduction

*32   Moody, R. A. (1975), *Life after Life: The Investigation of a Phenomenon – Survival of Bodily Death*, New York: Bantam Books; London: Corgi

*33   Moody, R. A. (1977), *Reflections on Life after Life*, New York: Mockingbird Books; London: Corgi

Chapter 4   Isolation

*1   Lilly, J. C. (1956), 'Mental effects of reduction of ordinary levels of physical stimuli on intact healthy persons', *Psychiatric Research Reports* (American Psychiatric Assn.), **5**, 1–28

2   Bexton, W. H., Heron, W., and Scott, T. H. (1954), 'Effects of decreased variation in the sensory environment', *Canadian Psychology*. **8**, 70–6

*3   Zubek, P, (ed.) (1969), *Sensory Deprivation: Fifteen Years of Research*, New York: Meredith Corporation

*4   Brownfield, C. A. (1965), *Isolation: Clinical and Experimental Approaches*, New York: Random House

5   Courtauld, A. (1935), 'Living alone under polar conditions', *The Polar Record*, No. 4, 66–74

6   Wollaston, N. (1980), *The Man on the Ice Cap: The Life of August Courtauld*, London: Constable

*7   *British Medical Journal* (1966), '130 days in isolation', **3**, 373

8   Siffre, M. (1964), *Beyond Time*, London: Chatto & Windus

9   Bone, E. (1957), *Seven Years Solitary*, London: Hamish Hamilton

*10   Vernon, J. A. (1966), *Inside the Black Room*, Harmondsworth: Penguin, p. 39; New York: C. N. Potter.

11   Willis, W. (1956), *The Epic Voyage of the 'Seven Little Sisters'*, London: Hutchinson

12   Bombard, A. (1953), *The Bombard Story*, London: André Deutsch, p. 144

*13   Hay, D., and Oken, D. (1972), 'The psychological stresses of intensive care unit nursing', *Psychosomatic Medicine*, **34**, 109–18

*14   Baxter, S. (1974), 'Psychological problems of intensive care', *British Journal of Hospital Medicine*, **11**, 875–85

*15   Bennet, G. (1979), *Patients and their Doctors: the Journey through Medical Care*, London: Bailliere Tindall, p. 81

16   Weisman, A. D., and Hackett, T. P. (1958), 'Psychosis after eye surgery', *New England Journal of Medicine*, **258**, 1284–9

17   Lewis, D. (1975), *Ice Bird*, London: Collins, p. 42

18   Huxley, A. (1954), *The Doors of Perception*, London: Chatto and Windus; (St Alban's: Granada, 1977)
19   Burney, C. (1959), *Solitary Confinement*, London: Clerke and Cockeran, p. 150
20   Tomalin, N., and Hall, R., (1970), *The Strange Voyage of Donald Crowhurst*, London: Hodder and Stoughton (Harmondsworth: Penguin, 1971)
21   Bennet, G. (1974), 'Psychological breakdown at sea: hazards of singlehanded ocean sailing', *British Journal of Medical Psychology*, **47**, 189–210

Chapter 5   Isolated Groups

1   Read, P. P. (1974), *Alive: The Story of the Andes Survivors*, London: Secker and Warburg (London: Pan, 1975)
2   Defayolle and Dietlin (1969), 'Etude psychologique de petits groupes de sujets isolés en haute montagne', *Revue de Corps de Santé des Armées*, **10**, 169–81
3   Lester, J. T. (1969), 'Personality and Everest', *Alpine Journal*, **74**, 101–7
4   Kinsey, J. L. (1959), 'Psychologic aspects of the "Nautilis" transpolar cruise', *US Armed Forces Medical Journal*, **10**, 451–62
5   Serxner, J. L. (1968), 'An experience in submarine psychiatry', *American Journal of Psychiatry*, **125**, 25–30
*6   Radloff, R., and Helmreich, R. (1968) *Groups Under Stress: Psychological Research in Sealab 11*, New York: Appleton-Century-Crofts
7   Day, R. M. (1967), *Authority in the Sailing Navy*, Fort Worth, Texas: Texas Christian University Institute of Behavioural Research
8   Mullin, C. S. (1960), 'Some psychological aspects of isolated Antarctic living', *American Journal of Psychiatry*, **117**, 323–5
9   Smith, W. A. (1966), 'Observations over the lifetime of a small isolated group: structure, danger, boredom and vision', *Psychological Reports*, **19**, 475–514
*10 Edholm, O. G., and Gunderson, E. K. E. (eds) (1973), *Polar Human Biology. The Proceedings of the SCAR/IUPS/IUBS Symposium on Human Biology and Medicine in the Antarctic*, London: Heinemann Medical Books
11   Law, P. (1960), 'Personality problems in Antarctica', *Medical Journal of Australia*, **1**, 273–82
12   Strange, R. E., and Klein, W. J. (1973), 'Emotional and social adjustment of recent US winter-over parties on isolated Antarctic stations', in *Polar Human Biology*, eds O. G. Edholm and E. K. E. Gunderson, London: Heinemann Medical Books
*13 Space Science Board (1972), *Human Factors in Long-Duration Spaceflight*, Washington, D.C.: National Academy of Sciences
*14 Wright, D. S., *et al.* (1970), *Introducing Psychology: an Experimental Approach*, Harmondsworth: Penguin, p. 627
15   Sherif, M. (1964), *The Psychology of Social Norms*, New York: Harper and Row (Octagon Books, 1965)
16   Asch, S. E. (1952), *Social Psychology*, New York: Prentice-Hall (also in *Attitudes*, eds M. Jahoda and N. Warren, Harmondsworth: Penguin)
17   Lansing, A. (1959), *Endurance: Shackleton's Incredible Voyage*, New York: McGraw-Hill; London: Hodder and Stoughton (Granada, 1980)
18   Banks, R. (1962), *The Unrelenting Ice*, London: Constable, p. 193
*19 McKee, A. (1975), *Death Raft: One Human Drama of the Medusa Shipwreck*, London: Souvenir Press, p. 151

Chapter 6   Physical Conditions

*1   Poulton, E. C. (1970), *Environment and Human Efficiency*, Springfield, Ill.: C. C. Thomas

*2   Holmstorm, F. M. G. (1971), 'Hypoxia', in *Aerospace Medicine*, ed. H. W. Randel, 2nd edn, Baltimore: Williams and Wilkins

*3   Ward, M. (1975), *Mountain Medicine: a clinical study of cold at high altitude*, London: Crosby Lockwood Staples

*4   Heath, D., and Williams, D. R. (1981), *Man at High Altitude: the Pathophysiology of Acclimatisation and Adaptation*, London: Churchill Livingstone.

*5   Dhenin, G. (1978), *Aviation Medicine*: (vol. 1) *Physiology and Human Factors*, London: Tri-Med Books

6   Habeler, P. (1979), *Everest: Impossible Victory*, London: Arlington Books; Munich: Wilhelm Goldmann (1978)

*7   Edholm, O. G., and Gunderson, E. K. E. (eds) (1973), *Polar Human Biology*, London: Heinemann Medical Books. See also O. G. Edholm (1978), *Man – Hot and Cold*, London: E. Arnold

8   Golden, F. St C. (1972), 'Accidental hypothermia', *Journal Royal Naval Medical Service*, **58**, 196–206

*9   Keating, W. R. (1969), *Survival in Cold Water: the Physiology and Treatment of Immersion Hypothermia and of Drowning*, Oxford: Blackwell

10   Golden, F., St C. (1973), 'Death after rescue from immersion in cold water', *Journal Royal Naval Medical Service*, **59**, 5–8

11   Pugh, L. G. C. E. (1963), 'Tolerance to extreme cold at altitude in a Nepalese pilgrim', *Journal of Applied Physiology*, **18**, 1234–8

12   Evans-Wentz, W. Y. (1958), *Tibetan Yoga and Secret Doctrines*, 2nd edn, London: Oxford, p. 172

*13   Mackworth, J. F. (1969), *Vigilance and Habituation: a Neuropsychological Approach*, Harmondsworth: Penguin

*14   *Lancet* (1979), **1**, 910–11

15   Wilkinson, R. T. (1969), 'Sleep deprivation and behaviour', in *Progress in Clinical Psychology*, eds B. F. Riess and L. A. Abt, New York: Grune

*16   Wilkinson, R. T. (1966), 'Sleep and dreams', in *New Horizons in Psychology*, ed. B. M. Foss, Harmondsworth: Penguin

*17   Colquhoun, W. P. (ed.) (1972), *Aspects of Human Efficiency: Diurnal Rhythm and Loss of Sleep*, London: English Universities Press (as *Biological Rhythms and Human Performance*, New York: Academic Press, 1971)

*18   Williams, H. L., Morris, G. O., and Ardie, L. (1962), 'Illusions, hallucinations and sleep loss', in *Hallucinations*, ed. L. J. West, New York and London: Grune and Stratton

*19   Luce, G. G., and Segal, J. (1967), *Sleep*, London: Heinemann (as *Sleep and Dreams*, Panther, 1969)

20   Broadbent, D. E. (1955), 'Variations in performance arising from continuous work', paper presented to Conference on Industrial Efficiency in Industry, Medical Research Council, Cambridge, England, MRC 55/195

21   Blagden, D. (1973), *Very Willing Griffin*, London: Peter Davies, p. 167

*22   Stepney, R. (1980), 'Doctors without sleep', *World Medicine*, **15**, 29–35

*23   Hawkins, F. H. (1981), 'Sleep and body rhythm disturbance amongst flight crews in long-range aviation', M.Phil. thesis in Department of Applied Psychology, University of Aston, Birmingham, England

24 Minors, D. S., and Waterhouse, J. M. (1981), *Circadian Rhythms and the Human*, Boston: P. S. G. Publishing; Bristol: John Wright

*25 Luce, G. G. (1971), *Body Time*, New York: Pantheon Books

*26 Luce, G. G. (1974), 'Biological rhythms in health and disease', in *Ways of Health*, ed. D. Sobel, New York: Harcourt Brace Jovanovich, 1978 (also in *Britannica Yearbook of Science and the Future*, 1974)

27 Wolcott, J. H., *et al.* (1977), 'Correlation of general aviation accidents with the biorhythm theory', *Human Factors*, **19**, 283–93

*28 Keys, A., *et al.* (1950), *The Biology of Human Starvation*, vols 1 and 2, Minneapolis: University of Minnesota Press

*29 Edholm, O. G., Bacharach, A. L. (eds) (1965), *The Physiology of Human Survival*, London and New York: Academic Press

*30 Hocking, F. (1969), *Starvation: Social and Psychological Aspects of a Basic Biological Stress*, Mervyn Archdall Medical Monograph, No. 6, Australian Medical Association, Sydney: Australasian Medical Publishing Company

31 Benedict, R. (1935), *Patterns of Culture*, London: Routledge and Kegan Paul

32 Huxley, A. (1956), *Heaven and Hell*, London: Chatto and Windus, p. 59 (St Alban's: Granada, 1977)

33 Read, P. P. (1974), *Alive: The Story of the Andes Survivors*, London: Secker and Warburg (London: Pan, 1975)

*34 Arens, W. (1979), *The Man-Eating Myth*, Oxford: Oxford University Press

*35 Shepherd, M. (1975), 'Pollution, noise, and mental health', *Lancet*, **1**, 322–3

*36 McLean, E. K., and Tarnopolsky, A. (1977), 'Noise, discomfort and mental health: a review of the socio-medical implications of disturbance by noise', *Psychological Medicine*, **7**, 19–62

37 Tarnopolsky, A., and Morton-Williams, J. (1980), *Aircraft Noise and Prevalence of Psychiatric Disorders*, Social and Community Planning Research, 35 Northampton Square, London EC1

38 Herridge, C. F. (1974), 'Aircraft noise and mental health', *Journal of Psychosomatic Research*, **18**, 239–43, ch. 5

*39 Shinar, D. (1978), *Psychology on the Road: The Human Factor in Traffic Safety*, New York: Wiley

*40 Raffle, P. A. B. (1981), 'Drugs and driving', *Prescribers' Journal*. **21**, 197–204

*41 Havard, J. D. J. (1970), 'Drugs and driving', *British Journal of Hospital Medicine*, **4**, 455–8

42 Klonoff, H. (1974), 'Marijuana and driving in real-life situations', *Science*, **186**, 317–24

Chapter 7   The People

1 Gray, D. (1968), 'Personality and climbing', *Alpine Journal*, **73**, 167–73

2 Ryn, Z. (1971), 'Psychopathology in alpinism', *Acta Medica Polona*, **12**, 453–67

3 Lester, J. T. (1969), 'Personality and Everest', *Alpine Journal*, **74**, 101-7

4 Bennet, G. (1978), 'Why I didn't sail the Atlantic singlehanded', *Cruising World* (Newport, RI) August, 60–2

5 Jung, C. G. (1964), *Man and his Symbols*, London: Aldus and Paladin

6 von Franz, M. L. (1970), *Puer Aeternus*, Santa Monica, California: Sigo Press

*7 McGuire, F. L. (1976), 'Personality factors in highway accidents', *Human Factors*, **18**, 433–42

*8 Shinar, D. (1978), *Psychology on the Road: The Human Factor in Traffic Safety*, New York: Wiley

9   Tillman, W. A., and Hobbs, G. E. (1949), 'The accident-prone automobile driver: a study of the psychiatric and social background', *American Journal of Psychiatry*, **106**, 321–31

10   Hinkle, L. E., and Wolff, H. G. (1958), 'Ecologic investigation of the relationship between illness, life experiences and the social environment,' *Annals of Internal Medicine*, **49**, 1373–88

11   Nicholi, A. M. (1970), 'The motorcycle syndrome', *American Journal of Psychiatry*, **126**, 1588–95

*12   Black, S. (1966), *Man and Motor Cars*, London: Secker and Warburg

*13   Gregory, R. L. (1970), *The Intelligent Eye*, London: Weidenfeld and Nicolson

*14   Gregory, R. L. (1973), *Eye and Brain: the Psychology of Seeing*, 2nd edn, London: Weidenfeld and Nicolson

*15   Bennet, G. (1979), *Patients and their Doctors: the Journey through Medical Care*, London: Bailliere Tindall

*16   Goodenough, D. R. (1976), 'A review of individual differences in field dependence as a factor in auto safety', *Human Factors*, **18**, 53–62

*17   Beaty, D. (1969), *The Human Factor in Aircraft Accidents*, London: Secker and Warburg

*18   Poulton, E. C. (1970), *Environment and Human Efficiency*, Springfield, Ill.: C. C. Thomas

*19   Reed, G. (1972), *The Psychology of Anomalous Experience: A Cognitive Approach*, London: Hutchinson

20   Berkun, M. M., et al. (1962), 'Experimental studies of psychological stress in man', *Psychological Monographs*, **15**, No. 534

*21   Ross, H. E. (1974), *Behaviour and Perception in Strange Environments*, London: Allen and Unwin

22   Reid, D. D. (1945), 'Fluctuations in navigator performance during operational sorties', in *Aircrew Stress in Wartime Operations*, eds E. J. Dearnaley and P. B. Warr, London: Academic Press (1979)

*23   Rachman, S. J. (1978), *Fear and Courage*, San Francisco: W. H. Freeman

*24   Bourne, P. G. (1970), *Men, Stress and Vietnam*, Boston: Little Brown

25   Hacket, T. P., Cassem, N. H., and Wishnie, H. A. (1968), 'The coronary care unit: an appraisal of its psychological hazards', *New England Journal of Medicine*, **279**, 1365–70

26   Egbert, L. D., et al. (1964), 'Reduction in postoperative pain by encouragement and instruction of patients', *New England Journal of Medicine*, **270**, 825–7

*27   Kübler-Ross, E. (1969), *On Death and Dying*, New York: Macmillan; London: Tavistock

28   Naydler, M. (1968), *The Penance Way: The Mystery of Puffin's Atlantic Voyage*, London: Hutchinson

29   Ridgway, J., and Blyth, C. (1966), *A Fighting Chance*, London: Hamlyn

Chapter 8   Simple Errors, Poor Concentration and Forgetfulness

1   Friedman, R. C., Bigger, J. T., and Kornfeld, D. S. (1971), 'The intern and sleep loss', *New England Journal of Medicine*, **285**, 201–3

2   Chichester, F. (1961), *Alone Across the Atlantic*, London: Allen and Unwin

*3   Shinar, D. (1978), *Psychology on the Road: The Human Factor in Traffic Safety*, New York: Wiley, p. 41

4   Byrd, R. E. (1938), *Alone*, New York and London: Putnam

*5   Patrick, D. (1981). *Fetch Felix: The Fight Against the Ulster Bombers,* London: Hamish Hamilton

6   Garrison, P. (1981), 'High expectations and high terrain', *Flying,* **108,** 72–74

7   Brown, D. A. (1981), 'Incorrect computer route cited in Antarctic crash', *Aviation Week and Space Technology,* **114,** 18 May, 26–7; 11 May, 34

8   Report on the Accident to Boeing 727 G-BDAN on Tenerife, Canary Islands, on 25 April 1980 (1981), 20 London: Her Majesty's Stationery Office.

9   *Panorama,* BBC 1, 6 July 1981

Chapter 9   Faulty Judgements and Perceptions

1   Davis, D. Russell, and Cullen, J. H. (1958), 'Disorganisation of perception in neurosis and psychosis', *American Journal of Psychology,* **71,** 229–38

2   Langley, C. A. (1958), *Railway Accidents: Report on the Collision which Occurred on 4th December, 1957, near St. John's Station, Lewisham in the Southern Region of British Railways,* London: Her Majesty's Stationery Office

*3   Davis, D. Russell (1958), 'Human errors and transport accidents', *Ergonomics,* **2,** 24–33

*4   Rolt, L. T. C. (1955), *Red for Danger: A History of Railway Accidents and Railway Safety Precautions,* London: John Lane The Bodley Head (Pan, 1960, p. 250)

5   Hayter, A. (1965), *Business in Great Waters,* London: Hodder and Stoughton, p. 87

6   Pye, P. (1952), *Red Mains'l,* London: Herbert Jenkins (Hart Davis, Mariner's Library, 1961, p. 134)

7   Bennet, G. (1974), 'Psychological breakdown at sea: hazards of singlehanded ocean sailing', *British Journal of Medical Psychology,* **47,** 189–210

8   Mulville, F. (1972), 'The loneliness of the long-distance sailor', *Yachting Monthly* (London) May

*9   Danaher, J. W. (1980), 'Human error in ATC systems operations', *Human Factors,* **22,** 535–45 (also of interest: pp. 521–670)

10   Davis, D. Russell (1946), 'The disorganisation of behaviour in fatigue', *Journal of Neurology and Psychiatry,* **9,** 23–9

11   *The Times,* 5 January 1973

12   *The Times,* 3 December 1981

13   Wilson, G. R. S. (1953), *Railway Accidents: Report on the Double Collision which occurred on 8th October, 1952, at Harrow and Wealdstone Station in the London Midland Region British Railways,* London: Her Majesty's Stationery Office

Chapter 10   Illusion and Misinterpretations

*1   Gregory, R. (1973), *Eye and Brain: the Psychology of Seeing,* 2nd edn, London: Weidenfeld and Nicolson

2   Davison, A. (1951), *Last Voyage,* London: Heinemann, p. 162

*3   Ross, H. E. (1974), *Behaviour and Perception in Strange Environments,* London: George Allen and Unwin

*4   Roscoe, S. N. (1979), 'When day is done and shadows fall, we miss the airport most of all', *Human Factors,* **21,** 721–31

5   Byrd, R. E. (1938), *Alone,* New York and London: Putnam, p. 84

6   Smith, W. M. (1966), 'Observations over the lifetime of a small isolated group: structure, danger, boredom, and vision', *Psychological Reports*, **19**, 475–514

7   Bonatti, W. (1964), *On the Heights*, London: Hart Davis (Diadem, 1979)

8   Gillman, P., and Haston, D. (1966), *Eiger Direct*, London: Collins

9   Chichester, F. (1967), *'Gipsy Moth' Circles the World*, London: Hodder and Stoughton (Pan, 1969, p. 127)

*10   Shinar, D. (1978), *Psychology of the Road: The Human Factor in Traffic Safety*, New York: Wiley

11   Smythe, F. (1934), in *Everest 1933*, by H. Ruttledge, London: Hodder and Stoughton, ch. 8

12   Murray, W. H. (1947), cited by H. E. Ross (1974), in *Behaviour and Perception in Strange Environments*, London: Allen and Unwin (see also W. H. Murray, *Mountaineering in Scotland*, London: Diadem, 1979)

13   Benson, A. J. (1978), 'Spatial disorientation – common illusions', in *Aviation Medicine: Physiology and Human Factors*, ed. J. Ernsting, London: Tri-Med Books

14   Stave, A. M. (1979), 'The effects of cockpit environment on long-term pilot performance', *Human Factors*, **19**, 503–14

15   Garrison, P. (1981), 'Help me fly the airplane', *Flying*, February, pp. 88, 90

16   Smythe, F. (1937), *Camp Six: an Account of the 1933 Mount Everest Expedition*, London: Hodder and Stoughton, p. 270

17   Davison, A. (1951), *Last Voyage*, London: Heinemann, p. 172

18   Lewis, D. H. (1961), *The Ship Would Not Travel Due West*, London: Temple Press, p. 48 (Hart Davis, Mariners' Library, 1963, p. 70)

19   Chichester, F. (1967), *'Gypsy Moth' Circles the World*, London: Hodder and Stoughton (Pan, 1969, p. 238)

20   Manry, R. (1966), *Tinkerbelle*, New York: Harper & Row; London: Collins (1967), pp. 116–18

21   Lewis, D. (1975), *Ice Bird*, London: Collins, p. 57

Chapter 11   Hallucinations and 'The Other Person'

*1   Slade, P. (1976), 'Hallucinations', *Psychological Medicine*, **6**, 7–13

2   Dumas, V. (1960), *Alone Through the Roaring Forties*, London: Adlard Coles

3   Shackleton, E. H. (1919), *South*, London: Heinemann; New York: Macmillan

4   Worsley, F. A. (1977), *The Great Antarctic Rescue: Shackleton's Boat Journey*, London: Sphere; New York: Norton (first published as *Shackleton's Boat Journey*, London: Hodder and Stoughton, 1940)

5   Smythe, F. (1937), *Camp Six: an Account of the 1933 Mount Everest Expedition*, London: Hodder and Stoughton, p. 268

6   Buhl, H. (1954), in *Nanga Parbat*, by K. M. Herrligkoffer, London: Elek

7   Bonington, C. (1977), *Everest, the Hard Way*, Harmondsworth: Penguin (this extract not in English edition published by Hodder and Stoughton, 1976); New York: Random House

8   Lindberg, C. A. (1953), *The Spirit of St. Louis*, New York: Scribners

9   Davison, A. (1956), *My Ship is so Small*, London: Peter Davies, p. 81

10   Slocum, J. (1900), *Sailing Alone Around the World*, New York: Sheridan House; London: Hart Davis, Mariners' Library, 1948

11   Manry, R. (1967), *Tinkerbelle*, London: Collins, p. 117

12 Bailey, M. and M. (1973), *117 Days Adrift*, Lymington, England: Nautical Publishing Co., p. 167

13 Robertson, D. (1973), *Survive the Savage Sea*, London: Elek, p. 120

14 Lewis, D. H. (1960), 'Notes on some reactions to solitude and fatigue', *Journal of the Royal College of General Practitioners*, **3**, 129–30

15 Scott, D, and Haston, D. (1976), in *Everest, the Hard Way*, by C. Bonington, London: Hodder and Stoughton (Penguin, 1977); New York: Random House

16 Koestler, A. (1954), *The Invisible Writing*, London: Collins, p. 350

*17 Moody, R. A. (1975), *Life After Life*, New York: Mockingbird, Bantam

18 L'Hermitte, J. (1951), 'Visual hallucinations of the self', *British Medical Journal*, **1**, 431–3

19 Bennet, E. A. (1955), 'The double', in *Studien zur Analytischen Psychologie C. G. Jungs*, vol. 1 (Festschrift for C. G. Jung's eightieth birthday), Zurich: Rascher

*20 Keppler, C. F. (1972), *The Literature of the Second Self*, Tucson, Arizona: University of Arizona Press

21 Kovalevsky, S. (1895), *Reminiscences of Childhood*, London: Macmillan

*22 Kübler-Ross, E. (1975), in *Life After Life* (foreword), by R. A. Moody, New York: Mockingbird, Bantam

*23 Critchley, M. (1953), *The Parietal Lobes*, London: E. Arnold

*24 Bennet, G. (1968), 'LSD: 1967', *British Journal of Psychiatry*, **114**, 1219–22

*25 Sacks, O. W. (1973), *Awakenings*, London: Duckworth (Harmondsworth: Penguin, 1976)

26 Benedict, R. (1935), *Patterns of Culture*, London: Routledge and Kegan Paul

27 Huxley, A. (1956), *Heaven and Hell*, London: Chatto and Windus, p. 59

*28 Williams, H. L., Morris, G. O., and Ardie, L. (1962), 'Illusions, hallucinations and sleep loss', in *Hallucinations*, ed. L. J. West, New York and London: Grune and Stratton

29 Bexton, W. H., Heron, W., and Scott, T. H. (1954), 'Effects of decreased variation in the sensory environment', *Canadian Journal of Psychiatry*, **8**, 70–6

Chapter 12   Ecstasy to Black Despair

1 Williams, G. (1969), 'Sir Thomas Lipton' Wins, London: Peter Davies, p. 115

2 Byrd, R. E. (1938), *Alone*, New York and London: Putnam, p. 85

3 Lester, J. T. (1975) 'Stress, self-transcendence, and dreams on Mount Everest' (unpublished)

*4 Murphy, M., and White, R. A. (1978), *The Psychic Side of Sports*, Reading, Mass.: Addison-Wesley

5 Ritter, C. (1954), *Woman in the Polar Night*, London: George Allen and Unwin

6 Mulville, F. (1972), 'The loneliness of the long distance sailor', *Yachting Monthly*, **132**, May, 686–8

7 Blagden, D. (1973), *Very Willing Griffin*, London: Peter Davies

8 Byrd, R. E. (1938), *Alone*, New York and London: Putnam, p. 199

Chapter 13   Disorganised Behaviour And Psychological Breakdown

1 Davis, D. Russell (1946), 'The disorganisation of behaviour in fatigue', *Journal of Neurology and Psychiatry*, **9**, 23–9

2 Davis, D. Russell (1946), 'Neurotic predisposition and the disorganisation observed in experiments with the Cambridge cockpit', *Journal of Neurology and Psychiatry*, **9**, 119–24

*3 Wolfenstein, M. (1957), *Disaster, A Psychological Essay*, London: Routledge and Kegan Paul, p. 77

4 Scott, D. (1972), 'To rest is not to conquer', *Mountain*, **23**, 10–18

*5 Wallace, A. F. C. (1956), *Tornado in Worcester: An Exploratory Study of Individual and Community Behavior in an Extreme Situation*, Disaster Study No. 3, Washington, D.C.: National Academy of Sciences, National Research Council.

*6 Hersey, J. (1946), *Hiroshima*, New York: Bantam (1959); Harmondsworth: Penguin (1946), pp. 43, 73

7 Friedman, P., and Linn, L. (1952), 'Some psychiatric notes on the *Andrea Doria* disaster', *American Journal of Psychiatry*, **114**, 426–32

8 *The Times*, 22 February 1971

9 See also: *Observer*, 11 November 1979; *Daily Telegraph*, 10 and 11 June 1980

*10 Davis, D. Russell (1966), 'Railway signals passed at danger: the drivers, circumstances and psychological processes', *Ergonomics*, **9**, 211–22

11 Robertson, J. R. H. (1964), *Railway Accident: Report on the Collision that occurred on 3rd June 1964 at Bradford (Exchange) Station*, London: Her Majesty's Stationery Office

*12 Beach, H. D. (1967), *Management of Human Behaviour in Disaster*, Ottawa: Department of National Health and Welfare

13 Faxon, N. F. (1943), 'Problems of hospital administration: the Cocoanut Grove disaster', *Annals of Surgery*, **117**, 803–8

14 Danzig, E. R., Thayer, P. W., and Galanter, L. R. (1958), *The Effects of Threatening Rumour on a Disaster-Stricken Community*, Disaster Study No. 10, Washington, D.C.: National Academy of Sciences, National Research Council

15 Heim, A. St G. (1892), 'Remarks on fatal falls', in 'The experience of dying from falls', by R. Noyes and R. Kletti (1972), *Omega*, **3**, 45–52. Also in *The Games Climbers Play*, ed. K. Wilson, London: Diadem (1978)

16 Williams, N. (1978), in *Accidents Happen*, A. Welch, London: John Murray, p. 26. See also *Aerobatics* by N. Williams, Shrewsbury (UK): Airlife Publications

17 Popović, M, and Petrović, D. (1964), 'After the earthquake', *Lancet*, **2**, 1169–71

*18 Perry, H. S., and Perry, S. F. (1959), *The Schoolhouse Disasters: Family and Community as Determinants of the Child's Response to Disaster*, Disaster Study No. 5, Washington, D.C.: National Academy of Sciences, National Research Council

*19 Prince, S. H. (1920), *Catastrophe and Social Change*, New York: Columbia University Press, p. 77

*20 Janis, I. L. (1951), *Air War and Emotional Stress*, New York: McGraw-Hill, p. 133

21 Wolfenstein, M. (1957), *Disaster: a Psychological Essay*, London: Routledge and Kegan Paul, p. 213

22 Bennet, G. (1975), 'Community disaster in Britain', in *The Yearbook of Social Policy in Britain 1973*, ed. K. Jones, London: Routledge and Kegan Paul. See also G. Bennet, *Community Disaster in Britain: The Role of the General Practitioner* (1970), British Medical Association library

23 Davison, A. (1951), *Last Voyage*, London: Heinemann

24 Bennet, G. (1974), 'Psychological breakdown at sea: hazards of singlehanded ocean sailing', *British Journal of Medical Psychology*, **47**, 189–210

25 Tomalin, N., and Hall, R. (1970), *The Strange Voyage of Donald Crowhurst*, London: Hodder and Stoughton (Harmondsworth: Penguin, 1971)

Chapter 14   Surviving Against the Odds

*1 Bettelheim, B. (1960), *The Informed Heart: The Human Condition in Mass Society*, London: Thames and Hudson; Illinois: Free Press

*2 Bettelheim, B. (1943), 'Individual and mass behaviour in extreme situations', *Journal of Abnormal and Social Psychology*, **38**, 417–52

*3 Matussek, P. (1975), *Internment in Concentration Camps and its Consequences*, Berlin: Springer Verlag

*4 McClure, B. (1979), 'Hostage survival', in *International Terrorism in the Contemporary World*, ed. M. H. Livingston. Contributions in Political Science, No. 3, Westport, Conn.: Greenwood Press

5 Gibson, W. (1953), *The Boat*, Boston: Houghton Mifflin; London: W. H. Allen (Star Books, 1979)

6 Bailey, M. and M. (1974), *117 Days Adrift*, Lymington, Hampshire: Nautical Publishing Co.

7 Courtauld, A. (1935), 'Living alone under polar conditions', *The Polar Record*, No. 4, 66–74

8 *Illustrated London News* (1931), 'Rescuing a six weeks buried explorer from Greenland snow'. (London) 6 June

9 Jung, C. G. (1931), Seminar: 'Interpretation of visions', unpublished transcript, spring 1931 (in C. G. Jung Institute, Zurich)

*10 Friedman, M., and Rosenman, R. H. (1974), *Type A Behaviour and Your Heart*, New York: A. A. Knopf and Fawcett Crest; London: Wildwood House

11 Timerman, J. (1981), *Prisoner Without a Name, Cell Without a Number*, London: Weidenfeld and Nicolson

12 Jackson, G. (1973), *People's Prison*, London: Faber and Faber, p. 173

13 Henderson, S., and Bostock, T. (1977), 'Coping behaviour after shipwreck', *British Journal of Psychiatry*, **131**, 15–20

*14 Watts, A. (1957), *The Way of Zen*, New York: Pantheon and Mentor (Harmondsworth: Penguin, 1962)

15 Shackleton, E. H. (1919), *South*, London: Heinemann; New York: Macmillan

16 Worsley, F. A. (1977), *The Great Antarctic Rescue: Shackleton's Boat Journey*, London: Sphere; New York: Norton (first published as *Shackleton's Boat Journey*, London: Hodder and Stoughton, 1940)

17 Lansing, A. (1959), *Endurance: Shackleton's Incredible Voyage*, London: Hodder and Stoughton (Granada, 1980); New York: McGraw-Hill

*18 Furse, C. (1979), *Elephant Island: An Antarctic Expedition*, Shrewsbury (UK): Anthony Nelson

19 Thomson, D. (1977), *Scott's Men*, London: Allen Lane, p. 120

*20 Tyhurst, J. S. (1958), 'Problems of leadership: in the disaster situation and in the clinical team', in *Symposium on Preventive and Social Psychiatry*, p. 33. Sponsored by Walter Reed Army Institute of Research and National Research Council, Washington, D.C.: Superintendent of Documents, US Government Printing Office.

21   Bech, H. D., and Lucas, R. A. (1960), *Individual and Group Behavior in a Coal Mine Disaster*, Disaster Study No. 13, National Academy of Science, National Research Council

*22   Keys, A., et al. (1950), *The Biology of Human Starvation*, vols 1 and 2, Minneapolis: University of Minneapolis Press

*23   McKee, A. (1975), *Death Raft: The Human Drama of the Medusa Shipwreck*, London: Souvenir Press

24   Warner, L. and Sandilands, J. (1982), *Women Beyond the Wire: a Story of Prisoners of the Japanese 1942–45*, London: Michael Joseph

25   Mawson, D. (1915), *The Home of the Blizzard*, vol. 1, London: Heinemann

26   Bickel, L. (1977), *This Accursed Land*, London: Macmillan

Chapter 15   Investigating and Understanding

*1   Boulding, J. G., Belton, R. O., and Cullen, S. A. (1978), 'Accident investigation and air safety', in *Aviation Medicine: vol 2 Health and Clinical Aspects*, ed. G. Dhenin, London: Tri-Med Books

*2   Shinar, D. (1978), *Psychology on the Road: The Human Factor in Traffic Safety*, New York: Wiley

3   *Daily Telegraph*, 28 November 1972

4   Lane, G. (1973), *Trident I G–ARPI, Report of the Public Inquiry into the causes and Circumstances of the Accident near Staines on 18th June 1972*, Civil Aircraft Accident Report 4/73, London: Her Majesty's Stationery Office

5   McNaughton, I. K. A. (1976), *Railway Accident: Report on the Accident that occurred on 28th February 1975 at Moorgate Station, on the Northern Line London Transport Railways*, London: Her Majesty's Stationery Office

6   Marks, L. (1976), 'Was it Suicide?', *Sunday Times*, 29 February

7   Forbes, H., Laing, M., and Myatt, J. (1979), *1979 Fastnet Race Inquiry*, London: Royal Ocean Racing Club, 20 St James's Place, London SW1

*8   Fisher, B. (1980), *The Fastnet Disaster and After*, London: Pelham Books

*9   Rousmaniere, J. (1980), *Fastnet Force 10*, Lymington, Hampshire: Nautical Publishing Co.

*10   Gardner, L. T. (1979), *Fastnet '79*, London: George Godwin

*11   Bennet, G. (1973), 'The singlehanders', *Yachting Monthly* (London), **133**, 47–54; *Sail* (Boston) **4**, No. 8, 80–5 and No. 9, 106–11

*12   Bennet, G. (1974), 'Scientific medicine?', *Lancet*, **2**, 453–6

*13   Bennet, G. (1979), *Patients and their Doctors: the Journey through Medical Care*, London: Bailliere Tindall

14   Calvert, E. S. (1969), 'Human factors and the collision problem', *Journal of the Institute of Navigation*, **22**, 48–55

*15   Godson, J. (1974), *Papa India: The Trident Tragedy*, Salisbury, England: Compton Press

*16   Davis, D. Russell (1966), 'Railway signals passed at danger: the drivers, circumstances and psychological processes', *Ergonomics*, **9**, 211–22

*17   Hawkins, F. H. (1981), 'Sleep and body rhythm disturbance amongst flight crews in long-range aviation', M.Phil. thesis in Department of Applied Psychology, University of Aston, Birmingham, England

18   Banks, R. (1962), *The Unrelenting Ice*, London: Constable

*19   Nicholl, G. W. R. (1960), *Survival at Sea: The Development, Operation and Design of Inflatable Marine Lifesaving Equipment*, London: Adlard Coles and Harrap

20 Venning, G. R. (1982), 'Validity of anecdotal reports of suspected adverse drug reactions: the problem of false alarms', *British Medical Journal*, **284**, 249–52

21 Department of Health and Social Security (periodically from 1952), *Report on Confidential Enquiries into Maternal Deaths in England and Wales*, London: Her Majesty's Stationery Office

Chapter 16   Drawing It All Together

*1 McMullen, M. (1975), *Multihull Seamanship*, Lymington, Hampshire: Nautical Publishing Co. See also 'The loss of *Three Cheers*', *Yachting Monthly* (London), **143**, 350–2, 1982

2 Blagden, D. (1973), *Very Willing Griffin*, London: Peter Davies

*3 Brown, G. W., and Harris, T. (1979), *Social Origins of Depression*, London: Tavistock

4 Cobb, S., and Rose, R. M. (1973), 'Hypertension, peptic ulcer, and diabetes in air traffic controllers', *Journal of the American Medical Association*, **224**, 489–92

*5 Davis, D. Russell (1970), 'Depression as adaptation to crisis', *British Journal of Medical Psychology*, **43**, 109–16

*6 Cooper, W., and Smith, T. (1981), *Human Potential: the Limits and Beyond*, Newton Abbot, Devon: David and Charles

Index

Principal entries are shown in **bold** type

The Author

Dr Glin Bennet works in the Department of Mental Health, Bristol University, and is a consultant psychiatrist and a psychotherapist. He holds MA, MD, FRCS and MRCPsych. Before taking up psychiatry he worked as a surgeon, and his previous book, *Patients and their Doctors*, is about the reactions of people to illness, to hospitalisation and to surgical operations. His present book also derives from personal involvement, this time in disasters, sailing and outdoor activities, as well as experience of working with people of all kinds who are in personal crisis. He lives in Bristol and has four children.